BOUND TO BOND

BOUND TO BOND

Gender, Genre, and the Hollywood Romantic Comedy

Mark D. Rubinfeld

Westport, Connecticut
London

Library of Congress Cataloging-in-Publication Data

Rubinfeld, Mark D., 1956–
    Bound to bond : gender, genre, and the Hollywood romantic comedy / by Mark D.
Rubinfeld.
      p. cm.
    Includes bibliographical references and index.
    ISBN 0–275–97271–2 (alk. paper)
    1. Comedy films—United States—History and criticism. 2. Love in motion
pictures. 3. Sex role in motion pictures. I. Title.
PN1995.9.C55R83   2001
791.43′617—dc21   00–069899

British Library Cataloguing in Publication Data is available.

Library of Congress Catalog Card Number: 00–069899
ISBN: 0–275–97271–2

First published in 2001

Praeger Publishers, 88 Post Road West, Westport, CT 06881
An imprint of Greenwood Publishing Group, Inc.
www.praeger.com

Printed in the United States of America

The paper used in this book complies with the
Permanent Paper Standard issued by the National
Information Standards Organization (Z39.48–1984).

10 9 8 7 6 5 4 3 2 1

To my mother and father

Contents

Illustrations

TABLES

FIGURES

Acknowledgments

This book would not have been possible without the gracious support of so many important people in my life. My former advisors at the University of Massachusetts Amherst—particularly N. J. Demerath, Robert Faulkner, Gene Fisher, Lisa Henderson, John Hewitt, Christopher Hurn, Suzanne Modell, and Randall Stokes—guided me through the early stages of this project. My former colleagues in the sociology and anthropology department at Assumption College—Linda Ammons, Charles Estus, and Susan Melia—graciously offered me their assistance, encouragement, and friendship. My past and current colleagues in the sociology department at Loyola University, New Orleans—Dee Harper, Anne Hornsby, Laurie Joyner, Anthony Ladd, Marcus Mahmood, Edward McCaughan, Jerrol Seaman, Brian Smith, Lydia Voigt, and Richard Wilson—provided me with an intellectually dynamic and emotionally supportive working environment. Additionally, Katherine Adams, Kim Ernst, Eric Gorham, Conrad Raabe, and Frank Scully at Loyola University; David Johnson at Massachusetts College of Liberal Arts; Kathleen Johnson at Keene State College; Seymour Leventman at Boston College; Alex Reichl at Queens College; and Jerry Watts at Trinity College offered me their advice and support through various stages of this project. Likewise, I am indebted to Paul Dergarabedian at Exhibitor Relations Company for his assistance in tracking the Hollywood movies, and to Eric Levy and Pamela St. Clair at Greenwood Publishing Group for their confidence in this book. I am equally grateful to my many supportive friends and peers over the years. Among others, Jennifer Beam, Jennie Bear, Lisa Conboy, Eda diBiccari, Melissa Embser-Herbert, Caroline Gayer, Sarah Gayer, Katrin Haertel, Julie Jansen, Elizabeth Keithley, Sarah Kelbaugh, Donna McCardell, R. Lee Questad, Denise Rezende, Lara Rutskin, Olivia Vaughn, and Kristin Violette were sources of inspiration and encouragement. Furthermore, I want to thank all of my students, first at the University of Massachusetts, then at Assumption College, and currently at Loyola University. They were—and continue to be—bright, energetic, and generous; and they make me optimistic about the future. Finally, I want to thank my late mother and my late stepfather who meant so much to me; my father who still means so much to me; all the members of the Rubinfeld family, still forever New Yorkers; and all the members of the Rose family, blooming now, from coast to coast.

Introduction

Popular culture, like all culture, is a set of signifying practices, and no narrative would be compelling unless its meaning(s) resonated with some buried aspect of our cultural unconscious.

Diane Raymond[1]

Your desire shall be for your husband, and he shall rule over you.

Genesis 3:16

Balls, said the queen, if I had them I'd be king.

Jill Clayburgh in *An Unmarried Woman*

By any measure, the last five years of the twentieth century were an astonishing five years for the Hollywood romantic comedy. Excluding all Hollywood romantic comedies that bombed so badly at the box office that they were in and out of the movie theaters faster than their coming attractions, the five years from 1995–1999 were a time of record new releases and ticket sales for the genre.[2] They were, in the parlance of Hollywood, blockbuster years. In 1999 alone, there were fifteen Hollywood romantic comedies that sold more than 3.398 million tickets at the box office. These fifteen movies easily broke the old record number of ten Hollywood romantic comedies released in a single year, first set in 1987 and then tied in 1998. As a matter of fact, there were more new

Hollywood romantic comedies released in the five-year period from 1995–1999 than there were in the entire fourteen-year period from 1970–1983.[3]

Furthermore, in the last four years of the twentieth century, there were eight Hollywood romantic comedies that grossed over $100 million (the "gold record" figure for Hollywood movies). These movies included: *There's Something About Mary* ($176 million), *Jerry Maguire* ($154 million), *Runaway Bride* ($150 million), *As Good As It Gets* ($147 million), *My Best Friend's Wedding* ($127 million), *Notting Hill* ($116 million), *You've Got Mail* ($115 million), and *Shakespeare in Love* ($100 million). As the old adage states, everybody, it seems, loves a love story. And when it comes to the Hollywood love story, these numbers indicate that there may be more people in love with the Hollywood love story today than ever before.[4]

It should come as no surprise that most of these people are women. After all, women are socialized from the earliest ages to love the Hollywood love story. One cannot understand the popular appeal of a blockbuster like *Pretty Woman*, for example, without also understanding the popular appeal of a fairy tale like *Cinderella*; one cannot understand the popular appeal of hits like *Moonstruck* and *Groundhog Day* without also understanding the popular appeal of a fairy tale like *The Frog Prince*. Furthermore, one cannot understand the popular appeal of fairy tales like *Cinderella* and *The Frog Prince* without first understanding how these fairy tales are passed on to children, mostly daughters, in sweet bedtime stories composing some of the most intimate moments ever shared between parents and children, and then reinforced, again, in adolescence and adulthood through the rituals of social regeneration: the first date, the first kiss, the first (and ideally, last) wedding.[5]

This said, men cannot be completely left out of the picture. The study of gender, after all, involves the study of men just as much as it involves the study of women. And to the degree that this book uses the Hollywood romantic comedy to examine contemporary gender roles and relationships, this book involves the study of men as much as it involves the study of women. On the one hand, it is a fact that more women than men go to see Hollywood romantic comedies. Although a few Hollywood romantic comedies have scored reasonably well with men over the years (*There's Something About Mary*, for example, was a big hit with teenage boys and *Jerry Maguire* drew as many men to the theaters as women), overall, females make up fifty-five to sixty percent of the genre's audience.[6] On the other hand, the Hollywood romantic comedy has been one of the most enduring of all Hollywood genres. It has outlasted, among others, such Hollywood staples as the western and the musical. It is as strong, if not stronger, today as it was during the so-called golden era of Hollywood romantic comedies in the mid- to late 1930s and early 1940s. And it could not have endured, nor could it continue to thrive, without the forty to forty-five percent of the males in the audience, many of whom, it would appear, are also moved by the Hollywood love story, even if they are not always willing to admit it.

Utilizing the tools of both literary criticism and social science—textual analysis and content analysis—this book looks at thirty years of the Hollywood love story. As we will soon see, the term "Hollywood love story" is a bit of a misnomer since there are actually four Hollywood love stories, not one. These four Hollywood love stories are driven by four basic plots intrinsic to all Hollywood romantic comedies. Every Hollywood romantic comedy utilizes at least one of these four plots; most Hollywood romantic comedies combine two or more of them. Because narrative is central to the Hollywood romantic comedy, one has to understand how these four Hollywood love stories work in order to understand the genre's popular appeal and its ideological implications.[7] In Part I, I identify these four basic Hollywood romantic comedy plots as *pursuit plots*, *redemption plots*, *foil plots*, and *permission plots*. Furthermore, through structural analysis, I interpret the conceptual symbolism of each of these four plots while demonstrating—through scores of critical readings—how they are structured into conventional Hollywood romantic comedies so as to construct a subject that is aligned with patriarchal ideology. In so doing, I show how these four Hollywood love stories, as they are embedded in the four Hollywood romantic comedy plots, are essentially stories of masculinity and femininity with roles and rules that ensure femininity is subordinated to masculinity.

In Part II, I shift from textual analysis to content analysis to empirically support my critical readings, as well as to introduce a time element that ensures that narrative text is not privileged over historical context. In so doing, I present a list—constituting my sample—of the "top" 155 Hollywood romantic comedies released from 1970–1999; a typology of the four Hollywood romantic comedy plots; and a series of percentage distribution tables that illustrate how the four plots play across popularity categories (blockbusters, hits, marginally successful movies, disappointments, and bombs), as well as across time. I then proceed to identify five different Hollywood romantic comedy genre types (i.e., five different ways that Hollywood romantic comedies tell their four love stories), and three different Hollywood romantic comedy themes (i.e., three different central ideas that Hollywood romantic comedies communicate through their four love stories and five genre types). These differentiations enable me to construct a baseline that, in turn, allows me to identify any structural and ideological changes in the genre from 1970–1999.

In Part III, I shift back to textual analysis: illustrating how the Hollywood romantic comedy, for a brief period of time during the 1970s and, to a lesser degree, the early 1980s, played with its plot conventions to challenge, rather than reinforce, traditional gender roles and relationships. In the later 1980s, and throughout the 1990s, the Hollywood romantic comedy then reversed course, using its plot conventions to reinforce traditional gender roles and relationships. Later, I will discuss how quickly, and how completely, this reversal occurred, as well as explore some of the reasons why it occurred. But for now, consider this: from 1984–1999, there were a total of 109 Hollywood romantic comedies that sold over 3.398 million tickets. Out of these 109 movies, only *one* dared to thematically argue that women can survive, and even thrive, without men, marriage, and motherhood. And that 1989 movie, *She-Devil*, bombed at the box office.

In the Conclusion, I tie together all my findings about the Hollywood romantic comedy, while linking those findings to some of the cultural changes and failures to change that characterize contemporary gender roles and relationships. After addressing questions of "why narratives matter" and "how narratives change," I end this book by projecting ahead—imagining what particular forms and functions the Hollywood romantic comedy narrative may assume in the twenty-first century.

Before proceeding, some cautions are in order. In offering this structural study of the Hollywood romantic comedy, I am well aware of the poststructuralist critique of structural analysis. As poststructuralists have clearly demonstrated in recent years, all texts are polysemic; that is, they contain multiple, and often contradictory, meanings. Different people can, and do, interpret the same texts differently, in ways that suit their social needs or fit in with their social experiences.[8] Therefore, in terms of the Hollywood romantic comedy, not all moviegoers are going to perceive the binary oppositions and sequences of action in any given movie the same way. Without incorporating ethnography into this study, we cannot know for sure what any particular Hollywood romantic comedy may mean to any particular individual.

Subject positions are theoretical constructs; they are not real people. So while I occasionally use terms such as "the male" and "the female" in this book, I certainly recognize that there is no such thing as a monolithic male or female. Instead, I am referring to ideal types, which, admittedly, make little allowance for race, ethnicity, class, age, religion, or sexual preference.[9] Indeed, since the Hollywood romantic comedy is both aimed at and consumed by audiences who are overwhelmingly white, it must be noted that the gender constructions discussed in this book are, for the most part, white gender constructions.[10] Of course, there are many cultural overlaps between different racial and ethnic groups. But there are also undeniable cultural differences, and these differences do make a difference.

This said, I would not have written this book if I believed that structural analysis has outlived its methodological usefulness for both exploring and affecting social relationships. To the contrary, despite its limitations, structural analysis remains a vital tool for understanding social structures, as well as for prompting social change. To point out the dominant structures and meanings in American popular culture texts, after all, is to point out some of the central social inequalities in American society. Once identified, these dominant structures and meanings can be more readily recognized and resisted.[11] While not everyone, of course, needs the assistance of textual analysis to recognize and resist these dominant structures and meanings, there are nevertheless tens of millions of people in the United States who are not quite as actively engaged as they can be with the popular culture texts they consume. Instead, they all too readily accept these texts' social constructions as ontological givens.[12] And while it is true that these texts may have multiple meanings, that does not mean they have infinite meanings. Nor does it mean that all of their meanings can be equally applied. There are, as cultural studies pioneer Stuart Hall notes, preferred textual meanings that elicit dominant readings.[13] And there are some popular culture texts with preferred meanings so blatant that polysemy ceases to be a critical issue.

Consider, for example, an advertisement for a soft drink that depicts a woman drinking a soda. On one level, the text—in this case, an advertisement—is exactly what it is: a picture of a woman drinking a soft drink connoting the message: "Buy this drink." But what if the woman is half-naked? And her body is soaked in sweat? And her face is tilted up? And her eyes are dreamily closed? And her lips are heavily lipsticked? And her mouth is open into an oval? And the shape of the bottle containing the soft drink is, of course, phallic? And the bottle is shoved so far down the woman's throat that only the lower half of the bottle is visible? And there is soda dripping down her chin? And the words underneath the picture of the woman, read: "YES!"? With such a text, does it really matter if the viewer is male or female; rich or poor; black, white, Latino, or Asian?

Well, on the one hand, it certainly does matter. Depending on the viewer, such a text may elicit emotional anger or sexual arousal. It may move one viewer into protesting, and another into masturbating. On the other hand, despite what the text may elicit from one viewer to the next, are there any connotations but sexual connotations that can be reasonably read into such a text? And what if the text is not one text, but tens of millions of such texts, strung all across this country, with nearly identical depictions? Do we really need to incorporate ethnography into our textual analysis to determine from these tens of millions of texts that the sexual objectification of women is a social problem in this country?

Furthermore, what if nearly all the women that are pictured in these tens of millions of texts are young: under thirty? And what if *not a single woman* who is pictured in these tens of millions of texts is over fifty? Doesn't that say something about how this country defines which females are sexually desirable and which females are not? What if, in addition, nearly all the women who are pictured in these tens of millions of texts are white? And thin? And unblemished? And beautiful? Are, in short, what most women are not? Doesn't that, too, say something about how this country defines which females are sexually desirable and which females are not?

Because texts *are* polysemic, not everyone has to, nor do they, buy into these definitions. But this does not mean that millions of Americans are not affected by these definitions. After all, millions of American women do buy beauty products. Do try to lose weight. Do get cosmetic surgery. Do what they can to match an image that, because they did not make, is not them. And not only women, but men, too, are affected. After all, there are millions of American men who are not as happy as they can be because their wives no longer look like they once did. So at a certain age, some of these men begin collecting "trophy wives," and, in the process, break apart families. Furthermore, there are millions of single (and married) men who, for whatever reason, do not get to "sexually connect" with the "girl of their dreams." So their lust (and, occasionally, their resentment) is sated through pornography: one of the most popular texts in America. And doesn't that, too, say something about the social relationships between men and women in this country?

In other words, ethnography is important. And there are many studies that must interview and/or observe people to learn more about their social relationships. But there is a great deal that can be learned about these social relationships through textual analysis, as well. After all, texts are data. They can be critically read in ways that uncover their hidden, and sometimes not so hidden, meanings. They can be linked to the social contexts and social processes that give all texts their meanings. They can provide great insights into the ongoing struggles for social power between a society's subordinates and superordinates. They can, at any given point in time, suggest who may be winning and who may be losing these struggles. Furthermore, when the analysis of a single text— a word, a picture, an advertisement, or a movie—is expanded into an analysis of a collection of similar texts, these texts can provide even more information. Such an analysis, or *genre study*, can be used to track many similar texts over an extended period of time to examine how, if at all, the balance of social power in a given society sometimes shifts, and whether such shifts are transitory or permanent.

The analytical value of a genre is that, like any text, it can be critically read to decipher the processes of signification at work in a given society. Moreover, if we were to think of a genre along the lines of film scholar Barry Keith Grant as "a system of conventions structured according to cultural values," then its analytical value is twofold.[14] First, examining a genre enables us to explore one of

the many ways that a society consciously and unconsciously manages to produce and reproduce its most fundamental values and beliefs. And, second,
since the processes of cultural production and reproduction are always affected
by competing discourses—and because the study of a genre is, in large part, the
study of such competing discourses—examining a genre also enables us to explore those social conflicts that periodically inhibit and occasionally alter a society's ability to produce and reproduce its most fundamental values and
beliefs.

On a deeper level, a genre is more than simply a distinct group of popular
stories consisting of well-known characters, formulaic plots, repetitious
themes, and satisfying resolutions. And a genre does more than simply enter-
tain audiences. As genre analyst Arthur Asa Berger points out, a genre has social
and political implications. It offers us "roles to imitate and generate[s] world
views that shape our social and political behavior."[15] And, as genre analyst
Gina Marchetti suggests, it may also provide a valuable social function:

> Particular genres tend to be popular at certain points in time because they
> somehow embody and work through those social contradictions the cul-
> ture needs to come to grips with and may not be able to deal with except
> in the realm of fantasy. As such, popular genres often function in a way
> similar to the way myth functions—to work through social contradic-
> tions in the form of a narrative so that very real problems can be trans-
> posed to the realm of fantasy and apparently solved there.[16]

In *Mythologies*, the noted literary critic and semiotician Roland Barthes argues
that the function of myth is to "transform history into nature."[17] One of the
"great myths" that Barthes asks us to question concludes that "women are on
the earth to give children to men."[18] To Barthes's credit, he recognizes myths
for what they are: social constructions posing as natural truths. The goal of
semiology, for Barthes, is to cut through these natural truths. Toward that end,
this book seeks to cut through the natural truth of the Hollywood romantic
comedy—to denaturalize its narrative assertion that *men and women are, without question, and without questioning their assigned roles in the familial economy,
bound to bond.*

In attempting to cut through this natural truth, it goes without saying that
not everyone will agree with all of my critical readings. Like all interpretations,
mine are open to alternate interpretations. In opting to offer a large number of
critical readings rather than a small number, I am well aware that I am increas-
ing the likelihood of offending some readers. How could I attack this particular
movie and not attack that particular movie? Why did I include this particular
movie in my sample and leave out that particular movie? How can I spend so

much time focusing on this particular reactionary aspect of this particular movie, while ignoring that particular progressive aspect of that particular movie? Where do I get off reading so much into a single line of dialogue, and reading it so wrongly?

To quickly address some of these points, I am, admittedly, harsh in some of my critical readings. It is not that I do not recognize the ideological gaps and contradictions in some of these movies. But I am focusing on the "preferred textual meanings that elicit dominant messages." There are undoubtedly some people, after all, who may read the advertisement of the young, half-naked woman with the soda bottle shoved halfway down her throat, discussed earlier, as an act of female sexual power. Look at her—after all, she is looking right at the male viewer and saying, "This turns you on, doesn't it?" And there are undoubtedly some people who may read a movie like *Pretty Woman* as a similar celebration of female sexual power. Look at her—after all, she got what she most desired, the billionaire and the fairy tale. But such readings are arguably a stretch. Certainly, people can read ideological resistance into anything they want. The question is, *on balance*, does the image and/or the story reinforce traditional notions of femininity or masculinity, or do they challenge them? In what ways? To what effects?

Furthermore, because this is a structural analysis of the Hollywood romantic comedy, I am primarily focusing on the narrative elements of the Hollywood romantic comedy: the binary oppositions and sequences of actions from which the movie's thematic meanings are largely forged.[19] There are, of course, many other crucial components that make up a movie and these can serve as ideological counterpoints to the stories.[20] Unfortunately, an analysis of these ideological counterpoints is outside the scope of this book. This said, I do recognize that narrative, though central to the pleasures of the Hollywood romantic comedy, is not the only pleasure that the genre provides.[21]

Finally, when it comes to analyzing the four Hollywood love stories, it goes without saying that any narrative action, whether we are talking about a single line of dialogue or multiple crises and resolutions, can be read in many different ways, and there is always a danger of misreading and/or over-reading meaning(s) if all that we are looking at are just a few narrative actions from a few movies. However, I would argue that when the same narrative actions appear over and over—in the same context—in Hollywood romantic comedy after Hollywood romantic comedy, then at some point we are no longer drawing inferences from a few isolated narrative actions that can mean just about anything. Instead, we are now observing and recording an established, identifiable, and quantifiable pattern of culturally meaningful signifying practices.

The very word "quantifiable," of course, raises a final issue of methodology. Although I do include numerous statistical analyses and methodological observations in my chapters (particularly in Part II), I have tried as much as possible to relegate the more detailed methodological and theoretical commentaries to the endnotes. This does not in any way diminish their importance. They are there in the endnotes to be scrutinized and analyzed. But, whenever possible, I've left them out of my chapters so as not to clutter the narrative flow or substitute methodology for clarity. For those who are more methodologically inclined, the three most important tables in this book are this study's sample of the "top" 155 Hollywood romantic comedies released from 1970–1999 (presented in Part II), and this study's two data collection tables (presented in the Appendix).

In presenting this book, it is not my intention to ruin the pleasures of the Hollywood romantic comedy for anybody. After more than forty years of watching Hollywood romantic comedies, I am still a sucker for the Hollywood romantic comedy happy ending. Just as they do in the fairy tales, I want the hero and the heroine to live happily ever after. I am not ashamed to admit that my eyes were wet at the end of *Tootsie*. They were equally wet at the end of *When Harry Met Sally*. And they were just as wet at the end of *Pretty Woman*. To this day, the Hollywood romantic comedy continues to be my favorite Hollywood genre. Its love stories still resonate with me despite my critical reservations. Nor is it my intention in presenting this book to condemn the institution of marriage, which, for the majority of people in this world, provides warmth, safety, love, and happiness. I do question, however, whether the institution of marriage, as it is presented in the four Hollywood love stories, is the *only* route to these ends. And I do question whether there is room—even with all the progress that has been made in recent years—for turning the institution of marriage and, by extension, the institution of the family, into a more equal partnership. In raising these questions, I am not asking those of you who love the Hollywood romantic comedy, as I do, to love it any less. I am asking you, however, to understand it, and its social implications, a lot more.

Part I

The Four Hollywood Love Stories

Chapter 1

The Pursuit Plot

> The man should be strong and active; the woman should be weak and passive; the one must have the power and the will; it is enough that the other should offer little resistance. . . . I grant you this is not the law of love, but it is the law of nature, which is older than love itself.
>
> Jean-Jacques Rousseau[1]

Hollywood romantic comedies certainly did not invent sexual inequality, nor are they the first art form to reflect and reinforce sexual inequality. Such inequality, after all, is as old as stories. And, like stories, such inequality comes in many forms. Some contemporary forms, like slasher films, assume the form of violence against women. Graphic scene after graphic scene depicting half-naked teenage girls being chased, tortured, and/or killed for the sexual thrill of male viewers.[2] A generation of teenage boys learning early what their culture teaches them: to funnel their frustrations toward females, and to use sex as a purge and a sedative.[3] Other contemporary forms, however, are less visible, but perhaps equally harmful. What follows, then, is an examination of one such form: the Hollywood romantic comedy, which, at first glance, appears to the most gentle and loving of all Hollywood genres. However, if the study of popular culture teaches us anything, it teaches us that appearances are often deceiving. The task of textual analysis is to get us to see—really *see*—beneath these appearances. To critically read popular culture texts for their unspoken messages. To dig out, in this case, what the Hollywood romantic comedy may really be saying about men, women, and the relationships between them in this society.

It goes without saying that the Hollywood romantic comedy is, like all Hollywood genres, conservative and traditional in its values. The purpose here, however, is to go a step further—to show exactly *how* and *how much* the Hollywood romantic comedy is conservative and traditional in its values and, equally important, to show how this wasn't always the case and, therefore, needn't always be the case. As previously noted, Hollywood romantic comedies utilize four basic plots—pursuit plots, redemption plots, foil plots, and permission plots—that are intrinsic to all Hollywood romantic comedies. Each of these plots depicts a different love story. And each of these love stories has different prescriptions—one for men and one for women—for finding and sustaining a loving relationship. The first type of Hollywood romantic comedy plot, the *pursuit plot*, involves a "quest of conquest" in which a hero is attracted to a heroine; courts her; encounters resistance from her; and, being a "real man," refuses to take "no" for an answer. Ultimately, the hero woos her, wows her, and wins her.

The narrative pleasures of the pursuit plot demand female submission since, simply put, these are stories of male "wants" and, more important, of males getting what they want. For example, in the 1991 Hollywood romantic comedy *L.A. Story*, the hero—a mild-mannered television weatherman—desperately wants a heroine whose ability to resist, from the beginning, is doomed. If power is the ability to take what one wants no matter what (whether it be property or another human being who, in being taken, is transformed into property), then the climactic sequence in *L.A. Story* epitomizes the power of males in patriarchy to *take* females. At the same time, the climactic sequence also epitomizes the power of fictional narratives in patriarchy to naturalize male dominance in order to neutralize female resistance. Toward the end of *L.A. Story*, the heroine, Sara (Victoria Tennant), is faced with a choice: whether to stay with the hero, Harris (Steve Martin), or to go back home, by herself, to London. Begging her to stay, Harris proposes a future that includes: "marriage, kids, old age, and death." But Sara is reluctant. She asks what will happen if she chooses, instead, to go. "All I know," Harris answers in a wistful voice that masks the threatening nature of his words, "is if I had the power, I would turn the winds around, I would roll in the fog, I would bring in storms, I would change the polarity of the earth so compasses couldn't work—so your plane couldn't take off." Sara glares at him. "This is everything I didn't want," she snaps. "Pain, lying, complications!"

The next morning, Sara chooses to go. Harris desperately chases after her. "I know there is something that would make you stay!" he pleads. "There's some move I can make, the right word, attitude, plan. But these are all tricks. These are all just things I would think up and try. So let's forego all that. Let's assume that whatever that thing is—that whatever it is that would make you stay has occurred—that it has happened, and that my hand has already gone down your throat and grabbed your heart!"

The particular choice of words—*that my hand has already gone down your throat and grabbed your heart*—may be unintentional, but it is no accident. For whether the screenwriter consciously knew, or didn't know, the symbolic import of the words when he wrote them down, they capture the eventual outcome of all conventional pursuit plots.[4] As the words intimate, everything that the heroine says and does in the course of the pursuit plot means nothing because the ending, from the beginning, is inevitable. And, as the words also inadvertently reveal, the male pursuit of female love is occasionally tinged in Hollywood romantic comedies with violence and/or threats of violence. Sara's answer to Harris's plea is to shut him out. She slams a door in his face. Harris leaves, but, like the narrative, he is not finished. The leaving is only a detour.

That detour, however, is essential. For while the ending may be inevitable, the Hollywood romantic comedy narrative constructs its subject positions through a series of delays that create emotional tension (in the action) and personal investment (in the outcome).[5] In the pursuit plot, the primary source of these delays is the heroine's resistance; the pursuit plot narrative, therefore, not only dichotomizes males and females into culturally acceptable ideals of masculinity and femininity, it also poses masculinity (i.e., male dominance) as the solution to femininity while picturing the female, and the actions of the female, as problematic. Sara (the problem) tries to leave (also the problem). In the climactic scene of *L.A. Story*, the narrative deals with its problem(s) by symbolically transforming its hero's hand into the "hand of God" through an electronic freeway sign that—throughout the movie—taps into, displays, and unleashes the hero's unconscious desires. The sequence that depicts Harris's climactic conquest is remarkable: a succession of fifty parallel action crosscuts between the hero and the heroine that affirm with a vengeance the primacy of male power.[6]

Cutting between Sara and Harris, the climactic shots picture Sara attempting to leave the United States, boarding a jet, and glancing out the window as the jet rolls toward the runway. Halfway across the city, the electronic freeway sign blinks to life. The camera cuts to Harris sitting alone in his study. As Harris unconsciously wishes for the weather to change, the needle on his barometer turns from "very dry" to "cloudy." Suddenly, a gust of wind blows through the room. Outside, fog rolls in. Storm clouds obliterate the sun. There are flashes of lightning. Cracks of thunder. Rain. The camera cuts to Sara's jet, pelted by rain, aborting its takeoff. Then the camera cuts back to Harris, stepping out of his house into the pouring rain. A taxi pulls up. Sara gets out. She runs to Harris, dropping her suitcases as she runs. The two of them passionately embrace. And then the two of them kiss the *key kiss*, which, completing the scene, punctuates the successful completion of the pursuit plot.[7]

Of course, there may be many kisses between a hero and a heroine in the typical Hollywood romantic comedy signifying everything from friendship to foreplay. But there is usually only one key kiss toward, or at, the end of the love story that signifies an end to resistance, a recognition of romantic love, a declaration of commitment, a portent of permanent union, and a pleasurable closure to the narrative. The key kiss is defined by conventions: by music, lighting, mood, and by the emotions it elicits. In *L.A. Story*, the key kiss is shown five times from five different camera angles, while the hero's voice, as narrator, informs the audience: "A kiss may not be the truth, but it is what we *wish* were true." Meanwhile, the background music; the pouring rain; the shot-reverse-shot of the embracing lovers; the backlighting; the close-up of Sara's face in soft focus, head tilted back, eyes fluttering closed, mouth open, jugular exposed, heavy breathing; the voice of Harris as narrator defining the meaning of the key kiss, all conspire to ensure that the key kiss is seen as a sign of love—and all that love signifies: social regeneration through marriage, kids, old age, and death.

In a final analysis, the climactic sequence in *L.A. Story* is emblematic and symptomatic with all the framing devices of story and spectacle coming together to naturalize romantic coupling while, in the process, dismissing the heroine's earlier declaration that "*this is everything I didn't want!*" In short, the conventions of the love story ensure that when the key kiss finally occurs, it is interpreted by moviegoers as a sign of female desire rather than a sign of female capitulation. Ultimately, the tricks and tropes of the pursuit plot serve their purpose. In a movie that opens, after all, with a shot of a flying advertising balloon shaped like a giant frankfurter, that transforms its weak hero from a "weenie" into a god, that neuters its resisting heroine into the compliant role of the redemptive wife, and that closes with a happy ending that satisfies all desires, the tricks and tropes work to mitigate against re-visioning those desires to ask: at what price; on whose terms?

Although the climactic sequence in *L.A. Story* provides one of the more vivid examples of the pursuit plot in action, it is by no means the only example. The "hand of God" metaphor, for example, is also played out in *I.Q.* (1994), which, like *L.A. Story*, simultaneously manages to empower its befuddled hero while taming its ambitious, career-minded heroine. From the moment that the hero, Ed (Tim Robbins), first spots the heroine, Catherine (Meg Ryan), early in the narrative, her fate is fixed. Lined up in his sights, she is, literally, a sitting duck. "I'm going to marry her!" Ed blurts out to his fellow garage mechanics. "I

Taking his cue from an electronic freeway sign, Steve Martin kisses Victoria Tennant in *L.A. Story*. Courtesy of Photofest.

looked at her, she looked at me and it was, you could feel it, it was like death but in a good way . . . pop, pop, pop, pop, pop, it was electric, and then I kissed her—in the future!" But to get Catherine to marry him, Ed first has to get Catherine to notice him, then like him, and finally desire him. The pursuit plot is constructed, after all, around an impulse and an imperative. The hero wants the heroine. And the movie, in order to "work," has to position its viewers into wanting the heroine to want the hero (even if wanting him is—as it was with the heroine of *L.A. Story*—"everything I didn't want").

To help Ed win Catherine, *I.Q.* employs Albert Einstein (Walter Matthau) as the ultimate father figure, picturing him as the heroine's wise "Uncle Albert."[8] In the opening scenes of the movie, one of Uncle Albert's scientific cronies ponders whether we are "all victims of some comic, cosmic accident or is it a grand design." Uncle Albert, in turn, professes that "I, for one, will never believe that God plays dice with the universe." Once again, the choice of words is significant, especially when viewed in the context of a script that loads the dice, from the beginning, in favor of female submission.[9] To ensure that Catherine makes the right choice (i.e., wanting the hero), Uncle Albert conspires with his cronies to ensure that she does. Furthermore, to ensure that its viewers go along with the conspiracy, the movie pictures its heroine's resistance as repression. "When was the last time you went 'wahoo'?" Ed asks Catherine. "Well I'm sure I don't know," Catherine curtly replies, indicating that she has no desire to go "wahoo."

That lack of desire is, of course, depicted as the problem. The heroine of *I.Q.* may be initially introduced to viewers as a "brilliant mathematician," but female brilliance, the narrative eventually argues, is not particularly desirable. As Uncle Albert laments, "Catherine should be having more fun." And as Uncle Albert tells Ed, "What she needs is to go out with someone like you. The problem is, she would never go out with someone like you." So to nudge his niece along, Uncle Albert arranges a series of chance encounters between Catherine and Ed. "I think she wants to leave," Ed observes to Uncle Albert during one of those encounters. "*She doesn't know what she wants,*" Uncle Albert whispers back to Ed with words that, yet again, may be unintentional but are no accident. For the choice of words reinforces a recurring theme that pops up, repeatedly, in Hollywood romantic comedy pursuit plots. *Men know, more than women know, what women really want. And it is up to men to give women what they really want, whether they want it or not, because men know that it is what they really want.* In this sense, male dominance is thematically transformed into an act of loving paternalism.

As Catherine struggles with her mixed feelings, Uncle Albert begs her: "Don't let your brain interfere with your heart." But he could just as easily implore her, as the electronic freeway sign—through the hero—implores the heroine of *L.A. Story*: "Let your mind go and your body will follow." For in both movies, the same message keys the heroine's eventual surrender. *Women should not think.* An object, after all, has no will/power. In the climactic scene of *L.A. Story*, it is Harris's willpower, embodied in the electronic freeway sign, that stops Sara's jet from taking off, ensuring that she cannot flee, and bringing her back for the key kiss. And in the climactic scene of *I.Q.*, it is Albert Einstein's ingenious invention, a remote control, that stalls Catherine's car, ensuring that she cannot flee, and bringing her back to Ed for the key kiss. That the key kiss signifies capture as much as it signifies love is captured in *I.Q.*'s final two shots: a picture of Catherine responding to the key kiss by whispering "wahoo," and a picture of Uncle Albert, peering through his telescope at Catherine's response, and affirming: "wahoo."

While the Hollywood romantic comedy pursuit plot plays a major role in both *L.A. Story* and *I.Q.*, it makes a late, more subdued appearance in the 1998 remake of the 1961 Disney classic *The Parent Trap*. It is important to note, however, that this late showing does not necessarily diminish its symbolic import. The 1998 version of *The Parent Trap* opens sweetly enough where most Hollywood romantic comedies end: with the "happy coupling" of the hero, Nick (Dennis Quaid), and the heroine, Elizabeth (Natasha Richardson), aboard the *Queen Elizabeth 2*. There are fireworks, dancing, love songs, and a bottle of wine with a label that reads: "Where the Dreams have no end." It is a perfect beginning to a love story, and it lasts just till the end of the opening credits.

The credits completed, *The Parent Trap* quickly skips ahead eleven years and nine months to reveal in bits and pieces how Nick and Elizabeth ended up divorcing soon after the birth of their identical twin daughters. And worse, in divorcing, they split up their daughters: one moving to London with her mother; the other to the Napa Valley with her father. True to the original 1961 version of *The Parent Trap*, the twins accidentally meet in summer camp, discover that they are sisters, and conspire to bring their mother and father back together. To rekindle the romance, the twins arrange a dinner date for Nick and Elizabeth aboard a beautiful boat. The lights dim. Mood music kicks up. Bubbly pours. Nick and Elizabeth begin to reminisce. Nick asks what went wrong between the two of them all those years ago. Elizabeth answers.

That answer, in turn, marks a turning point for the movie. For in using Elizabeth's answer to address what went wrong between the hero and the heroine, the 1998 remake of *The Parent Trap* significantly deviates from the original version of the movie: introducing a pursuit plot that was never a part of the Disney classic. Elizabeth tells Nick that, yes, she loved him, but the love was "just too much, and much too soon." Overwhelmed, and not ready to be overwhelmed, she had to leave. "I packed," Elizabeth tells Nick. "*And you didn't come after me.*" Stunned, Nick replies, "I didn't know you wanted me to."

This exchange, never included in the original version, is crucial. For it blames the hero and his failure to pursue for ripping apart a family and, in the process, breaking four hearts. Having failed once to fulfill the narrative pleasures of the pursuit plot, the hero is given a second chance to make amends. In the movie's climactic sequence, Nick assures Elizabeth that now that he is back in the picture, she doesn't need "to be so brave." But Elizabeth, still wary of dependency, leaves again. Like the heroine in *L.A. Story*, she boards a jet bound for London. And like the heroine in *L.A. Story*, her "flight" provides only a temporary reprieve, a last delay, before the inevitable recoupling, played to the hilt with tears and pouring rain. When Elizabeth's plane touches down in London, Nick is already there, waiting for her. "I made the mistake of not coming after you once, Lizzie," he tells her in no uncertain terms. "I'm not going to do that again, no matter how brave you are." It is left, then, to Elizabeth's tears of joy in the film's final shots to help viewers read between the heroine's en/gendered lines: "*No matter what I say or do, chase me, catch me, never let me go.*"

This insistence on male persistence, of course, reinforces male dominance, just as the heroine's "giving in" reinforces female deference. To successfully reaffirm these traditional gender roles, the Hollywood romantic comedy pursuit plot must close on either one of two notes: the hero's persistence overcomes the heroine's resistance in order to get what he wants or the heroine, if she succeeds in her resistance, pays a steep price for not "giving in" and/or "putting out." In other words, the pursuit plot forces its heroine to co-star in a narrative that either dismisses her or punishes her. In *Doc Hollywood* (1991), for example, the hero, Ben (Michael J. Fox), wagers ten dollars that he can separate the heroine, Lou (Julie Warner), "from her panties within a week." It takes him two weeks. "You lost that bet," Lou tells Ben in the film's final shots as the two of them, happily coupled, walk off together. "Says who?" Ben asks. "Says me," Lou quips. "Says you!" Ben answers. "You have no say in this bet, *you are the bet!*"[10]

The hero of *Moonstruck* (1987) is even quicker in his conquest: it takes him only two days. "You're a wolf," the heroine, Loretta (Cher), tells the hero, Ronny (Nicolas Cage), before sleeping with him. But when Ronny tells Loretta that he loves her, she reminds him that she is engaged to marry his brother, tells him that they can never see each other again, and slaps his face. In response, Ronny begs Loretta to accompany him to the opera promising, if she agrees, to never bother her again. She agrees. He, however, can't keep his promise. "I'm a wolf," Ronny points out to her after the opera. "You run to the wolf in me," he adds. " Now, I want you to come upstairs with me and get in my bed!" Blown away by his persistence, Loretta nods, takes his hand, and follows him upstairs.

In both movies, the heroine is an object *and* an objective. And in both movies, the message is the same: men take what they want; women respect men who take what they want. If there are any doubts as to *whose* wants most propel the pursuit plot, consider the dilemma of the hero of *Blume in Love* (1973). "She is the only woman I will ever love," the hero, Blume (George Segal), mumbles to himself after his wife, Nina (Susan Anspach), catches him cheating on her and divorces him. "I will die if I don't get her back. I do not want to die. Therefore, I will have to get her back." The particular choice of words, yet again, exposes another hidden truth about the Hollywood romantic comedy: the male pursuit of female love is propelled, more often than not, by self-love. Eventually, the heroine, Nina, pays dearly for her resistance. Toward the end of the narrative, Blume rapes—and impregnates—her while crying out: "I love you so much my heart is breaking."[11] In the final scenes of the movie, he also wins her back.[12]

Just as the Hollywood romantic comedy pursuit plot occasionally depicts female resistance as a mistake, it also pictures male persistence—in the face of female resistance—as heroic. Even rape, if it is accompanied by "love," is understandable. Male betrayal, after all, is forgivable as long as the male promises to change. What is unforgivable is deviance: a man who won't go after what he wants, or a female who refuses to defer. Of the four Hollywood romantic comedy plots, the pursuit plot most epitomizes the "genderization" in our culture of males and females into active subjects and passive objects. But since most moviegoers would be unwilling to empathize with a narrative that so blatantly subjugates females, the Hollywood romantic comedy has to broaden its appeal. And this entails shifting the focus of the love story from a narrative that emphasizes what the male most wants to a narrative that emphasizes what the male most needs.

Chapter 2

The Coldhearted Redemption Plot

To broaden its appeal, the Hollywood romantic comedy almost always combines the pursuit plot with one or more of its other plots.[1] In most cases, the other plot turns out to be the second type of Hollywood romantic comedy plot: the *redemption plot*. Of the four Hollywood romantic comedy plots, the pursuit plot and the redemption plot are, by far, the most ideologically significant. In essence, these two plots key all the love stories. Furthermore, when analyzed together, these two plots also key our understanding of why these love stories are so popular even if they are occasionally hurtful and harmful.

While the pursuit plot is almost always teamed up with other plots, the redemption plot may appear in combination with other plots or by itself. Of the four Hollywood romantic comedy plots, the redemption plot is the most frequently utilized and, as we will later see, the most polysemically appealing. There are two variations of the redemption plot: the *coldhearted redemption plot* and the *brokenhearted redemption plot*. Although these two variations tend to differ slightly in terms of motivation and point of view, both serve similar commercial and ideological functions: to emotionally appeal to females by emphasizing the female's emotional appeal.

Simply put, the first variation of the redemption plot, the coldhearted redemption plot, features a bitter hero who is incapable of love. He is heartsick. He is, also, too heartless to know that he is heartsick. Just as the pursuit plot positions its viewers to know more than the heroine knows about what the heroine really desires (i.e., to be taken by the hero), the coldhearted redemption plot positions its viewers to know more than the hero knows about what the hero most needs. And what the hero most needs, it turns out, is a redemptive heroine. As "nurse and nurturer," the redemptive heroine is synonymous with the "good wife" who, like all good wives, is a "good mother." And like all good mothers, the redemptive heroine is also a "good deferrer."

Occasionally, the hero of the coldhearted redemption plot is only mildly coldhearted: unintentionally neglecting, mistreating, and/or betraying a heroine who loves him or wants to love him. More typically, however, the hero is knowingly cruel. Like the beast in *Beauty and the Beast*, he is consumed by hate until he is touched by love. To put it another way, the hero of the coldhearted redemption plot is a heel. The role of the redemptive heroine is to heal the heel. In *Moonstruck*, for example, the heroine, Loretta, doesn't simply fall prey to the hero, Ronny, because he is a "wolf" who happens to want her. But rather, she eventually succumbs to him because he is a "wolf" whose paw, it turns out, is caught in a trap. "This is the most tormented man I have ever known," a female co-worker whispers to Loretta after Ronny, in his introductory scene, bitterly storms out on them. "I'm in love with this man," she continues; a tear trickling down her face. "But he doesn't know that. I never told him because he could never love anybody since he lost his hand and his girl."

The female co-worker in *Moonstruck* is a plot device; she appears in only one scene and delivers only a couple of lines. But those lines, occurring when they do in the narrative, serve their purpose. For they immediately position both the heroine and viewers into sympathizing with a needy hero. Touched by his torment, Loretta runs after Ronny, counsels him, calms him down, and then sleeps with him. Afterwards, she finds herself torn between her desire for Ronny and her loyalty to her fiancé. When they return from the opera, Loretta insists that she can control herself—that she can say "no." But Ronny won't buy it. "The storybooks are bullshit!" he tells Loretta. "Now, I want you to come upstairs with me and get in my bed!" Loretta hesitates. "Come on," Ronny pleads: his outstretched hand reaching out to her. "Come on," he pleads again. And then softer, a third time, "Come on." Loretta nods and, as detailed earlier, takes his hand and follows him upstairs. But as much as Loretta may be blown away by his persistence, her tears—captured by the camera—reveal that she is also blown away by his needs.

A similar "animal" analogy occurs in *Green Card* (1990), which, like *Moonstruck*, works to humanize its hero. "If you push me to be a beast, I can be a beast," the hero, George (Gérard Depardieu), threatens the heroine, Bronte (Andie MacDowell), early in the narrative. "I am the gutter, but you need a bit of the gutter in your life." However, Bronte—"seeing" through George—views it differently. "He says he's not sensitive. That's not true. He's a very sensitive man," she tells an immigration officer who is charged toward the end of the narrative with deciding George's fate. "He's had a hard life. In a way, he hasn't learned how to give. But he's got so much to give." Eventually, Bronte's love overcomes George's hate. And while the inevitable happy ending may be slightly tempered in *Green Card*, it nevertheless complies with closing conventions. As George is forced to leave the country in the final scene, George and Bronte exchange gold rings and wedding vows while the soundtrack promises viewers: "Everything is going to be all right."

In both films, as in all coldhearted redemption plots, the heroine's love transforms the hero into a complete man who is capable of loving. In so doing, the female "softens" both the male and cultural signifiers of masculinity. But at the same time, she is also trapped in a narrative that, while downplaying the dominant male, nevertheless manages to reinforce male domination. Or, to put it another way: the coldhearted redemption plot is basically a warmhearted fairy tale that manages to suggest equality while typically en/gendering inequality.

Two movies in particular—*Groundhog Day* and *Pretty Woman*—illustrate different ways that similar fairy tales can produce such inequality: gently and not so gently. In the more gentle of the two movies, *Groundhog Day* (1993), a coldhearted hero learns that he is doomed to live Groundhog Day over and over for profaning the sacred (i.e., belittling Groundhog Day on Groundhog Day in Punxsutawney, Pennsylvania). Taking advantage of his predicament, he uses "all the time in the world" to try to sexually score with a kindhearted heroine. At the last second, however, the kindhearted heroine, Rita (Andie MacDowell), sees through the hero, Phil (Bill Murray), and slaps his face. Phil learns his lesson. Toward the end of the narrative, he turns his curse into a gift, using his second chances to become a better human being. Eventually, the reluctant Rita is bowled over by the "new" Phil: touched to tears by his compassion, sensitivity, and talent. Closing out the pleasures of the love story, Rita kisses Phil on the mouth. As soon as she does, the snow begins to fall again; her willing kiss breaks the evil spell. The movie's final scene depicts the hero and the heroine embracing the pleasures of a new morning after a chaste night of sleeping together. And the movie's final shot, symbolizing the "promise of a wedding," pictures the hero sweeping the heroine up into his arms, carrying her over a white gate, through a white archway, and into the white, snow covered landscape.

As in *Moonstruck* and *Green Card*, the narrative downplays, even denounces, the dominant male in order to affirm the redemptive female. But even though it is a nicer guy who wins the heroine in the end, *Groundhog Day's* final coupling can still be interpreted as a capture when viewed in the context of countless pursuit plots in which the male wants the female at the beginning of the narrative and gets the female at the end of it. Furthermore, the final coupling can still be interpreted as a capture when viewed in the context of countless coldhearted redemption plots in which the male needs the female at the beginning of the narrative and gets the female at the end of it.

Although these gender imbalances are sugarcoated in *Groundhog Day*, there is little that is sweet about how *Pretty Woman* (1990) en/genders inequality. The highest grossing Hollywood romantic comedy of the twentieth century, *Pretty Woman* is essentially a thinly disguised fairy tale that is structured around male fantasies of conquest and female fantasies of rescue. Ostensibly, a love story between a coldhearted billionaire businessman and a warmhearted Hollywood hooker, *Pretty Woman* manages to delight in its disgust for women.[2] Its females characters, for example, are consistently portrayed as either prostitutes, clerks, secretaries, or servants who eagerly take orders from the men around them. Wives are depicted as catty bitches. Salesladies are pictured as social snobs. Women are told that while they cannot be trusted with money, they certainly can be bought. And in one particularly disturbing scene early in the movie, the death of a prostitute is twisted into a cheap joke, serving to warn the heroine and viewers of what happens to women who do not have male protectors.

Although *Pretty Woman* ends with a suggestion of equality (i.e., males rescue females who, in turn, rescue them right back), that ending is built on a narrative that reinforces inequality at every step of the way. The construction of that inequality is most readily observed in the stark contrast between the male quest in *Pretty Woman* and the female quest in *Pretty Woman*. From the moment that the heroine, Vivian (Julia Roberts), informs the hero, Edward (Richard Gere), that she does everything except kiss on the mouth, Edward's quest is to get Vivian to kiss him on the mouth. The kissing on the mouth is an imperative; the pleasures of the narrative depend on the heroine's emotional surrender. Or, to put it another way, the male quest in *Pretty Woman*—as in most pursuit plots—is female conquest. Eventually—inevitably—Vivian's prohibition against kissing on the mouth must be—and is—overturned by a series of heroic actions that work in *Pretty Woman* to literally beat her into submission.

There is emotional abuse: small taunts that serve over and over to reinforce the heroine's insecurity. When Vivian inquires why Edward picked her to spend the week with him out of all the women he could have picked, Edward coldly answers: "I wanted a professional." When Vivian mentions how she refuses to get emotionally involved with her clients, Edward remarks: "You and I are such similar creatures, we both screw for money." And when Vivian angrily tells Edward, "Nobody ever made me feel so cheap," Edward fires back: "Somehow, I find that hard to believe."

There are the constant orders, establishing paternal authority while infantilizing the heroine in the process. "Put this on," Edward tells Vivian.

"Stop fidgeting." "Try a strawberry." "Why don't you sit and have something to eat." "I want you to buy some clothes." "Never ever pick up the phone." "I want you to come down from there." "Time to shop." "Get rid of your gum." "Come back here, I'm speaking to you." In essence, Edward spends as much time in *Pretty Woman* telling Vivian what to do as he spends talking to her. And while all of this may not seem like much, it takes on a greater significance when contrasted with the fact that once, only once, throughout the narrative does Vivian ever give Edward a direct order in return. Only after he betrays her, after she tries to leave him, after he begs for forgiveness, Vivian whispers to him: "You hurt me." Then she warns: "Don't do it again."

There is the act of isolating the heroine from the outside world. As soon as Vivian is whisked up to Edward's penthouse suite, she is literally the princess trapped in the tower: an allusion that she herself acknowledges later in the narrative. The spell that traps Vivian, however, is not cast by any wicked witch, but by a billionaire's riches. It includes nearly every female fantasy that money can buy from limitless shopping sprees, to the one magnificent gown that turns every man's head, to the $250,000 diamond necklace gently strung around the heroine's neck, to a private jet ride into a magical sunset, to a "Prince Charming" who can—and does—read Shakespeare in the park, to the possibility of transcendence—and social mobility—through the magic of love, to a fairy-tale ending that culminates in the promise of a perfect marriage. The female fantasies, however, come at a price. For whenever Vivian is not with Edward, the narrative depicts her with nothing to do but sit around and wait for him. In the two key scenes in which Vivian is forced to interact with people on her own, the narrative ensures that she is brutalized: first by the saleswomen on Rodeo Drive and then by Edward's personal lawyer, Philip. Furthermore, in another key scene in which Vivian dares to drift from Edward's side during a polo match in order to talk—*just talk*—to another man, the narrative ensures that she is brutalized for that act of independence by Edward.

There is the weapon of economic control and coercion. Every chance that *Pretty Woman* gets, it reminds Vivian and viewers that Vivian's fate is tied to Edward's money. She can either stay with him, overlooking his contempt, or end up like the dead prostitute she witnesses early in the movie getting dragged out of the trash bin. In light of the relationship between representations of reality and reality, it is no accident that the very first spoken words in *Pretty Woman* are: "No matter what they say, it's all about money." Nor is it an accident that the very first visual image in *Pretty Woman* depicts a man with money standing between two women with outstretched hands while another man (the "villain," Phillip) suggestively jests: "A penny for your thoughts, how much for the rest of you?" In *Pretty Woman*, as in real life, the bottom line is the top dollar, controlled primarily by men. Moreover, it is no accident that just as *Pretty*

Woman's heroine is pictured preparing to venture forth on her own in the film's final scene (telling her girlfriend of her plans to move to a new city and go back to school), the narrative ensures that its hero arrives just in time to rescue her from such an "unhappy ending."

Finally, there is the threat of physical violence, underscoring female vulnerability while accentuating the heroine's need for masculine protection. In *Pretty Woman*, as in real life, violence against women serves as the ultimate weapon of male control. When Edward sees Vivian talking to David Morse (a potential romantic rival), he gets back at her by telling Philip that she is a prostitute. Later, when Philip learns that Edward has reneged on their business deal by entering into a partnership with James Morse, his former business rival, he gets back at Edward by sexually assaulting Vivian (i.e., Edward's "whore"). As the scene plays out, Edward arrives just in the nick of time to rescue Vivian from rape. Significantly, the narrative then immediately entrusts him, not Vivian, with the patriarchal prerogative of dispensing justice (punching Philip in the nose) and determining punishment (presumably firing him). The cathartic punch in the nose works to contain two key ideological contradictions leading up to and following the sexual assault. First, it covers up the fact that it is Edward's anger at Vivian (for talking to David Morse) and Edward's betrayal of Philip (in financially embracing James Morse) that provides Philip with the ammunition and, in his mind, the motive to rape Vivian. And, second, it covers up the fact that after Edward rescues Vivian from rape, he allows Philip to walk out the door completely free to sexually assault other women. In short, the functional logic of the sexual assault scene in *Pretty Woman* implies, among other things, that when men cannot exact direct revenge on other men, they can always target women; that it is all right after a hard day at the office to kick dogs and beat wives; that the real impropriety of rape is that it is a violation of men's property rights; and, finally, that women are more than happy to serve as spectacle in a world where they must wait to be rescued by men . . . from men.

All of these "heroic actions" in *Pretty Woman* conspire to reverse the heroine's prohibition against kissing on the mouth, which, in turn, leads to a fairy-tale ending that completes the male quest for female conquest. But equally significant, the fairy tale ending also completes the female quest for male rescue. For in addition to reinforcing male dominance, the fairy tale also needs to reinforce female passivity in the face of male dominance: a reinforcement accomplished time and time again through countless depictions of females that want and need to be rescued. "When I was a little girl," Vivian tells Edward toward the end of *Pretty Woman*, "my momma used to lock me in the attic when I was bad, which was pretty often. And I would—I would—pretend I was a princess trapped in the tower by a wicked queen. And then suddenly, this knight on a white horse with these colors flying would come charging up and draw his sword. And I would wave. And he would climb up the tower and rescue me."

"What is it you want?" Edward asks her. "I want the fairy tale," Vivian answers. Significantly, the fairy tale that Vivian wants is marriage; it is the only demand that she makes in the entire narrative other than telling Edward not to hurt her again. The wedding ring serves in *Pretty Woman* as the heroine's ultimate vehicle of rescue. It is her ticket out of nowhere, her claim to legitimacy, and her right to male protection. And it is the fulfillment of the wedding fantasy, symbolized by the climactic embrace in *Pretty Woman*'s final scene, that completes both the male and female quest—conquest and rescue—while tying up all narrative loose ends into a neat illusion of equality and reciprocity.

That illusion implodes, however, in a careful comparison of the hero's actions leading to his conquest of the heroine, and the heroine's actions leading to her rescue by the hero. For to get the gold ring that she so desperately wants, the narrative forces Vivian to pass three tests of chastity and charity, proving that she is worthy of rescue. The first test occurs early in the narrative when Edward follows Vivian into the bathroom and forces open her hand to see if she is concealing drugs. At first glance, his actions seem ludicrous, smacking as they do of double standards. After all, in the preceding twenty-five minutes of the movie, Edward dumps his live-in girlfriend; conspires to bankrupt his competitor's company; steals his lawyer's Lotus; picks up a prostitute on Hollywood Boulevard, and offers her $300 to stay the night. After closing the deal, Edward corners Vivian in the bathroom; treats her like a child; orders her to open her hand and, assuming a moral high ground, threatens to kick her out if she is hiding drugs. Absurd as his actions may seem, however, that absurdity is essential to the patriarchal logic of the fairy tale. The heroine, after all, cannot do heroin. When Vivian opens her hands, she reveals a packet of dental floss. "You shouldn't neglect your gums," she tells Edward. The "revelation" is key; it serves to inform Edward and viewers that Vivian may be a prostitute, but she is clean: literally and figuratively unpricked.

Vivian's second test is rooted in more contemporary concerns. After Edward betrays her for talking to another man, Vivian tries to leave him. "Give me my money," she cries, "I want to get out of here." Edward flings a fistful of hundred dollar bills on the bed. Vivian looks at him; looks at the money; looks back at him; and then without taking a single bill, leaves. Edward watches Vivian walk out; glances over his shoulder; spots the untouched money; and then, only then, chases after her to apologize. In an era of prenuptial agreements, common-law marriages, and palimony suits, Vivian's refusal of the money serves to reassure Edward and viewers that Vivian loves Edward, not Edward's money. Furthermore, it implies that she is willing to be left penniless if Edward ever chooses to leave her. To prove herself worthy of rescue, Vivian must submit to financial dependency. And yet it is precisely that financial dependency that makes Vivian the ideal object for rescue.[3] In other words, the fairy tale strips women of their sexual power, denies them any economic power, deprives them of social power, and presents true heroines as those who willingly submit to total dependency in the name of love.

Essentially, the fairy-tale narrative is, for the heroine, a test of love. If Vivian fails her first test, Edward kicks her out. If Vivian fails her second test, Edward lets her go. The two tests taken together prove that Vivian is not a "prostitute." However, it is Vivian's third test, her final test, that is key. For this is the test she must pass to prove that she is not only "not a prostitute," but that she is also—in the classic sense of the word—a *Lady*. Toward the end of the narrative, Edward flies Vivian to San Francisco for a night at the opera. Guiding her to their reserved box, he tells her that music is a powerful force. "People's reactions to opera the first time they see it are very dramatic," Edward whispers. "People love it or they hate it. If they love it, they will always love it. If they don't, they may learn to appreciate it but it will never become a part of their soul." The opera starts. We hear it; see scenes flash by; watch Vivian watching in awe; smiling and enchanted. The camera zooms in on Vivian. Her eyes well with tears. Then the camera turns to Edward—*Edward watching Vivian*—as Vivian watches the opera, lost in rapture and touched to tears.[4]

It is those tears—women's tears—that are key to the narrative's construction of femininity. For they signify not only Vivian's ability to acculturate into Edward's world but also her assigned role in that world—everything that tenderness and gentleness imply—the "innate" capacity of women to nurture, forgive, and heal. Once signified, the tears defuse the threat of Vivian's sexuality, stripping her, in essence, of her sexual power by shifting the focus of the "male gaze" from sex to love. As we will later see, it is precisely this transformation—from sex object to love object—from hard to soft—that symbolizes the heroine's journey in many Hollywood romantic comedies from a position of relative independence to a position of near total dependency.[5] After passing her third and final test, Vivian's quest in *Pretty Woman* is nearly complete. Simply put, she is ready for rescue, primed for marriage, and prepared for motherhood. She is also, as it turns out, ready to be kissed on the mouth.

Both movies—*Groundhog Day* and *Pretty Woman*—are based on classic fairy tales: the first updates *The Frog Prince* and the second modernizes *Cinderella*. Furthermore, the happy ending in both movies hinges on the heroine's willing kiss, which, because it is repeatedly delayed, serves as both a cure for the hero and a catharsis for the audience identifying with the hero. Finally, and most important, the hero changes in both movies; the heroine's love transforms him into a better human being. Toward the end of *Groundhog Day*, for example, Phil tries to save a homeless old man whom he disdainfully ignored

Wrapping up all loose ends into a neat illusion of equality, Richard Gere and Julia Roberts "rescue" each other in the final scene of *Pretty Woman*. Courtesy of Photofest.

earlier. When the old man dies in his arms, Phil's eyes swell with tears and, imploringly, he looks up to God.[6] Similarly, toward the end of *Pretty Woman*, Edward abandons his plans to take over Morse Enterprises; instead, he symbolically reunites with his own late father by teaming up with the fatherly James Morse. Cleansed of his bitterness, the "new" Edward then walks barefoot in the grass, appreciating life for the first time in his life (or, at least, for the first time since the start of the movie).

What both *Groundhog Day* and *Pretty Woman* do, and do quite well, is to combine the pursuit plot with the coldhearted redemption plot to make the pursuit plot more palatable. This combination enables moviegoers to negotiate an ambivalent engagement with the dominant ideology of the film's text. In other words, viewers can choose which story line they wish to most identify with. Male viewers, for example, may derive narrative pleasure from watching the psychological and sexual surrender of a desirable female: thrilling at the male power to whittle away female resistance. Female viewers, on the other hand, may derive narrative pleasure from watching the "softening" of a desirable male: thrilling at the female power to contain male dominance.[7] The love story may be mired in misogyny, as it is in *Pretty Woman*, but the coldhearted redemption plot allows viewers to overlook even the most obvious sexual stereotypes and inequalities.

Whether real viewers (including which group or groups of real viewers) do, or do not, overlook these sexual stereotypes and inequalities is, of course, an ethnographic question. What textual analysis can demonstrate, however, is how the "natural" sexual hierarchy of the coldhearted redemption plot typically serves men at the expense of women.[8] In reinforcing that sexual hierarchy, the coldhearted redemption plot turns the love story into an oxymoron. Downplaying the dominant male, it nevertheless reaffirms the deferential female. The heroine may or may not succumb to the hero's wants, depending on whether or not the coldhearted redemption plot is combined with the pursuit plot, but she certainly yields to his needs. And while the hero changes in the course of the love story, her role remains forever fixed. Time and time again, she is forced to defer her desires to save him, which, the narrative suggests, is everything she desires.

In a final analysis, the hero all too often *is* the story while the heroine is the "vehicle" that makes the story possible. Consider, for example, how the respective roles play out in the 1995 Hollywood remake of the 1954 classic *Sabrina*. After learning that even his friends refer to him as "the world's only living heart donor," the hero, Linus (Harrison Ford), asks the heroine, Sabrina (Julia Ormond), if she thinks he is a lost cause. "I don't like to think of anyone as a lost cause," Sabrina gently reassures him. Forced to decide whether his love of money is worth a life without love, Linus finally acknowledges that "some things are missing in my life . . . like a life." The particular choice of words, yet again, is significant. For the redemptive heroine functions in Hollywood romantic comedies as a lifeline. In *Sabrina's* final scene, the hero reaches for *it* (her). "Save me, Sabrina Fair," he begs. "You're the only one who can." The plea underscores the symbolic significance of all coldhearted redemption plots; the key kiss that quickly follows punctuates the deferential female role that keys most Hollywood romantic comedies.

The metaphor of the heroine as a lifeline is repeated again in the 1996 Hollywood romantic comedy blockbuster *Jerry Maguire*. "Great at friendship but really bad at intimacy," the hero, Jerry (Tom Cruise), cannot completely give himself to a woman. "I'm just not built that way," he admits to himself late in the narrative while realizing, unless he can become that way, he will forever hate himself. It is up to the redemptive heroine, of course, to change him. "I love him! I love him for the man he wants to be . . . and I love him for the man he almost is!" the heroine, Dorothy (Renee Zellweger), cries out to her disapproving sister after spending her first night together with Jerry. And, indeed, Dorothy loves the hero enough in the end to "let him go," which, it turns out, is just enough for him to realize that without her, he is lost. "You complete me," Jerry finally recognizes—his needs met, his soul saved, his heart transformed.

With similar blockbuster results and ideological ramifications, the metaphor of the heroine as a lifeline reemerges, once again, in the 1997 Hollywood romantic comedy *As Good As It Gets* when yet another coldhearted hero, Melvin (Jack Nicholson), is thrown his lifeline. This time, the redemptive heroine is Carol (Helen Hunt), an absolute angel of a human being who is forced to tap into the "devil's" missing humanity. As in all coldhearted redemption plots, it is a tough job—requiring the redemptive heroine to be both savior and masochist—and, time and time again in *As Good As It Gets*, Carol tries to quit. Disgusted by Melvin's constant contempt for women, as well as all things feminine, she finally tells him: "I don't think I want to know you, anymore. All you do is make me feel bad about myself." But Carol's problem is that *she makes Melvin feel good about himself.* And Carol's flaw, thematically reconfigured into an asset, is that she ultimately cannot deny Melvin his one last chance at happiness even if it means forever coupling with a man who, no matter how hard he tries, will always make her feel bad about herself. "I'm not the answer for you," she informs Melvin in the film's final shots. But her words—signifying one last attempt at resistance—quickly fall on deaf ears as moments later another key kiss signifies, once again, that this "happy coupling" is as good as it gets.

A year after the happy coupling in *As Good As It Gets*, still another redemptive heroine is forced to tap into another coldhearted hero's missing humanity in the 1998 Hollywood romantic comedy hit *You've Got Mail*. This time, the devilish hero, Joe (Tom Hanks), is a much nicer "devil": younger, more charm-

Her love providing a lifeline, Julia Ormond "saves" a coldhearted Harrison Ford in the 1995 remake of *Sabrina*. Courtesy of Photofest.

Chapter 3

The Brokenhearted Redemption Plot

The second variation of the Hollywood romantic comedy redemption plot, the *brokenhearted redemption plot*, is similar to the coldhearted redemption plot in its ideological functions even if the tale it tells is slightly different. While the role of the healing heroine remains constant in both variations, the hero of the brokenhearted redemption plot is more loveless than heartless; his wounds stem from loneliness, not bitterness. Instead of being softened, the brokenhearted hero is introduced as already soft. He is aware that something is missing; something has been missed. While the coldhearted hero is scared to death of commitment and struggles to say "I love you," the brokenhearted hero longs for commitment and is scared to death he'll never get the chance to say "I love you." As the brokenhearted hero of *Splash* (1984) notes in one of that movie's early scenes: "I don't ask for that much. . . . I just want to meet a woman, and I want to fall in love, and I want to get married, and I want to have a kid, and I want to see him play a tooth in the school play." Then after a momentary pause, he adds: "But I'm kidding myself. This is never going to happen. I'm going to grow old, and I'm going to grow lonely, and I'm going to die, and I'm going to be surrounded by a bunch of rotten fruit."

What the brokenhearted hero of *Splash* seeks is what most uncoupled people in America seek: a Hollywood romantic comedy happy ending. His initial observation conveys to viewers what he wants. His follow-up observation conveys to viewers what will happen to him if he doesn't get what he wants and, in so doing, redefines those wants as needs. It is up to the heroine, of course, to fulfill those needs; her desire to be there for him is what makes her a heroine. At the same time, it is up to the Hollywood romantic comedy to get its viewers to accept that desire as natural: positioning the heroine and viewers into sympathizing with a sympathetic male.

Like the coldhearted redemption plot, the brokenhearted redemption plot accomplishes this naturalization through both gentle and not so gentle narratives. For example, the 1993 Hollywood romantic comedy blockbuster *Sleepless in Seattle* epitomizes, to many, the ideal date movie. Gentle, sweet, and unapologetically romantic, the movie could easily serve as a sermon for family values. But in its own disarming way, *Sleepless in Seattle* may reinforce the deferential female gender role and the sexual hierarchy it is based on every bit as much as the Hollywood romantic comedy blockbuster that most immediately preceded it: the not so gentle *Pretty Woman*.

Early in *Sleepless in Seattle*, the movie's grief-stricken hero recounts for a radio talk show host all the things that he most loved about his late wife. As Sam (Tom Hanks) painfully describes how much he misses her, *Sleepless in Seattle* cuts back and forth between Sam, talking on the phone to a nationwide radio audience, and the heroine, Annie (Meg Ryan), driving her car, listening to his voice on her car radio. Hanging on to Sam's every word, Annie begins to cry: touched to tears by this brokenhearted man's need for a good wife. In time, she drops everything—including her impending marriage—to find, meet, and save Sam. After a series of comic misconnections, Annie and Sam finally connect in the film's final scene with their romantic coupling, atop the Empire State Building, fulfilling the hero's need for a heroine, the heroine's need to be needed, and the audience's need for a happy ending.

To its credit, *Sleepless in Seattle* never feels compelled to empower its hero or to break its heroine as many other Hollywood romantic comedies tend to do. Instead, it simply depicts its hero as a gentle sort of guy who needs a woman to complete his life and who, by virtue of that need, gets Annie. But even as the narrative manages to question popular perceptions of masculinity through its gentle hero, it nevertheless reaffirms popular perceptions of femininity. For whenever Annie is not being portrayed in *Sleepless in Seattle* as either emotional, irrational, or hysterical, she is alternatively depicted as the good wife (and the good mother) who just needs the right husband (and the right child) to complete her destiny. In other words, she serves as the love object. Sam doesn't have to chase *it* down. *It* comes to him. In the end, *Sleepless in Seattle* may very well reaffirm family values but the family that it values gently reinforces patriarchal conventions in its assertion that heroines serve only to heal; that even the best of wives are interchangeable; and that true heroes, after a brief period of mourning, need to get "back in the saddle" and recouple.

As in *Sleepless in Seattle*, the role of the healing heroine also keys the brokenhearted redemption plot in *Defending Your Life* (1991), which, by propelling the Hollywood romantic comedy into the afterlife, suggests that female deference transcends even death. In the movie's opening scene, the hero, Daniel (Albert Brooks), is pictured as a "weenie." For his birthday, he treats himself to a brand new BMW that he promptly drives into a bus. Then before he knows what hit him or, to be more precise, what he hit, Daniel finds himself in Judgement City—a sort of way station between heaven and earth—where he is forced to defend his life. If the cowardly Daniel can prove he is no longer a "weenie," he can move on. If he can't, however, he will have to go back to earth and start over.

During Daniel's trial, he is forced to watch all the times in his life that he failed to be a real man in a series of flashbacks that further expose to viewers the hero as a zero. To help Daniel out, the narrative introduces a heroine, Julia (Meryl Streep), depicting her as the ideal woman at the ideal time. On cue, Julia laughs at all of Daniel's jokes. On cue, Julia tells Daniel how wonderful she thinks he is. On cue, Julia makes Daniel feel that despite his shortcomings, he is no zero. And on cue, Julia falls in love with Daniel. In other words, she is a caricature: a plot device that functions, on the periphery, as a vehicle for heroic redemption.

In the film's final scene, Julia's love transforms Daniel into a real man. When he loses his trial, Daniel is placed on a tram bound for earth. Settling into his seat, he hears Julia crying out to him from another tram destined for heaven. Realizing that he will lose his angel forever if he doesn't do something, Daniel finally acts. He leaps out of his seat, forces open the doors to his tram, races over to Julia's tram, grabs a hold of it, and hangs on for dear life. Impressed by Daniel's newfound bravery, the higher powers in Judgement City bow to an even higher power, which, in this case, is the imperative of the narrative. Popping open the doors to Julia's tram, they allow Daniel to enter: ensuring that the hero and heroine can, in the film's final shots, heroically move on.

That these journeys are primarily heroic journeys fulfilling male needs is vividly illustrated yet again in the 1999 Hollywood romantic comedy *Blast From the Past*. Living up to its title, the movie begins, appropriately enough, with a blast from the past. At the height of the 1962 Cuban Missile Crisis, a husband and wife—erroneously believing that Los Angeles is under nuclear attack—bury themselves in their impenetrable, underground, fallout shelter. As they scurry to safety, a military training jet accidentally crashes into their house. The husband, fearing the worst, sets the time-locks on the fallout shelter, sealing him and his wife underground for thirty-five years. As it turns out, the husband doesn't seem to mind all that much. After all, he has equipped the fallout shelter with all the amenities of home—even constructed it to physically mirror, in every way, the house he left behind. A scientific genius who is also a bit of a social misfit, the husband is quite content without society. He has his adoring wife; his beautiful house, which, even replicated, contains all the comforts of home; and, after a couple of months of living underground, he acquires yet another perfect addition: his wife "presents" him with a baby boy whom they name, appropriately enough, Adam.

For the husband, basking in the warm glow of his "nuclear family," life is bliss. For the husband's wife, however, one man's bliss is another woman's hell. Stir-crazy from being cut off from the outside world, she begins to sneak nips from the bottle. Perpetually numb from the booze, she dutifully resumes her role as the good wife: endlessly doting on her child, while deferring all the major decisions to her husband who, because he is so self-centered, has no idea that his wife is perpetually numb from the booze. "The acorn does not fall very far from the tree!" the husband proudly proclaims as Adam, growing up, begins to take after his father. Adam (Brendan Fraser), however, is more interested in pollination than he is in trees. "I wish I can meet a girl," he announces to his parents.

Noting that their thirty-five years of living underground will soon be up, Adam's parents begin advising Adam on the outside world. "Go find a girl," they tell him, "one who is preferably not a mutant." And "when you do," they add, "bring her back down." So as soon as the time-locks unseal, Adam ventures forth to "find a girl who doesn't glow in the dark." Once outside, however, he quickly finds himself lost and vulnerable in post-Apocalyptic Los Angeles until, by chance, he stumbles into a woman named Eve (Alicia Silverstone).

All of this, of course, is just a prelude to the Hollywood love story, which begins here, at this point, with the chance meeting of the hero, Adam, and the heroine, Eve. And while the names Adam and Eve may evoke images of parody, the classical narrative form of the Hollywood love story, faithfully adhered to in *Blast From the Past*, manages to quickly transform any potential for parody into parable. As she is initially presented, *this* Eve is a self-described nineties woman who, in her own words, "can't keep her mouth shut." She is feisty, tough, opinionated, sexually assertive, and not afraid, from time to time, to take a swig from the bottle in public. She is, in short, everything that femininity isn't supposed to be. And the last thing that *this* Eve professes to want or need is to get involved with a brokenhearted man like Adam who desperately wants and needs a good wife who is just like his mother.

"You're like a lost puppy," Eve tells the clueless Adam. "I should've taken the money and run."

"Don't even think about it!" she later snaps at him, sensing that he is after something more serious from her than friendship. "Forget it!" she further tells Adam after he reveals how desperately he wants to get married. "Marriage bites!" But Adam, of course, can't forget it. "I fell in love with you the very moment that I saw you," he eventually confesses to Eve, who, despite her protestations, softens more and more into a leading *Lady*. By the end of the love story, Eve is not only ready, she is dying, to be the good wife. And if being the good wife also entails being a sacrificial female, the sting of that sacrifice is lessened by the revelation that Adam's father's stock portfolio from the early 1960s is worth, by 1999, tens of millions of dollars. In other words, marriage no longer bites when the brokenhearted man that needs her is, as the movie puts it, "the kindest, most polite, most incredibly rich guy" in the world. And just to show how the acorn does not fall very far from the tree, *Blast From the Past* finishes with a series of scenes that bring the acorn right back to its Oedipal roots. Fulfilling his parents' wishes, the prodigal son returns to the nest, wife in tow. Accepting his rightful inheritance, he escorts his parents out of their fallout shelter; finances the rebuilding of their old house; happily reunites with his father—both of them bursting with pride—while reclaiming, through his new wife, his old mother. And if there is still any question that the genesis of *this* Genesis is Oedipus, Eve's final lines, closing out the love story, eliminate any doubts.

"Adam says," Eve conveys in voice-over, "that this is simply how things work. First the parents take care of the children, and then the children take care of the parents." Completing her closing narration over moving images of the picture perfect family, Eve's final comments indicate, however, that although she knows better, her role as the good wife is to never let on. "Whenever Adam gives me such obviously incorrect information," Eve remarks, "I just smile, slap him on the knee, and look out the window. Why spoil his dreams? They're such wonderful dreams."

The operative word in Eve's closing narration is, of course, "his." *His* dreams. *His* stories. Earlier, I mentioned that the Hollywood romantic comedy pursuit plot and the Hollywood romantic comedy redemption plot (both variations) are the most ideologically significant of the four Hollywood romantic comedy plots; in essence, these two plots key all the love stories. To the degree that this is true, we can also conclude that most of these love stories are really stories about men's power to control and/or possess women. With the pursuit plot, that power is manifest. With the redemption plot, it's modified, relying more on subtle manipulation (including pity and guilt) than on brute force. In either case, what is ultimately defeated or marginalized in most of these love stories is female resistance to the love story.

"I know it's New Year's Eve. I know you're feeling lonely," the heroine of *When Harry Met Sally* (1989) acknowledges to the hero in that movie's climactic scene. "But you just can't show up here, tell me that you love me, and expect that to make everything all right. It just doesn't work that way!" As it turns out, however, the heroine is wrong. For that is exactly how it does work in most Hollywood romantic comedies. The hero, Harry (Billy Crystal), responds to the heroine, Sally (Meg Ryan), by listing all the wonderful things he loves about her. "You see," Sally cries, "that's just like you, Harry, you say things like that and you make it impossible for me to hate you! And I hate you, Harry. I really hate you. I hate you," she continues to cry just before her key kiss in the scene's final shot indicates that she loves him with all her heart.

The music, the words, the actions, and the outcome in the climactic scene of *When Harry Met Sally* all capture the critical role that the redemption plot plays in Hollywood romantic comedies. For what the redemption plot does in a final analysis is to make it impossible for females to hate the love story without appearing heartless. The pleasures of the narrative demand the key kiss, which, in turn, demands that the heroine doesn't have the heart to say *no*. "Marry me, Gwen, I'm lost without you," the hero, Davis (Steve Martin), begs the heroine, Gwen (Goldie Hawn), in the final scene of *Housesitter* (1992). Gwen mouths "Yes!" before leaping, in slow motion, into Davis's open arms.

"I am thinking . . . I want you," the hero, Luc (Kevin Kline), tells the heroine, Kate (Meg Ryan), in the final scene of *French Kiss* (1995). "You want me?" a grateful Kate asks. "That's all, I want you," Luc answers in the film's final exchange.

"Can I have the last dance?" the hero, Zack (Freddie Prinze, Jr.), asks the heroine, Laney (Rachael Leigh Cook), in the final scene of *She's All That* (1999). Forgiving Zack for his earlier deceptions, Laney answers: "No, you can have the first." Then just before Zack kisses her, Laney happily adds: "I feel just like Julia Roberts in *Pretty Woman*, except for that whole hooker thing."

"I need you," the hero, Billy (Kevin Costner), tells the heroine, Jane (Kelly Preston), in the final scene of *For Love of the Game* (1999). About to leave for a new job and life in London, Jane is stopped dead by his words. "I love you," Billy finally admits. "I never believed it," Jane tearfully whispers. "Believe it," Billy tearfully whispers back.

In touching love story after love story, it is this simple. And as the enduring popularity of the Hollywood romantic comedy seems to suggest, at least for now, this simplicity works.

Chapter 4

The Prick Foil Plot

Although the pursuit plot and the redemption plot (both variations) are the most ideologically significant of the four Hollywood romantic comedy plots, the third type of Hollywood romantic comedy plot, the *foil plot*, has the potential to be equally ideologically significant. But that potential is quickly quashed in most Hollywood romantic comedies. For instead of making its own ideological statements, the foil plot simply supplements the conservative ideology of the pursuit plot and the redemption plot by making sure that the "choice" it offers—adding a romantic foil into the mix—precludes any real choice.

There are four variations of the foil plot: the prick foil plot, the dweeb foil plot, the bitch foil plot, and the temptress foil plot. In the first two variations—the prick foil plot and the dweeb foil plot—the heroine has to choose between two men who love her or profess to love her. In the second two variations—the bitch foil plot and the temptress foil plot—the hero, likewise, has to choose between two women who love him or profess to love him. Although Hollywood certainly did not invent the eternal triangle along with all its propensities for conflict (confusion, betrayal, pain, grief, guilt, doubt—in short, all of the necessary combustible ingredients for ideological disruption), in the four Hollywood romantic comedy foil plots, Hollywood nevertheless has found a most effective way to contain and co-opt it.

The first variation of the Hollywood romantic comedy foil plot, the *prick foil plot*, depicts two men who are in love with or profess to be in love with the same woman. The heroine must eventually choose between the two suitors: figuring out for herself which one is the hero and which one is the prick foil. Typically, in the prick foil plot, the hero is depicted as a "regular sort of guy" who although not always in the same social class as the heroine, genuinely loves her. The prick foil, on the other hand, is typically pictured as a romantic rival who is economically and/or socially better positioned than the hero, knows it, and flaunts it. To put it another way, the heroine often gets to pick between a "down-to-earth Joe" and an "upper-class dick." And indeed, much of the popular appeal of the prick foil plot lies in watching the "upper-class dick" finally get whipped. In exploiting that particular appeal, it appears that the Hollywood romantic comedy prick foil plot challenges dominant conventions by maintaining that the real size of a man has little, if anything, to do with his social standing. But, more often than not, such class implications are merely a front with the prick foil serving as nothing but a straw man.

In other words, to focus on the hero/villain binary opposition is to miss the point. For the relationship that most counts in the prick foil plot is the relationship between the hero and the heroine, not the relationship between the hero and the prick foil. And in terms of that relationship, the prick foil plot has but one ideological function: to help out the hero by ensuring the successful completion of the pursuit plot and/or the redemption plot.[1] Consider, for example, how the prick foil plot plays right into the hands of the pursuit plot in *Crossing Delancey* (1988), helping to ensure, once again, that everybody (including the audience) knows *more than the heroine knows* about what is best for the heroine. Also consider how when the different plots begin to team up in Hollywood romantic comedies, the long-running debate over whether women do or do not have a voice in Hollywood cinema remains as unresolvable as ever. Like the tree that falls in the forest: if a woman speaks and nobody listens, does a woman speak?

"Listen to me, Bubbie," the thirty-three-year-old heroine of *Crossing Delancey* begs her grandmother early in the narrative. "I'm a happy person. I have everything . . . I have a wonderful, wonderful job . . . I know lots of famous writers and editors and publishers . . . [I] don't need a man to feel complete!" But Bubbie knows better. "She lives in a room like a dog," she observes about her granddaughter. So, out of love, Bubbie employs the services of a matchmaker to fix Isabelle (Amy Irving) up with a "good man" who happens to sell pickles for a living. "Maybe I don't want a husband," Isabelle squawks to Bubbie. "And if I did, he wouldn't be a pickle man!"

The heroine's words serve as declaration of resistance that is quickly quashed in *Crossing Delancey* by the joint conventions of the prick foil plot and the pursuit plot.[2] Before the movie is over, Isabelle will, of course, want a husband.

And before the movie is over, Isabelle will, of course, want the hero, Sam (Peter Reigert), the pickle man, to be that husband. After all, in using the prick foil plot to complete the pursuit plot, the conventional Hollywood romantic comedy is as much about quashing a woman's resistance—and women's resistance— as it is about love.

When Sam meets Isabelle, he likes what he sees. But, unfortunately for Sam, Isabelle only has eyes for Anton (Jeroen Krabbe), a self-absorbed European poet who, she feels, is more her type (i.e., he doesn't sell pickles for a living). Bubbie, however, won't be deterred; she implores Sam not to give up. "You want to catch the wild monkey," she advises, "then you got to climb the tree!" So Sam dutifully climbs. In the movie's climactic scene, Isabelle leaves Sam hanging so she can consummate her relationship with Anton. But when Anton reveals to Isabelle his idea of love—that she serve as his part-time secretary and on-call mistress—the heroine comes to realize that her prince is a prick: a bard with words who is a bastard with women. "How could I have been so stupid!" she cries to herself. "Stupid! Stupid! Stupid!"

This realization serves in *Crossing Delancey*, as it serves in most prick foil plots, to empower the hero who cannot help but shine in comparison to the prick foil. And this realization also serves in *Crossing Delancey*, as it serves in most prick foil plots, to shake the wild monkey out of the tree by getting her to fall off her high horse. In the film's final scene, Isabelle runs back to Sam, tearfully apologizes, and finally acknowledges that, yes, indeed, she needs a man, just like Sam, to feel complete. The secession enjoined, the key kiss closes out the pleasures of the pursuit plot.

Like the prick foil plot in *Crossing Delancey*, most prick foil plots force the heroine to choose between the hero and the prick foil prior to marriage; the hero, in essence, rescues the heroine from foolishly marrying the wrong person. There are a few prick foil plots, however, that begin with a heroine *already* foolishly married to a prick foil who, eventually, she has to divorce.[3] In reversing the normal flow of the narrative by beginning with a marriage and ending with a divorce, it might appear that these movies critique the institution of marriage.[4] But this reversal is only a diversion for a bunch of movies that are ideologically quite conventional, typically ending with a new suitor/hero rescuing the heroine from a bad marriage by dangling the promise of a new marriage.

Take, for example, the 1993 Hollywood remake of the 1950 classic: *Born Yesterday*. The movie opens with its dim-witted heroine, Billie (Melanie Griffith), accompanying her filthy-rich, common-law husband, Harry (John Goodman), to Washington, D.C. where, to save his real estate ventures, the prick foil has to bribe some senators. "I'm crazy about her," Harry tells his financial aide, "I'm crazy when she is not around." But having Billie around becomes a liability for Harry when her intellectual deficiencies start turning her into a laughingstock.[5] So to smarten Billie up, Harry hires Paul (Don Johnson), an investigative reporter, to tutor her. "You be nice to him or I'll crack you one!" he warns. As it turns out, however, Billie doesn't need to be coaxed. "Maybe I can teach *you* some things," she seductively whispers into Paul's ear before adding: "I've got the hots for you, right off."

Of course, in order to successfully complete the pleasures of the prick foil plot, the heroine, Billie, and the hero, Paul, will have to couple. But before they can couple, the narrative must make Billie less stupid; make Billie less of a slut; and make Billie realize that her filthy-rich husband is a prick. To these ends, *Born Yesterday* soon pictures Billie working her heart out to beef up her brains. In addition to teaching herself how to walk, talk, and dress like a *Lady*, Billie begins reading Tocqueville's *Democracy in America*. When Harry sees her with it, he bursts out laughing; Paul, in turn, sends her a dictionary and gives her some flowers. "You worked really hard to make yourself smart," Paul tells her. "But?" Billie asks. "Well, a smart person knows who she is living with," Paul notes.

With Paul's encouragement, Billie finally begins to see Harry in a new light. "You're not as big as I used to think," she tells him. When Harry then orders her to sign off on some of his business documents, Billie refuses. "Sign the papers!" he barks. "No!" she shouts. So Harry belts her. Twice. Hard. Across the face. Billie then runs to Paul who, in turn, helps her get the goods on Harry. As it turns out, he has been sheltering all of his companies in Billie's name, which means, as Paul explains to Billie: "You own him." With all the pieces finally in place, all that is left is the happy ending. Paul proposes. And Harry, trying to make up for belting Billie, also proposes. In the film's final scene, Billie announces to everybody that she is going to marry Paul because, as she puts it, "I finally smartened up." As for Harry, she orders him to pay back all of his bribes and then promises, if he is good, to give him back his companies one by one, one year at a time. "You do what I'm telling ya!" she barks at him just before, in the film's final shot, walking out the door with Paul.

Despite its feminist pretensions, *Born Yesterday* is as mean-spirited a movie as any movie in the sample, presenting an hour and a half of unabashed woman bashing followed by a five-minute lecture, at the end, telling women not to let men treat them like doormats or punching bags. But if one overlooks, for a moment, the bad dialogue, bad acting, bad pacing, and bad everything else, *Born Yesterday* also happens to be a terrific movie. For it points out, terrifically, just what is going on in the prick foil plot. And this includes a reaffirmation of the institution of marriage; a diminution of women and the women's movement; and an ingenious justification, by implication, for the perpetuation of patriarchy.

First and foremost, the prick foil plot empowers the hero. The prick foil in the prick foil plot is nothing more than a narrative device that ensures whether the hero wants the heroine (pursuit plot) or the hero needs the heroine (redemption plot), the hero gets the heroine. For the characters are caricatures: the prick foil is such a cretinous creep that the heroine's choice is essentially "no choice." The hero cannot help but shine in comparison. To get the heroine, he does not even need to actively pursue her. All he needs to do is to *be there* and to *not be the prick foil.* The narrative then takes care of the rest: handing the heroine over to the hero and, more important, ensuring that viewers "root" for the heroine to be handed over to the hero.

Second, the prick foil plot reaffirms the institution of marriage by exposing and then containing the dangers that are embedded in the eternal triangle. Simply defined, the eternal triangle is one man who is attracted to two women, or one woman who is attracted to two men, and the emotional and sexual tensions that stem from such an attraction. The story of the eternal triangle continues to resonate in our popular culture, I would argue, because most human beings have known, or will know, what it means to be torn between two lovers: either forced to choose between two people who love them (hurting one), or told by the person they love that there is someone else (getting hurt themselves). To experience the eternal triangle, then, is to know that romantic love is often problematic.

Even more specifically, it is to know that the love story itself may be problematic. For the eternal triangle calls into question the viability of marriage. As the seventeen-year-old heroine of *Manhattan* (1979) keenly observes at one point in that movie's narrative: "Maybe people weren't meant to have one deep relationship. Maybe people were meant to have a series of relationships with different links." It is an observation that the conventional Hollywood romantic comedy, of course, has to reject. For to accept the heroine's words in *Manhattan* is to accept the notion that marriage—one time, one person, for life—may be both unnatural and confining. And it is to also accept the notion that separation—as hard as it often is—may be liberating.

To deal with the problem of the eternal triangle, the Hollywood romantic comedy confronts it head-on: utilizing the prick foil plot to assure viewers that the problem is "no problem." By depicting the characters as caricatures—the prick foil as such a mean-spirited prick—the Hollywood romantic comedy is able to transform the often heart-wrenching decision of who to choose and who to reject into a "no brainer." The eternal triangle, in other words, is disentangled: its three lines rearranged into the shape of an arrow. And that arrow—pointing the heroine straight to the hero—defuses all the conflict, confusion, betrayal, pain, grief, guilt, and doubt that, in real life, often accompanies love. As for the heroine, she winds up with a nicer guy. But she still *winds up with a guy*: in essence, shifting her dependency from one man to another.

The message of the prick foil plot, then, is that there is nothing wrong with the love story and, by implication, marriage. If it doesn't work, it is because one of the partners is not working. And since it is easy to separate the good partners from the bad partners, the solution is also easy: just change partners. What is almost always excluded from the prick foil plot, however, is the possibility of a third option: that the heroine can reject both the hero and the prick foil. For to allow for that third option is to allow for the unallowable: that a woman can go through her life, or at least part of her life, with the knowledge that she doesn't need a man or marriage to feel complete. Perhaps even worse, to allow for that third option is to allow for yet a fourth option: that a woman may choose to love more than one hero at a time, to desire and enjoy what millions of men have gotten away with ever since storytellers first began telling the story of the eternal triangle—the "pleasures" of promiscuity over the "monotony" of marriage.

But in addition to reaffirming the institution of marriage, the prick foil plot also reinforces the female's status as the weaker partner in the institution of marriage and, for that matter, all institutions. For it drives home the message that women are "not very bright." Less bright, as a matter of fact, than the average five year old. For when you strip down the Hollywood romantic comedy prick foil plot to its basics, it is essentially nothing more than a lengthier, slightly more sophisticated version of the old "Popeye the Sailor" cartoon. Once incorporated into a Hollywood romantic comedy such as *Crossing Delancey* or *Born Yesterday*, the cartoon plot line then becomes a narrative declaration with political overtones: females are inherently fickle and, more important, they aren't very smart. For as any five year old who has watched more than one episode of "Popeye" knows, the villain is no good. And yet in prick foil plot after prick foil plot, it takes the heroine nearly the entire movie to figure out what most preschoolers watching the cartoon version figure out in five minutes: to reject the prick foil.

How this cartoon typically plays out in Hollywood romantic comedies is anything but cartoonish in its social, economic, and political ramifications. Consider, for example, the actions of the heroine in the 1998 Hollywood romantic comedy hit *The Wedding Singer*. As pictured in the movie, the heroine, Julia (Drew Barrymore), may very well be the sweetest, kindest, nicest catch in the world, but she is only getting married because her mother warns her: "You've got to marry before your hips start spreading and you get facial hair." Never mind that she is barely into her twenties. And never mind that the guy she is marrying is a loud lout that treats her like an old sow. With Julia's smarts or, rather, lack of smarts, she deserves such humiliation. After all, it takes her the entire movie to figure out what is telegraphed in the movie's first few scenes: to forget the prick foil and get on, already, with the task of saving Robbie (Adam Sandler): a down-in-the-dumps wedding singer who desperately wants to wed the perfect female partner. As scripted, she will have to save the brokenhearted hero, which she finally does, through sweetness and kindness because, pardon the mixed metaphor, she doesn't have a brain to stand on.

Time and time again, the prick foil plot relies on this dumbing down to present its vision of the perfect female partner as pretty and pretty stupid. She may be a dim-witted waitress, as in *The Wedding Singer*. Or on the other end of the status strata, the heroine may be a female psychologist with a Ph.D., as in the 1996 Hollywood romantic comedy/sports movie *Tin Cup*. But whether she is a waitress or a doctor, the bottom line is still the same: to reduce the political and sexual threat of a female with brains and beauty, the prick foil plot eliminates the brains, thereby turning the beauty into an object of ridicule. It is no accident, for example, that the adult female psychologist in *Tin Cup* is transformed in the course of the love story from a strong-minded woman into a mindless cheerleader whose triumphs are limited, by the end of the love story, to her boyfriend's triumphs. As the film opens, Roy (Kevin Costner), the brokenhearted hero of the movie, is introduced as an aging, beaten, part-time golf instructor who, stuck in the middle of the Texas desert, spends his days guzzling beers, goofing on buddies, and gazing at armadillos. He desperately needs a redemptive heroine and so, enter Molly (Rene Russo). She is initially pictured as the picture of perfection: beautiful, successful, confident, and in charge. She is also in need of golf lessons to keep up with her current boyfriend, David (Don Johnson), a famous golf pro and infamous prick who was once Roy's biggest golf rival. A woman with wit—and a whiz with words—Molly is more than a match for Roy who, from the moment he sees her, sees her as the solution to his "really fucked up" existence. "I'm chock full of demons," Roy tells Molly, explaining how he ended up stuck in the middle of nowhere. "You're chock full of bullshit," Molly fires back—seeing right through him, which, in turn, makes the brokenhearted hero even more brokenhearted. Hopelessly in love with a "doctor lady" who is way out of his league, Roy quickly realizes that as things stand, any pursuit on his part is doomed to failure. So it is up to the narrative, then, to change the way things stand. To empower Roy. To belittle Molly. To restore the natural order in which femininity, once again, is subordinated to masculinity.

Tin Cup's solution is simple. For a few seconds, in a key scene, it lets its heroine talk about *her* feelings—to reveal a bit about herself. In the parlance of film theory, it gives her a "voice." And then it has its heroine use that voice against herself to communicate how utterly unimportant and, therefore, easily attainable she really is. "I'm a terrible shrink . . . I should have never gotten out of real estate. Actually, I should have never left Ohio for that cowboy in Amarillo," Molly babbles to Roy after he unexpectedly shows up at her office, requests psychological treatment, and confesses that he thinks he may be in love with her. "Fuck, I'm certifiable!" she continues to blabber, tearfully adding how she only became a "shrink" because she "needed a new gig." So to empower its lead male, *Tin Cup* turns on its lead female—turning her years of hard work in earning a doctorate and establishing a profession into a gig and a gag. From this point on, Roy's pursuit of the "doctor lady," now reduced to a "neurotic nut," is easy. And it is made even easier by the heroine's mindless devotion to a prick foil who, every chance he gets, further exposes her gullibility. By the time Molly finally gets around to realizing that the prick foil is, indeed, a prick, she has lost all credibility. On the other hand, she has found "a new gig": loving Roy. Meanwhile, Roy—cheered on by Molly—is eventually boosted into superstardom: scoring with the "doctor lady of his dreams" and, in the film's climactic scene, making a one-in-a-million golf shot in front of a national television audience on the final hole of the U.S. Open.

Just two years after mollifying Molly, the dumbing down of a female doctor occurs yet again—with a vengeance, times three—in the riotous Hollywood romantic comedy blockbuster *There's Something About Mary* (1998). Unlike *Tin Cup*, however, *There's Something About Mary* at least serves up a smorgasbord of stupidity: a heroine pursued by a hero and *three* prick foils who are all equally stupid. But while *There's Something About Mary* may be even-handed in its celebration of stupidity, there is nothing equal about the reasons for, and the effects of, the portrayal of that stupidity. For the hero of the love story, Ted (Ben Stiller), his desperate stupidity serves only to make him all the more sympathetic—all the more human. From the moment the dopey dip gets his dick caught in his zipper in the film's first of many hilarious sequences, Ted is the proverbial "every guy" who has ever been struck speechless by the sight of a sexy siren—who has ever been reduced into a mass of mush by a flash of female flesh. His every imperfection serves only to make him all the more lovable; he is a loser, all right, but he is a loser in a script with a purpose: to transform him into a winner by handing him the most perfect of all perfect women.

For the heroine of the love story, Mary (Cameron Diaz), on the other hand, her clueless stupidity matched by her drop-dead gorgeous looks serve only to dehumanize her. She is a male adolescent's dream in a male adolescent's wish fulfillment fantasy: even sweeter and kinder than Julia in *The Wedding Singer*, and twice as "sexually delicious" as Molly in *Tin Cup*. Mary is, in short, the girl who "every guy" dreams of and no girl can ever be. As long as she stays perfect (i.e., never gets old; never gets any blemishes; never talks back or, for that matter, talks at all—in essence, never does anything, or has anything happen to her, that can spoil her perfection)—she will be desirable. As a dream, she is ephemeral as a dream. Never allowed to develop into a real person, she is but a picture who, like all pictures of sexually posed sexual females, exists to be taken out; looked at; shown off; passed around; slobbered over; masturbated to; put aside;

and then taken out again, as necessary, to serve "every guy's" wants and/or needs.

This excess of female sexual desirability, of course, poses a problem for the hero in the narrative just as it often does for males in real life. After all, how does a "dopey dip" like Ted get such a sexually desirable heroine and, even if he does get her, how does he keep her? Or, to put it another way, how does a guy with nothing to offer (no profession, no money, no brains, no looks) continue to possess the one woman that "every guy" wants? So to ensure that the heroine has no choice in the matter, the movie consistently depicts her as too stupid to realize that the *something* in *There's Something About Mary* that every man in the movie desires is her body. She is pictured as so sweet, so kind, and *so* clueless that, as scripted, there is no way she ever would—or could—use the sexual power that she holds over men against the hero or, for that matter, the male viewer. The sexual threat is thus contained. Once again, then, the prick foil plot's depiction of the perfect female as pretty and pretty stupid furthers the female's initial objectification; in this case, by taking the emphasis off of her as a person (who just happens to be drop-dead gorgeous) with a mind and will of her own, and placing it, instead, on her "to-be-looked-at-ness," with enough upskirt and downshirt shots sprinkled about to arouse even the deadest of male libidos.

How stupid is the heroine in *There's Something About Mary?* As it turns out, so stupid that she can't figure out that one of the prick foils pursuing her is really a sleazeball who, after every lie, laughs at how easy it is to lie to her. So stupid that she can't figure out that another one of the prick foils pursuing her—a crippled architect whom she refers to as her dearest friend—is really a pizza delivery boy who has been pretending to be a crippled architect in order to scheme his way into her pants. So stupid that she can't figure out that yet another one of the prick foils pursuing her is her old college boyfriend—a nervous twit who, lurking in the background, has been sabotaging the other two prick foils in the hopes of also getting into her pants. And so stupid that she can't figure out that the hero, the one pursuer who is supposedly more interested in her than in her pants, is also obsessed with getting into her pants (even if he is, himself, too stupid to realize it).

Adding to all of this stupidity is the fact that the heroine is supposed to be a doctor (connoting economic power, as well as brainpower). But, as scripted, the heroine is a doctor (an orthopedic surgeon, no less) who cannot tell the difference between a crippled architect and a pizza delivery boy posing as a crippled architect. And she is a doctor who, in one of the film's funniest sequences, doesn't know the difference between a glob of hair gel and a glob of semen; totally clueless, she gleefully runs the gook through her hair, only to be pictured, in the next scene, with her bangs spiking stiffly up into the air. It is that picture, then, of the sexually delicious heroine with her bangs spiking stiffly in the air,

A clueless Cameron Diaz shows off her funky new hairdo in
There's Something About Mary. Courtesy of Photofest.

that is frozen for all time: adorning every advertisement, poster, and billboard for the film coast to coast and, indeed, around the world.

In all fairness, it must be noted that, as comedy, *There's Something About Mary* works. The movie has a wonderful sense of the ridiculous—playing, at times, more like a parody of a love story than a love story. And, indeed, there is room for reading rebelliousness, even ideological resistance, into the film's funniest sequences. But there is also a cruel undercurrent that undercuts much of that ideological resistance. For the narrative is still presented classically enough to ensure that viewers never forget that, despite the many bits of slapstick, *There's Something About Mary* is still very much a love story. Consistently told from the hero's point of view, the love story is, of course, the hero's love story, which, obsessed with the heroine, could care less about the heroine. For all that she represents, the heroine could be a blow-up sex doll. Never more than a projection of the hero's wants, needs, and desires, she is merely a conduit. Her wants, needs, and desires never matter.

Just how much they do not matter is revealed in a telling sequence late in the movie when, thirteen years after Ted's first date with Mary ends prematurely in zipper trouble, he finally gets his second chance: another big date with Mary. After dinner, they begin to catch up on the lost years. Ted, as usual, talks about Ted. And then it is Mary's turn to talk about herself: what *she* wants, needs, and desires. So she begins to tell Ted (and viewers) one of her love stories about a guy she once loved and, sadly, lost. One sentence into her story, however, the movie quickly cuts her off: cutting away from Mary to show, on the other side of town, two of the three prick foils throwing chunks of raw meat, laced with speed, at Mary's pet pooch in yet another dopey attempt to eventually get into Mary's pants. With the dog drugged and the diversion over, the movie finally cuts back to Mary just in time to catch her telling Ted (and viewers): "That's the end of the story."

As it turns out, the love story that Mary tells Ted and nobody hears is linked to another joke at the end of the movie. There is yet one more man after Mary: an ex-fiancé who is also a famous football player. That she chooses Ted over the football player in the film's final shots is, of course, dictated by conventions: what better way to cap off an adolescent's wish fulfillment fantasy than to not only have him get the most sexually desirable girl in the school, but to also beat out the star quarterback in the process? Still—and this is critically important—there is no reason why the film had to cut off Mary when it did. She could have easily been allowed to tell the audience her love story—honestly revealing her feelings—without necessarily revealing the punch line. But then, again, she couldn't. Because this would allow viewers, in turn, to get to know her as a real person, a subjective human being, and make it harder for them to rationalize using her as a sexual projection. Far better, then, to show the heroine off (and get off on showing her off) as a clueless bimbo or, as one of the prick foils refers to her: "a dumb shit."

And here, then, is the true symbolic significance of the prick foil plot as it plays out time and time again in conventional Hollywood romantic comedies. Like the dominant culture that it reflects and reinforces, all too often, it can barely contain its hostility toward women. Often combined with the brokenhearted redemption plot, the heroine has but one role in life: to emotionally serve the brokenhearted hero. And if one is to believe the narrative—that women are, indeed, this stupid—then the political implications, too, become a no-brainer. Heroines need the benevolence of heroes just as women need the benevolence of patriarchy to protect them from themselves.

Chapter 5

The Dweeb Foil Plot

The second type of Hollywood romantic comedy foil plot, the *dweeb foil plot*, serves many of the same ideological functions as the prick foil plot. Among other things, it empowers the hero. It ensures the successful completion of the pursuit plot and/or the redemption plot. It exposes and then contains the dangers embedded in the eternal triangle. It reaffirms the institution of marriage. It ridicules the fickle female. And it drills home, once again, the notion that women are, at the very least, a bit dim-witted.

Like the prick foil plot, the dweeb foil plot forces the heroine to choose between two men who love her or profess to love her. But instead of pitting the hero against a mean-spirited prick, the narrative, this time, pits the hero against a romantic foil who is such a dweeb—such a pinhead—such a schmo—that the heroine's choice, once again, is "no choice." Once again, the hero cannot help but shine in comparison. And once again, the audience—for most of the movie—knows more than the heroine knows about what most five year olds are able to figure out in five minutes: to reject the dweeb foil. The poor schnook, in the end, doesn't stand a chance since, simply put, the guy is all woo and no wow.

For example, as detailed earlier, the hero in *L.A. Story* is aided in his pursuit of the heroine by the "hand of God," which, through the medium of an electronic freeway sign, changes the weather, stops the heroine's plane from taking off, and brings the fleeing heroine back to him for the key kiss. But the hero in

L.A. Story is equally aided in his pursuit of the heroine by the injection into the narrative of a dweeb foil who, in *L.A. Story*, turns out to be the heroine's ex-husband: a geek named Roland who is so desperate to win his ex-wife back that he vows to cook for her and sew for her. When Roland finally gets around to kissing her, the poor dope makes the mistake of asking: "Well, how was that?" The heroine, giggling, offers: "It was very nice, thank you." Despite the heroine's underwhelming response, it nevertheless takes the dweeb foil and, for that matter, the heroine, nearly the rest of the movie to figure out what the hero and audience already know: whenever a woman describes a man, or his kiss, as "very nice" in a Hollywood romantic comedy, it is the kiss of death.

In *Moonstruck*, the hero is a "wolf" who wants the heroine. But also, as detailed earlier, he is a tortured soul who needs the heroine as much as he wants her. The heroine, because she is not heartless, has no choice but to surrender to the imperatives of the pursuit plot and the coldhearted redemption plot. To ensure, however, that the audience roots for that surrender, *Moonstruck* also adds a dweeb foil plot: initially picturing the heroine as romantically involved with a drip named Johnny who, even though he is in his forties, won't even think about getting married until after his dying mother in Sicily kicks the bucket. When it looks like the old bat is finally going to croak, Johnny gives the heroine an engagement ring, then flies to Sicily to be with momma (the old bat, as it turns out, makes a miraculous recovery). Meanwhile, back home, the heroine finally meets the hero who quickly proceeds to wow her in the bedroom; woo at the opera; and, for an encore, wow her again in the bedroom. By the time the dweeb foil finally returns at the end of the movie to announce that he can't marry the heroine (momma, after all, is still kicking), is it any wonder that nobody—least of all the heroine—really cares?

In *Doc Hollywood*, the hero has no problem winning his bet: separating the heroine from her panties. For his competition in the love story is a hayseed named Hank who, besides wearing slacks hiked up to his armpits, views the institution of marriage as an opportunity "to build equity in a future that has security." As the hero aptly mocks when the heroine describes Hank as decent and solid: "Very romantic."

In *Seems Like Old Times* (1980), the hero is the heroine's ex-husband, a loveable cad who vows to win the heroine back from her current husband: yet another poor schnook who doesn't stand a chance. "I love Ira. I have never been more content," the heroine tells the hero. "Content isn't excitement, content is content," the hero snaps back. One scene later, the heroine—choosing the loveable cad—manages to dump the dork.

In *Sleepless in Seattle* the heroine is engaged to a wimp named Walter who, as it turns out, has all of the charisma of a carrot. "It's destiny," she tells her mother, trying on her wedding gown. The gown rips. A few minutes later, the heroine only has to hear the sound of the hero's voice on the radio without even meeting him to realize that her "Mr. Right" is all wrong. When she finally gets around to telling the dweeb foil that there is "someone else," his response can only be described as the equivalent of: "Aw, shucks." As the hero of *Doc Hollywood* would put it: "Very romantic."

In *"Crocodile" Dundee* (1986), the dweeb foil is a supercilious snoot named Richard who is actually stupid enough to try to show up the hero in front of the heroine by tricking him into ordering from a menu that is written in Italian. The hero, answering the challenge, first diverts everyone's attention, and then punches the daylights out of the dumb schmuck. "You're not serious about this lemon?" he asks the heroine, nodding toward the unconscious dweeb foil. She tells the hero to "butt out!" By the end of the film, however, it is the lemon, not the hero, who is squeezed out of the picture.

In *French Kiss* (1995), the dweeb foil is a chump named Charlie. When the hero, trying to check out his competition, asks the heroine to tell him what it felt like when she first met Charlie, the heroine struggles for just the right words. "It wasn't exactly a thunderclap or lightning bolt," she imparts. "It was more like . . . like . . . like . . ." The hero, sensing her struggle, tries to help her. "Drizzle?" he offers. By the end of the movie, the right words come a lot easier for the heroine. "Sorry Charlie," she tells Charlie.

In *Six Days, Seven Nights* (1998), the dweeb foil is a whiny crybaby named Frank who is ready to kiss off his fiancée after she is lost at sea for six days and seven nights with a pilot named Quinn Harris—a "man's man" who, as played by Harrison Ford, is a dead ringer for the hero of all heroes: Indiana Jones. Faced, then, with a choice between a man or a mouse, the mouse gets the cheese while the heroine takes the ham.

In *Runaway Bride* (1999), the dweeb foil is a dull dud named Coach Bob (need we say more) who keeps giving the heroine visualizing exercises. "Visualize the end zone," he suggests in an effort to help the heroine get over her fear of marriage. "Visualize the ceremony," he further suggests at their wedding rehearsal, while asking the hero to stand in for him. With Coach Bob watching from the sidelines, the heroine first visualizes, and then French kisses the hero, kissing off Coach Bob.

The common thread in every one of these Hollywood romantic comedies is that the contest is, in the end, "no contest." Once again, the characters are caricatures: the dweeb foil, such a passionless pinhead that the hero—simply by virtue of not being the dweeb foil—winds up winning the heroine. Once again, the problem of the eternal triangle is pictured as "no problem." Once again, if the love story doesn't work, the solution is simple: just change partners. And once again, any female resistance toward the hero, the role, and/or the love story, is neutralized and nullified.

Chapter 6

The Bitch Foil Plot

Both the prick foil plot and the dweeb foil plot empower the hero, helping to ensure completion of the pursuit and/or the redemption plot. The final two Hollywood romantic comedy foil plots—the bitch foil plot and the temptress foil plot—reverse the eternal triangle: forcing the hero, rather than the heroine, to choose between two potential lovers. In so doing, both plots deify the good wife while defining as deviant any woman who does not live up to the idealized image of the good wife. And if it takes a healthy dose of women-bashing to drive home the message that there are only two kinds of girls—good girls and bad girls—then the message in both plots seems to be: bash away.

Of the two plots, the *bitch foil plot* is the most direct in its hostility toward women: pitting female against female in order to attack females. Consider, for example, the battle between the two female leads in the 1988 Hollywood romantic comedy hit *Working Girl*. As first depicted, the movie's heroine, Tess (Melanie Griffith), is a squeaky-voiced secretary with smart business ideas and a stupid-looking hairdo. When she is assigned to work for Katherine (Sigourney Weaver), a high-powered executive with stupid business ideas and a smart-looking hairdo, she is initially tentative. But when Katherine promises to teach Tess everything she needs to know to make it in a man's world and, on top of that, to listen to Tess's business ideas, *Working Girl*'s heroine can barely contain her enthusiasm. "It's so exciting," Tess exclaims. "She takes me seriously. And I think it's because she is a woman. There is none of the chasing around the desk crap. And it's like she wants to be my mentor, which is exactly what I needed."

Tess's bubble quickly bursts, however, when she discovers that Katherine is scheming to steal one of her smart business ideas. To get even, she poses as a corporate executive; teams up with Katherine's boyfriend, Jack (Harrison Ford); and works to turn her smart business idea into a done deal. In no time, the heroine, Tess, and the hero, Jack, begin clicking both on and off the job. When Katherine finally finds out what is going on, she storms into a critical executive meeting, exposes Tess as a fraud, and stakes her claim to Jack. In the movie's climactic scene, Jack is forced to choose between the kindhearted secretary with the squeaky voice or the bitch boss from hell.[1] Jack, of course, chooses Tess while Katherine ends up getting "the boot, but good." Using the exact words that the heroine, a few minutes earlier, directs at the bitch foil, Katherine's male boss (there are limits, after all, to how high up the corporate ladder an ambitious woman, even one with really great hair, can climb) orders Katherine to: "Get your bony ass out of my sight!" As she slinks out the door, one can almost hear the Munchkins from *The Wizard of Oz* singing: *Ding dong, the wicked witch is dead.*

With Katherine gone, Tess gets promoted to an executive position. Capping off the love story, the second to last scene in *Working Girl* depicts Jack presenting Tess with a lunch box, celebrating Tess's status as a working girl, while telling her to "make sure you're home before dark," signifying that even a working girl is not an independent woman. The final scene in *Working Girl* pictures Tess—cheered on by all the secretaries that she used to work with—making her triumphant entrance into her new office equipped, as it turns out, with her very own secretary. Like the ending of the love story, the heroine's final heroic entrance is full of mixed messages. For Tess's transformation from dreamy-eyed secretary to self-assured boss is more than matched by Katherine's transformation from self-assured boss to unemployed bitch. And while Tess's triumph can be interpreted as a victory for working girls, Katherine's humiliation can also be read as a defeat for working women who, playing in a man's world by men's rules, have the balls to try to make it to the top.

As the award-winning author and journalist Susan Faludi points out in her own critical reading of *Working Girl*, rather than truly supporting the women's movement, the movie simply co-opts it: wrapping its feminist tidbits around a conventional narrative that, appearing to challenge patriarchy, renders all significant challenges to patriarchy impotent.[2] In the conventional narrative, after all, the female mentor *must* be turned into a monster because the perpetuation of patriarchy demands the dissolution of sisterhood. The bitch foil plot contributes to that dissolution, suggesting that it is impossible for two women like Tess and Katherine to ever team up. For women are, by nature, predatory rivals. Without men around to separate them, they would cut one another to pieces. Once again, then, we have yet another narrative that leads to the same dead-end: heroines need the benevolence of heroes, just as women need the benevolence of patriarchy, to protect them from themselves. And once again, then, we have yet another plot that is a ploy. In turning the love story into a hate story, the Hollywood romantic comedy bitch foil plot works to ensure that whatever legitimate resentment, anger, and hatred women may feel toward patriarchy—including "the chasing around the desk crap"—is safely channeled toward other women.

Of course, *Working Girl* is certainly not alone in attacking women by having them attack each other. For example, the theme of female rivalry also keys the 1992 Hollywood romantic comedy *Housesitter*, which manages to deftly combine a pursuit plot, brokenhearted redemption plot, and bitch foil plot. In so doing, the movie reaffirms the role of the deferential female while reinforcing the message that a real man, if he is determined enough, can always win the woman he wants. He just needs to be sure that she is worth winning. In other words, he needs to be certain that she is the good wife who will support, nurture, and love him rather than the bitch foil who will emasculate him. The opposition between the good wife and the bitch foil powers *Housesitter*'s ideological construction of femininity by dividing women into two categories: those who defer and those who do not. Furthermore, by depicting its two leading female characters as caricatures of good and evil, *Housesitter* positions its viewers to identify with female deference over female defiance. Or, to put it another way, *Housesitter* positions its viewers to experience pleasure in watching an ambitious bitch foil get her ambitious ass kicked in by a kindhearted heroine whose ambitions, from the beginning, are limited to acquiring a husband and a house.

In the movie's opening scene, the hero, Davis (Steve Martin) has just finished building his dream house for Becky (Dana Delaney), the woman he desperately wants. "I have loved you since the ninth grade," he tells Becky. "Will you marry me?" But Becky turns him down. Heartbroken, Davis flees to New York City where he meets Gwen (Goldie Hawn), a waitress. "I'm stuck where I am, I can't change things," Davis whines to her. As it turns out, however, Davis won't have to change things; he has already found, in Gwen, the redemptive heroine who will change things for him. For unlike the bitch foil, Gwen is willing to love him for no other reason than he needs her to love him. "You're interesting, you're so average," Gwen tells Davis just before inviting him into her bed and giving him, in their first night together, what Becky has denied him for over twenty-five years. The sexual consummation, early in the narrative, is critical. For it defuses any and all sexual tensions between the hero and the heroine while constructing an opposition between a de-sexed Gwen, as love object, and Becky, as sex object. That opposition, in turn, serves to dictate the role of the love object, that is, to save the hero from the sex object.

In the course of the narrative, Gwen sneaks into Davis's dream house and—while he continues to recover out of town—pretends to be Davis's brand new wife; builds him up in Becky's eyes; and transforms him into a local hero through a bunch of lies about how successful he has become in New York City. When Davis finally returns to discover Gwen living in his house and posing as his wife, he is so excited about his sudden celebrity status that he agrees to continue the charade for as long as it takes to win Becky. "I didn't want to marry a dreamer," Becky confides to him. "But what I see through Gwen's eyes, you look very different to me . . . I can see how a dreamer with someone who believes in him can do great things."

As Gwen works her heart out to turn Davis into a real success, Becky schemes to get him back. First, she *almost* lets him make love to her. And then, at the last second, when he is already on top of her, she tells him that she can't allow him to do it; she won't be the one to ruin his marriage. Her message to Davis, of course, is clear: you can have me—and it—as soon as you get rid of the other woman. In the film's climactic scene, Davis is finally forced to choose: the redemptive heroine or the gold digger? But when he can't make up his mind, a sobbing Gwen chooses on her own to go. "I'm the one who found him," she tells Becky with Davis looking on. "And I'm the one who knows what he is worth, and you're the stuck-up one he wants!" As Gwen leaves, the camera—reinforcing the theme of female rivalry—cuts to a shot of a smirking Becky watching her go. Then staking her claim, Becky immediately moves in: sympathetically wrapping her arms around the dejected Davis. But Davis, just as quickly, ends up wiping the smirk off of Becky's face by finally realizing, after twenty-five years of sexual emasculation, it's time to ditch the bitch foil. The heroic action, of course, is forced. For once the sexual female is won, she is no longer worth winning. And once the redemptive heroine is lost, life is no longer worth living. Closing out the pleasures of the love story, Davis rejects Becky, chases after Gwen, catches up to her just as she is about to board a bus, apologizes, and proposes. "Marry me, Gwen, I'm lost without you," he begs. Gwen's answer—"Yes!"—is also forced. For the key kiss that follows, affirming the heroine's love, reaffirms another recurring theme in Hollywood romantic comedies. The good wife is, always, a forgiving wife.

Whether it occurs in *Working Girl* or *Housesitter* or, for that matter, any other Hollywood romantic comedy that includes a bitch foil plot, the "bitch-bashing" is a form of women-bashing. The mere word, of course, equates females with animals. And the fact that so many Hollywood romantic comedies use the word against their female characters and, more important, have their female characters use the word against each other, works to suggest that there are only two kinds of women: nice women and not nice women. Furthermore, it works to suggest that any woman who is not nice deserves what she gets: to be treated and punished like a dog. Finally, and perhaps most important, it works to suggest that male oppression is mostly a myth. To the contrary, women are women's worst enemies: females despising other females and, in the process, despising themselves.

But the bitch foil plot often does more than just exacerbate the theme of female rivalry. It also ensures that even when a bitch foil has something significant to say about the sometimes sorry state of gender relations in our society, nobody will listen to her. Her words will have no meaning. Her discontent will be discounted. Her voice will be silenced even as she shouts. Listen carefully, for example, to the words of the bitch foil in a key exchange between the hero and her in the Hollywood romantic comedy blockbuster *Jerry Maguire*. And then consider how easily the movie is able to turn the bitch foil's words against her. Furthermore, consider how the only way to hear—really hear—what the bitch foil is saying is to see her side of the story. And finally consider how hard it is to see her side of the story since *Jerry Maguire* is a movie about, well, Jerry Maguire.

"*It's all about you, isn't it?*" the bitch foil (Kelly Preston) rails at the hero, Jerry Maguire, when he turns to her for emotional support after losing his job and his star recruit. "*Soothe me! Save me! Love me!*" Continuing to vent, the bitch foil declares: "There is a sensitivity thing that some people have. I don't have it. I don't cry at movies! I don't gush over babies! I don't start celebrating Christmas five months early! And I don't tell a man who just screwed up both our lives 'oh, poor baby!' That's me, for better or worse."

In response to her tirade, the hero tells the bitch foil that their relationship is over. And to ensure that viewers sympathize with the hero and not the bitch foil, *Jerry Maguire* has the bitch foil respond to his response by informing him that "nobody dumps me," punching him in the nose, kicking him in the groin, screaming out "I'm too strong for you," and calling him "a loser!" As the bitch foil storms off the set leaving the hero to lick his wounds (as well as to find a good wife to lick his wounds for him), the underlying message is, of course, "good riddance!" That good riddance, in turn, completes what *Jerry Maguire* began in the bitch foil's very first scene when it introduced her to viewers as a sex-crazed nymphomaniac, butt naked, riding the hero like a horse at the Kentucky Derby, while shouting out at the top of her lungs: "Don't ever stop fucking me!" With two strikes against her—that she is an economically and sexually aggressive female—the bitch foil is sent packing. Defined by what she is not, she is cast as a bitch foil because she is not a lap dog. Lost in the bitch foil's good riddance, however, is the part of her that is most threatening. And that is her refusal to co-star in a narrative, ending with marriage, that is all about satisfying someone else's needs: soothing him, saving him, loving him.

An economically and sexually aggressive Kelly Preston turns out to be "too much"
for Tom Cruise in *Jerry Maguire*. Courtesy of Photofest.

Chapter 7

The Temptress Foil Plot

The way that bitch foils are consistently humiliated and/or punished in Hollywood romantic comedies points to a sense of something deeper going on than simple women-bashing. That "sense of something," which for the most part, so far, has only been alluded to, is exposed by the fourth and final type of Hollywood romantic comedy foil plot: the *temptress foil plot*. For it reveals how much the threat of female sexuality often drives the Hollywood romantic comedy. As a matter of fact, the genre is often obsessed with the threat of female sexuality. And along with that obsession, threading its way through the various narratives, is a warning for males. Simply stated: men who cannot control their erections cannot control their women.

Typically, the Hollywood romantic comedy deals with the threat of female sexuality in one of three ways. First, and most common, it introduces its heroine right from the beginning as a love object. Throughout the entire movie, she is pictured as sweet, kind, chaste, and, of course, conservatively clothed. Her role is to save the hero, not excite him. To that end, the camera emphasizes what film scholar James Conlon refers to as an Apollonian lust: "the safe and giving warmth of her, not a purging heat; her body as a home, not an adventure."[1] The second way that the Hollywood romantic comedy deals with the threat of female sexuality is to initially introduce its heroine as a sexually desirable female only to transform her in the course of the narrative from a sex object to a love object. By the end of the movie, she, too, is pictured as sweet, kind, chaste, and, of course, conservatively clothed.[2] The third, and final way, that the Hollywood romantic comedy deals with the threat of female sexuality is by employing the temptress foil plot. This involves hiding its heroine early in the narrative while focusing attention, instead, on a more sexually desirable female (i.e., the temptress) as a foil. Then after the narrative exposes that sexually desirable female as pitiful, pathetic, and once violated, anti-climactic, it entails refocusing attention on the heroine who, stepping forward, gets to assert herself as the good wife.[3]

Of the three ways that the Hollywood romantic comedy typically deals with the threat of female sexuality, the temptress foil plot provides the most direct assault; it not only rips opens the Pandora's box of female sexuality, it blows it apart. Consider, for example, how effectively the following two movies—*"10"* and *The Woman in Red*—combine the temptress foil plot with the pursuit plot and the coldhearted redemption plot to destroy the sexually desirable female, reaffirm the good wife, and reassert male control. In the opening scene of the 1979 Hollywood romantic comedy blockbuster *"10,"* the hero seems to have everything that any man could ever want: he is rich; he is successful; and he has a girlfriend who, in addition to looking just like Julie Andrews, absolutely adores him. But with all that George (Dudley Moore) has, it isn't enough. As in most redemption plots, something is missing. Something has been missed. "I feel betrayed," George moans to his girlfriend, Sam (Julie Andrews), when she asks him how he feels about turning forty-two years old. "I feel confused," he confides to his psychiatrist who suggests that his fixation on younger women may be related to his fear of death. George's answer to his midlife crisis is to spend most of his time getting drunk and peering through his telescope at naked young girls. Then driving around town one afternoon, George spots Jenny (Bo Derek) riding in a limousine. She is wearing a wedding veil, on her way to her wedding. And what George sees—what the camera shows—is the epitome of female contradiction: the bride as both a virginal angel and a sex-teasing whore. Capturing the enigmatic threat of the sexually desirable female, the visual codes embedded in that first shot (a slow-motion, soft-focus, close-up of Jenny's face and, in particular, her icy blue eyes coyly gazing into the camera in order to look both interested and disinterested at George) key all that follows in *"10."* For it is clear from the moment that Jenny's face, and later her body, steals the picture, that Jenny is a function, not a character, a come-on whose sole purpose is to tease George while, at the same time, arouse the "male gaze" in a way that Sam (the very name, sexually nonthreatening) can never arouse. From the moment that George spots Jenny, he is turned on. And to the degree that the male viewer is an extension of the hero, the male viewer is also turned

As the object of intense sexual desire, a "dangerous" Bo Derek must be properly dispensed with in *"10."* Courtesy of Photofest.

on. From the moment of that turn-on, the narrative has one, and only one, job to do: to find a way turn off the turn-on in order to reassert male control.

Bewitched by Jenny's face—helpless in the face of Jenny's sexual power—George tails her limousine and, distracted, plows right into the back of a parked police cruiser. After getting his ticket, he walks into Jenny's church; watches her get married; finds out where she is honeymooning; follows her to Mexico; accidentally rescues her husband from drowning and, while her husband is recuperating in the hospital, invites Jenny to dinner. After dinner, Jenny invites George up to her room so the two of them can, in her words, "fuck to 'Bolero.'" The temptress's sexual invitation more than halfway through *"10"* completes the pleasures of the pursuit plot. But just before the hero and temptress are able to sexually consummate, the narrative ensures that everything goes wrong. Jenny's hair winds up in George's mouth. The record needle gets stuck. Jenny's husband calls from the hospital. As George lies naked beside Jenny, she chats with her husband and then casually hands the phone over to George, telling him to say hello to her "old man." All the comedic action in the sex scene serves to defuse Jenny's sexual power. For once *"10"* gives its sexual vision a voice—in other words, lets the temptress speak—it exposes it/her as a fraud. "I thought you were something different, something special," George sadly whispers to Jenny after he finishes saying "hello to her old man." Then realizing that all Jenny sees in him is a one-night stand, George decides that she isn't good enough for him. He bolts for the door. The camera cuts from a long shot of George slipping out of the room to a full shot of Jenny's nude body lying in the bed to a medium shot of Sam, hundreds of miles away, fully dressed in a Victorian costume, on stage, singing her heart out.

Shots signify, cuts accentuate, and telephones don't just ring in movies, they ring for a reason. The ringing telephone in *"10"* serves as a plot device that enables the hero to pull out at the very last second: deflating the threat of female sexuality. The three plots work together brilliantly in *"10"* to restore male mastery over female mystery. First, by focusing on the pursuit plot, *"10"* enables the hero (and the male viewer) to sexually get off on stalking, stripping, and screwing the sexually desirable female who, as it turns out, is an easy lay. She is, in the end, nothing more than the sexually unattainable that in patriarchy is ultimately all too attainable. And second, by shifting the focus toward the end of the movie from the pursuit plot to the coldhearted redemption plot, *"10"* ensures that the hero gets to pull out just before sexually climaxing, an act that restores male control while reducing the sexually controlling female into a no/thing. Or, to put it another way, the deep structure of the two plots combining with the temptress foil plot work to transform the bombshell into a bimbo so the hero (and the male viewer) can fully concentrate on the far less threatening good wife waiting in the wings.

With Jenny's sexual hold over George finally broken, it is time for George to return to Sam. And all Sam has to do to complete the pleasures of the coldhearted redemption plot is accept George's apology, which, being a true heroine, she eventually does. In the film's final scene, George asks Sam to marry him, as if the absence of penetration somehow equals the absence of betrayal. She tells George she will think about it, demanding that they spend more time making love and less time arguing. George promises to change. Seen through a telescope, the film's final shot pictures George and Sam embracing to the soundtrack of "Bolero." As the music pushes toward a crescendo, they slip beneath the perimeter of the telescope sight in order to discreetly make love. The sexual intercourse with the heroine in the final shot is, of course, only implied. Out of sight, out of mind. Hidden from the viewer, it only goes to show, once again, "the safe and giving warmth of her, not a purging heat; her body as a home, not an adventure."

Like *"10,"* the 1984 Hollywood romantic comedy *The Woman in Red* also uses the temptress foil plot to destroy the sexually desirable female, reaffirm the "good wife," and reassert male control.[4] And like *"10,"* it does so because it is also obsessed with the threat of female sexuality. "How the hell did I get up here?" the hero, Ted (Gene Wilder), asks himself, stranded on a ledge a hundred feet above the ground in the movie's opening scene. "Just four weeks ago, I was a completely different person. I had no adventure in my life. I had a wife. I had a family. And I never looked twice when a pretty girl walked by ... never."

Leaving its hero hanging, *The Woman in Red* dissolves into a flashback showing Ted, four weeks earlier, sitting calmly in his car just before the temptress (Kelly LeBrock) enters his life. Dressed in red, she appears out of nowhere. As Ted stares, she casually steps over an air grate, which, à la Marilyn Monroe, blows her red dress up over her waist. Then to further taunt Ted (and the male viewer), she turns around; walks back over to the grate and flashing her bare legs, red panties, and bare belly a second time; dances on it.

Bewitched by the temptress, Ted obsessively pursues her, tracks her down, learns her name, and eventually charms her into dating him. But for all that she signifies in the narrative, Charlotte, the temptress, may as well be nameless. For like Jenny in *"10,"* Charlotte is a function, not a character. Like Jenny in *"10,"* Charlotte is the sexually unattainable that once again in patriarchy is all too attainable. Like Jenny in *"10,"* Charlotte turns out to be an easy lay. And like Jenny in *"10,"* the narrative ensures that Ted pulls out just in time so it can restore male control while reducing the sexually controlling female into a no/thing.

While the good wife waits patiently at home, Ted finally gets Charlotte alone in a hotel room. "I want you more than I ever wanted any other man," Charlotte whispers to Ted as she slips off his tie. As Charlotte continues to tell Ted how much she wants him, the camera cuts to a close-up of Charlotte's face so that, in effect, she is speaking to the male viewer as much as she is speaking to Ted. "You've been dreaming about this for a long time, haven't you?" she asks while her dripping wet hair, her bright red lipstick, the way she suggestively raises her eyebrow, the way the camera pans around her face so that her face remains centered at all times while everything around her spins in circles—all serve to depict Charlotte as, literally, a wet dream.

"This isn't a dream anymore," Charlotte says, her face filling the entire screen. "This is really happening." But, of course, it can't happen. The narrative cannot allow a sexual climax. To stop it, *The Woman in Red* cuts to a longer shot that includes the hero and heroine—snapping the male viewer out of his dream state while shifting the focus from spectacle to narrative. Then to completely turn off the turn-on, the narrative ensures that once again everything goes wrong. The water in the waterbed makes funny noises when Ted climbs into it. Ted's underwear lands on the lamp after he flings it aside. Charlotte makes him go get it before it catches on fire. The water in the waterbed makes more funny noise as Ted climbs back into it. Then just before sexual consummation, the intercom buzzes; Charlotte learns that her husband is on his way up to the room. She tosses Ted out of the bed and shoves him, half-naked, out on the ledge.

The movie's final scene picks up where its opening scene left off. Stranded on the ledge, Ted hears Charlotte moaning in sexual heat as she loudly copulates with her husband back in the hotel room. Thus, like Jenny in *"10,"* the narrative exposes the bombshell as a bimbo so that Ted, and the male gaze, can refocus on the good wife waiting in the wings. "What the hell am I doing?" Ted asks himself. "I have a wonderful wife. I could've thrown my whole life away. And for what? A pretty girl?" Then cured—redeemed—in control of his erection, the final shots of *The Woman in Red* depict Ted leaping off the ledge into a net held by firemen. On his way down, the movie's final shot depicts Ted struggling not to stare at a pretty female photographer who, in yet another Hollywood sex tease, suggestively winks at him.

While the heroine is typically offered a number of choices in the various Hollywood romantic comedy foil plots that are, in essence, no choice, note how the hero in both *The Woman in Red* and *"10"* gets to "have his cake and eat it, too." First, he gets to sexually conquer the sexually desirable female. Second, he gets to ridicule, then reject, the sexually desirable female for jerking him around. And, third, he gets to go back to the good wife as a better man for not having had sex with the sexually desirable female who, since sex is all she has to offer, has nothing to offer. Meanwhile, the sexually desirable female gets the crumbs (turned into a slut and a shit for no other reason than that she is a sexually desirable female) while the good wife gets the crumb (i.e., the hero).[5]

Furthermore, note how the negative portrayal of the sexually desirable female in these movies—as well as the positive portrayal of the mostly asexual good wife in these movies—seems to point to a cultural contradiction in America's sexual attitudes. On the one hand, women are constantly being bombarded with messages emphasizing female sexual accessibility and availability. Television commercials and magazine advertisements, for example, tell women that the way to get a man is to accentuate their sexuality. To look hot is to look good. On the other hand, Hollywood romantic comedies present a completely different message by downplaying and/or belittling female sexuality. The "discrepancy" begins to dissolve, however, as soon as we recognize that the different messages are aimed at different audiences: the former, at young women in their teens and early twenties; and the latter, at "older" women in their late twenties and beyond.

This adds a temporal dimension to the messages, as well as a more permanent admonition. Prior to marriage, young women must look hot to get a man. After marriage, "older" women may still look good, but they must never look hot. A hot wife, after all, threatens the institution of marriage: first, by inviting competition from other men who may sexually desire and go after the wife; and second, by inviting competition from the wife who, knowing that she is sexually desirable, may go after other men that she finds sexually desirable. In either case, female sexuality detracts women from their primary role in life: being good wives and good mothers. The cultural contradiction, then, is no contradiction at all. As women move from their teens to their twenties and then into their thirties and forties, the cultural messages aimed at them change. Their cultural worth is determined less and less by how they look sexually, and more and more by how they give emotionally. And if they don't give enough emotionally or if they look too good sexually, then the Hollywood romantic comedy, through its stories, adds to their cultural condemnation.

In looking over all four variations of the Hollywood romantic comedy foil plot, it is more than telling that the first two—the prick foil plot and the dweeb foil plot—empower the hero, and the second two—the bitch foil plot and the temptress foil plot—belittle females and, in the process, empower males.[6] To the degree that the Hollywood love story, as pointed out earlier, primarily feeds off the pursuit plot and the redemption plot, the Hollywood romantic comedy foil plot serves (at the risk of killing a metaphor) as the "icing on the cake."

Chapter 8

The Permission Plot

The fourth and final type of Hollywood romantic comedy plot, the *permission plot*, depicts a romantically involved hero and heroine encountering resistance from a parent and/or authority figure who vehemently disapproves of their courtship. Typically, the disapproving person is the father, although it can be both the mother and the father or, for that matter, any authority figure. However, in the cases when the disapproving person is a woman, such as a disapproving mother, grandmother, or aunt, it is usually a woman who has taken over the patriarchal role of the head of the family from an absent or impotent father. Faced with fierce resistance, the hero and/or the heroine (depending on whether both sides of the family disapprove or if only one side, which side) desperately try to get the parent and/or authority figure to approve of their romantic relationship. As with the redemption plot, there are two variations of the permission plot. In the first variation, the *acceptance permission plot*, the parent and/or authority figure eventually yields and the hero and/or the heroine are ultimately welcomed into the disapproving family. In the second variation, the *separation permission plot*, the hero and/or the heroine fail to win the parent and/or authority figure's approval and are forced into deciding whether to elope—betraying the family and losing their inheritance—or to break up. Faced with such a decision, the hero and heroine ultimately choose each other over everything else.

Both variations of the permission plot are riddled with ideological contradictions. In the acceptance variation, the hero and/or the heroine allow themselves to be joyously integrated into the very same family that, just a short time earlier, would not have them. Furthermore, the hero typically ends up bonding with the disapproving parent and/or authority figure. By the end of the narrative, the two of them wind up serving as the joint head of the family with the hero as the heir apparent. In the separation variation, the hero typically winds up replacing the parent and/or authority figure in the new family that he and his wife vow to build together. Whether the hero ultimately bonds with or replaces the parent and/or authority figure, both variations of the permission plot support patriarchal ideology while, at the same time, occasionally appearing to challenge it in their sympathetic depictions of a young couple trying to resist traditional authority.

The popular appeal of the permission plot might seem, at first, to lie in its suggestion that the lure of love is stronger than the dazzle of dollars. Yet in the two most popular Hollywood romantic comedies in the sample that have included a permission plot—*Coming to America* and *Arthur*—the hero winds up with both the heroine and millions of dollars. The viewer, then, gets to experience the pleasures of romantic coupling coupled with the pleasures of conspicuous consumption. As the hero of *Arthur* (1981) smugly puts it when, in that movie's final scene, he decides to accept his $750 million inheritance: "I took the money. I mean, I'm not crazy." Not to be outdone, the hero of *Coming to America* (1988) ends up inheriting his father's kingdom. When the heroine asks him if he really would have given up all of his riches just for her, the hero tells her, "Of course," then adds: "if you like, we can give it all up right now." The heroine takes all of three seconds to think about it and then, in the film's final line, shouts out: "Nah!" So much for ideological resistance.

What is far more ideologically significant, however, than what is said or not said in any particular movie, is the relative absence of permission plots in the sample. Out of the "top" 155 Hollywood romantic comedies produced from 1970–1999, only ten of these Hollywood romantic comedies include a permission plot. In other words, the permission plot has all but disappeared from a genre, that, for much of its history, keyed on the permission plot.[1] It might be tempting to argue that the permission plot no longer resonates simply because the companionate model of marriage has been firmly established in America since the end of World War II.[2] But as late as the late 1960s and the early 1970s, the permission plot still strongly resonated with American moviegoers. It played a key role, for example, in the most popular Hollywood romantic comedy of all time: *The Graduate* (1967).[3] And it also played a key role in three other Hollywood blockbusters that, while not all technically Hollywood romantic comedies, are all classifiable as Hollywood love stories: *West Side Story* (1961), *Guess Who's Coming to Dinner* (1968), and *Love Story* (1970).[4]

The demise of the Hollywood romantic comedy permission plot, then, is only a relatively recent phenomenon that reflects a significant change in American society since the early 1970s. Simply put: parents have lost much, if not most, of their say in who their children can, or cannot, marry. Of course, one can point to the record-breaking box office success of *Titanic* (1997) or, for that matter, the critically acclaimed Hollywood romantic comedy hit *Shakespeare in Love* (1998) as evidence that the permission plot occasionally still connects with American moviegoers. Both movies, after all, do include a permission plot. But both movies are also set in the distant past: *Titanic*, nearly a century ago; and *Shakespeare in Love*, centuries before that. And these settings are significant. For when presented as part of the distant past, the permission plot may still be credible. But when presented as part of the present, the relative absence of Hollywood love stories utilizing permission plots suggests that most American moviegoers, today, view the permission plot as no longer in touch with the times.[5]

To the degree that the four Hollywood romantic comedy plots represent the four love stories that we, as a society, tell each other over and over, one of our love stories (i.e., the permission plot) may very well be in danger of extinction. But as the continued popularity of pursuit plots, redemption plots, and foil plots indicate, our three other love stories are, for better or worse, doing just fine. Their messages continue to resonate as strongly as ever. It is a resonance, of course, not without ramifications. For as media scholar Susan J. Douglas poignantly observes in her study of how the mass media influence young girls:

> One of the most persistently conservative elements we women face is the story, the narrative, which continues to be structured around boys taking action, girls waiting for the boys, and girls rescued by the boys. In the stories, someone, usually the girl, is a victim, and someone else, usually the boy, is an actor in the world, while we feel ourselves to be both active agents and ongoing victims of stories we never wrote and images we never drew.[6]

A critical analysis of these stories, however, only tells half the story. There are other questions still left unanswered. If it is indeed true that one of the four Hollywood love stories, the permission plot, is currently on life support, how well are the three other love stories really doing? Have they, and must they, always reinforce traditional gender roles and sexual hierarchies? Are there any other love stories but these four Hollywood love stories embedded in the genre? Can we find either in the present or the past any other love stories embedded in the genre that may point the way toward a more equitable future between men and women?

Part II

The Numbers Also Tell Stories

Chapter 9

A Sample and a Typology

Textual analysis can describe; it cannot quantify.[1] To "find the other love stories," if such love stories do indeed exist, it is not enough to explore *how* the different Hollywood narratives may ideologically reinforce and/or challenge dominant gender conventions. We also need to examine *how often* they do so, and *how long* they have been doing so. To answer these questions, we need to temporarily shift our methodology from textual analysis to content analysis, as well as to better define our variables. And this entails looking at the numbers as well as the stories with the understanding that the numbers also tell stories.

Along these lines, all the critical readings presented so far in this book have been drawn from a universal sample of the "top" 155 Hollywood romantic comedies released from 1970–1999. All 155 of these movies have been viewed, re-viewed, coded, categorized, and quantified in terms of their plot structures and, as will be discussed later, in terms of their point of view, genre type, and theme. Appearing in the two data collection tables in the Appendix, these data sets provide a baseline for documenting the popular appeal of the Hollywood romantic comedy's structural, generic, and thematic variations, as well as for documenting any significant changes in these variations over time.

Of course, in presenting a universal sample of the "top" 155 Hollywood romantic comedies released from 1970–1999, we need to ask: "What exactly is a Hollywood romantic comedy?" And while this may seem like an easy enough question to answer, it is anything but. After all, definitions of genres vary from analyst to analyst with as many genre classifications, it seems, as there are classifiers.[2] So acknowledging the fact that there is no simple, nor single, answer as to what constitutes a Hollywood romantic comedy, I am nevertheless defining a genre for purposes of this book as "a collection of similarly structured texts that are presented in narrative form and linked by conventions (e.g., characters, plots, themes, settings, costumes) that readers can identify—and identify with—on a conscious and unconscious level." And I am defining a Hollywood romantic comedy for purposes of this book as a Hollywood movie that essentially focuses on romance and comedy with its romantic elements outweighing its comedic elements.[3] The love story is, of course, central to the narrative.[4] At a minimum, this entails: (1) a chance meeting between a hero and a heroine who together represent a potential heterosexual couple; (2) internal or external obstacles to the recognition, declaration, and legitimation of their mutual love; (3) the overcoming of these obstacles; and (4) a happy ending depicting a wedding or promise of a wedding.[5] These four ingredients, mixing together with other Hollywood romantic comedy conventions, solidly align the Hollywood romantic comedy within the dominant structural form (i.e., crisis, resolution, containment) that characterizes all Hollywood fictional narratives.[6] In this sense, to the degree that Hollywood romantic comedies are conventional in form, they are ideologically conservative in function.

However, not all Hollywood romantic comedies are conventional in form. For as film scholar Barry Keith Grant notes: "While it is true that genre movies tell familiar stories with familiar characters in familiar situations, it by no means follows that they do so in ways that are completely familiar."[7] Grant's observation is critical for, as we will soon see when we look at the different Hollywood romantic comedy genre types, a comprehensive genre analysis needs to identify not only the consistencies within a genre, but also the variations and variational excesses. Occasionally, these variations and variational excesses then coalesce into a counterconventional genre with countercultural implications. And it is only when we are able to identify this counterconventional genre; determine its form and function; and demonstrate how, when, and why it occasionally emerges into a dominant generic form that the concept of genre is fully vitalized.

With these genre definitions and qualifications in mind, the universal sample of the "top" 155 Hollywood romantic comedies that appears in Table 1 is all-inclusive—containing a listing and ranking of *all* Hollywood romantic comedies released from 1970–1999 with over 3.398 million admissions.[8] The size and diversity of this sample provide three significant advantages over more traditional, less systematic, studies of Hollywood genres. First, including all

Table 1

The "Top" 155 Hollywood Romantic Comedies, by Admissions,
Released from 1970–1999

RANK	TITLE OF MOVIE	ADMISSIONS	GROSS	YEAR
1	Tootsie	56,253,968	$177,200,000	1982
2	"Crocodile" Dundee	47,071,376	$174,634,806	1986
3	Heaven Can Wait	43,083,900	$100,816,327	1978
4	Pretty Woman	42,176,423	$178,406,268	1990
5	The Goodbye Girl	38,289,714	$85,386,061	1977
6	There's Something About Mary	37,627,486	$176,472,910	1998
7	Look Who's Talking	35,109,978	$140,088,813	1989
8	Jerry Maguire	34,834,654	$153,620,822	1996
9	Arthur	34,338,734	$95,461,682	1981
10	What's Up, Doc?	33,613,445	$57,142,857	1972
11	As Good As It Gets	32,348,151	$148,478,011	1997
12	Coming to America	31,180,609	$128,152,301	1988
13	"10"	30,570,933	$75,510,204	1979
14	Sleepless in Seattle	30,568,015	$126,551,583	1993
15	Runaway Bride	29,950,707	$152,149,590	1999
16	My Best Friend's Wedding	27,626,386	$126,805,112	1997
17	Shampoo	26,077,723	$52,937,778	1975
18	You've Got Mail	24,676,119	$115,731,542	1998
19	When Harry Met Sally	23,264,047	$92,823,546	1989
20	Notting Hill	22,852,299	$116,089,678	1999
21	Private Benjamin	22,304,833	$60,000,000	1980
22	The Main Event	21,812,774	$53,877,551	1979
23	Michael	21,594,014	$95,229,601	1996
24	Shakespeare in Love	21,373,416	$100,241,322	1998
25	The War of the Roses	21,113,160	$84,241,510	1989

Table 1 (continued)

RANK	TITLE OF MOVIE	ADMISSIONS	GROSS	YEAR
26	Semi-Tough	20,994,611	$46,817,982	1977
27	Splash	20,780,159	$69,821,334	1984
28	Moonstruck	20,400,317	$79,765,241	1987
29	Cocktail	18,803,966	$77,284,301	1988
30	While You Were Sleeping	18,632,726	$81,052,361	1995
31	Annie Hall	17,174,888	$38,300,000	1977
32	The Wedding Singer	17,105,438	$80,224,502	1998
33	Groundhog Day	17,100,031	$70,794,127	1993
34	Love at First Bite	17,020,573	$42,040,816	1979
35	Boomerang	16,867,470	$70,000,000	1992
36	Carnal Knowledge	16,404,518	$27,067,456	1971
37	Seems Like Old Times	16,355,360	$43,995,918	1980
38	Nine Months	16,020,461	$69,689,009	1995
39	Six Days, Seven Nights	15,850,596	$74,339,294	1998
40	Starting Over	15,781,211	$38,979,592	1979
41	Working Girl	15,122,247	$62,152,437	1988
42	The Owl and the Pussycat	14,853,316	$23,765,306	1970
43	The Parent Trap	14,138,277	$66,308,518	1998
44	Housesitter	14,096,539	$58,500,635	1992
45	The American President	13,795,286	$60,009,496	1995
46	Heroes	13,783,889	$30,738,071	1977
47	Bustin' Loose	13,758,993	$38,250,000	1981
48	Best Friends	13,188,949	$38,775,510	1982
49	Doc Hollywood	13,023,938	$54,830,779	1991
50	Hope Floats	12,800,380	$60,033,780	1998
51	Four Weddings and a Funeral	12,622,702	$52,636,671	1994

Table 1 (continued)

RANK	TITLE OF MOVIE	ADMISSIONS	GROSS	YEAR
52	Manhattan	12,602,230	$33,900,000	1979
53	Broadcast News	12,571,582	$49,154,886	1987
54	She's All That	12,464,470	$63,319,509	1999
55	House Calls	12,456,245	$29,147,612	1978
56	Sabrina	12,337,895	$53,669,845	1995
57	Chapter Two	12,325,629	$30,444,306	1979
58	Bull Durham	12,249,749	$50,346,467	1988
59	Tin Cup	12,219,704	$53,888,896	1996
60	Something to Talk About	11,686,391	$50,835,801	1995
61	Never Been Kissed	10,920,228	$55,474,756	1999
62	The Preacher's Wife	10,905,490	$48,093,211	1996
63	Pretty in Pink	10,880,397	$40,366,274	1986
64	Made in America	10,808,552	$44,747,407	1993
65	For Pete's Sake	10,582,011	$20,000,000	1974
66	All of Me	10,489,161	$35,243,581	1984
67	An Unmarried Woman	10,465,725	$24,489,796	1978
68	One Fine Day	10,456,358	$46,112,540	1996
69	About Last Night	10,431,889	$38,702,310	1986
70	Forces of Nature	10,413,520	$52,900,680	1999
71	Blind Date	10,056,705	$39,321,715	1987
72	Roxanne	10,012,318	$39,148,164	1987
73	Practical Magic	9,938,423	$46,611,204	1998
74	A Touch of Class	9,899,225	$17,323,644	1973
75	Mannequin	9,723,448	$38,018,682	1987
76	Joe Versus the Volcano	9,310,157	$39,381,963	1990
77	Alice Doesn't Live Here Anymore	9,288,654	$17,555,556	1974

Table 1 (continued)

RANK	TITLE OF MOVIE	ADMISSIONS	GROSS	YEAR
78	The Mirror Has Two Faces	9,261,939	$40,845,152	1996
79	It Could Happen to You	9,062,690	$37,791,414	1994
80	French Kiss	8,941,158	$38,894,036	1995
81	Pete 'n' Tillie	8,823,634	$15,000,178	1972
82	Murphy's Romance	8,616,199	$30,587,505	1985
83	Lovers and Other Strangers	8,609,694	$13,775,510	1970
84	Honeymoon in Vegas	8,487,229	$35,222,000	1992
85	Same Time, Next Year	8,420,121	$19,703,082	1978
86	Can't Buy Me Love	8,087,937	$31,623,833	1987
87	How Stella Got Her Groove Back	8,032,484	$37,672,350	1998
88	Night Shift	7,993,197	$23,500,000	1982
89	The Truth About Cats and Dogs	7,902,193	$34,848,673	1996
90	Micki and Maude	7,803,287	$26,219,045	1984
91	Desperately Seeking Susan	7,717,911	$27,398,584	1985
92	Forget Paris	7,627,056	$33,177,694	1995
93	Butterflies are Free	7,598,400	$12,917,280	1972
94	The Woman in Red	7,532,187	$25,308,147	1984
95	10 Things I Hate About You	7,514,982	$38,176,108	1999
96	Diary of a Mad Housewife	7,514,026	$12,022,441	1970
97	Addicted to Love	7,508,910	$34,465,895	1997
98	The Heartbreak Kid	7,229,359	$12,289,911	1972
99	Play it Again, Sam	7,058,824	$12,000,000	1972
100	For Love of the Game	6,922,912	$35,168,395	1999
101	For Richer or Poorer	6,893,899	$31,642,995	1997
102	L.A. Story	6,849,971	$28,838,380	1991

Table 1 (continued)

RANK	TITLE OF MOVIE	ADMISSIONS	GROSS	YEAR
103	A New Leaf	6,787,879	$11,200,000	1971
104	Green Card	6,755,791	$28,576,997	1990
105	Picture Perfect	6,716,497	$30,828,720	1997
106	The Best Man	6,707,656	$34,074,895	1999
107	Baby Boom	6,486,343	$25,361,603	1987
108	Fools Rush In	6,422,969	$29,481,428	1997
109	I.Q.	6,322,787	$26,366,022	1994
110	Overboard	6,279,947	$24,554,594	1987
111	Paternity	6,239,906	$17,346,939	1981
112	The Object of My Affection	6,206,127	$29,106,737	1998
113	Funny Farm	6,148,840	$25,271,734	1988
114	Grosse Pointe Blank	6,118,596	$28,084,357	1997
115	Sixteen Candles	6,098,333	$20,490,400	1984
116	Continental Divide	6,092,659	$16,937,592	1981
117	Other People's Money	6,086,580	$25,624,503	1991
118	Unfaithfully Yours	5,931,012	$19,928,200	1984
119	There's a Girl in My Soup	5,739,796	$9,183,673	1970
120	The Out-of-Towners	5,618,921	$28,544,120	1999
121	Blame It On Rio	5,548,979	$18,644,570	1984
122	The Other Sister	5,471,904	$27,797,271	1999
123	Cousins	5,440,410	$21,707,236	1989
124	The Story of Us	5,328,181	$27,067,160	1999
125	Valley Girl	5,301,587	$16,700,000	1983
126	The Last Married Couple in America	5,278,810	$14,200,000	1980
127	Kiss Me Goodbye	5,275,580	$15,510,204	1982
128	Frankie & Johnny	5,266,745	$22,172,996	1991
129	Blast From the Past	5,218,723	$26,511,114	1999

Table 1 (continued)

RANK	TITLE OF MOVIE	ADMISSIONS	GROSS	YEAR
130	The Sure Thing	5,108,600	$18,135,531	1985
131	Say Anything	5,021,739	$20,036,737	1989
132	Speechless	4,939,393	$20,597,269	1994
133	Only You	4,797,112	$20,003,957	1994
134	Multiplicity	4,794,103	$21,141,993	1996
135	Prelude to a Kiss	4,748,754	$19,707,328	1992
136	Some Kind of Wonderful	4,736,508	$18,519,745	1987
137	Only the Lonely	4,734,366	$19,931,682	1991
138	It's My Turn	4,442,000	$11,948,980	1980
139	Milk Money	4,349,559	$18,137,661	1994
140	Born Yesterday	4,336,439	$17,952,857	1993
141	First Monday in October	4,316,547	$12,000,000	1981
142	The Bachelor	4,277,756	$21,731,001	1999
143	Up the Sandbox	4,201,681	$7,142,857	1972
144	Used People	4,127,735	$17,130,101	1992
145	Heart and Souls	4,007,135	$16,589,540	1993
146	Defending Your Life	3,884,470	$16,353,618	1991
147	Crossing Delancey	3,868,501	$15,899,538	1988
148	She-Devil	3,750,645	$14,965,074	1989
149	Irreconcilable Differences	3,694,679	$12,414,120	1984
150	Educating Rita	3,692,816	$11,632,369	1983
151	An Ideal Husband	3,648,660	$18,535,191	1999
152	Threesome	3,563,897	$14,754,535	1994
153	Drive Me Crazy	3,512,862	$17,845,337	1999
154	Blume in Love	3,498,650	$6,122,449	1973
155	The Pick-up Artist	3,398,977	$13,290,000	1987

Hollywood romantic comedies with over 3.398 million admission minimizes the issue of selectivity bias.[9] Second, rather than just focusing on blockbusters and hits, the sample is large enough to be evenly proportioned between *blockbusters* (the movies ranked 1–15), *hits* (the movies ranked 16–50), *marginally successful Hollywood romantic comedies* (the movies ranked 51–105), *disappointments* (the movies ranked 106–140), and *bombs* (the movies ranked 141–155).[10] And, third, by basing the rankings on admission figures rather than gross, the sample is able to account for inflation. To avoid skewing the sample toward more recent movies that, charging more money, gross more money, the sample relies on admission figures as a more dependable indicator of a film's popularity while including gross for comparative purposes.[11]

From this universal sample of the "top" 155 Hollywood romantic comedies released from 1970–1999, we can draw up a typology of plot structures that, based on narrative quests, obstacles, and resolutions, is able to synthesize motivation, action, and ideological implication into more measurable variables (Table 2). In considering this typology, however, keep in mind that it relates only to conventional Hollywood romantic comedies and, as noted earlier, not all Hollywood romantic comedies are conventional. For as we will later see, although conventional Hollywood romantic comedies represent the dominant genre type, there have been periods of time when nonconventional genre types have taken over, playing with the conventional plot lines in such a way as to alter their ideological significance. Therefore, while the plot structures detailed in the typology are constant in the sense that they appear in all Hollywood romantic comedies, the ideological significance of these plot structures may be affected by genre type and, accordingly, should be viewed only as an ideal baseline by which we can measure and track for generic variance.

It is important to note that in some of these plot variations, the narrative action focuses primarily on the hero; in others, primarily on the hero and the heroine together; and yet in others, primarily on the heroine. This, in turn, raises the critical question of point of view. For if we are talking about Hollywood romantic comedies as love stories, well, whose love stories are they? Who are the defining characters? And who are the characters that are defined? In other words, who matters? And who matters less? If we are to follow the rules of linguistics that language is a social production, which, like all social productions, is constructed from an infinite array of symbols that are arbitrarily arranged into conventional meanings, the answers to these questions are, of course, completely arbitrary.[12] Top billings, like all symbolic orderings, are socially produced. And if we are to follow the "natural truth" of the Hollywood romantic comedy that men and women are equal partners in the romantic equation, then there can be no top billings when it comes to romantic love. Because females and males are equally divided in the population, it only follows that they

Table 2
The Narrative Structure and Ideological Significance of the Four Basic Hollywood Romantic Comedy Plots in Conventional Hollywood Romantic Comedies

	Quest	Obstacle	Resolution	Gender Roles	Family	Patriarchy
Pursuit Plots	Hero seeks to win heroine's heart.	Heroine resists hero's love.	Hero overcomes heroine's resistance and wins her heart.	Narrative supports traditional gender roles.	Narrative supports the traditional family.	Narrative supports patriarchal ideology.
Redemption Plots (Two variations: the *coldhearted* and *brokenhearted* redemption plot)	In the coldhearted variation, hero seeks salvation from a bitter life; in the brokenhearted variation, hero and/or heroine seek fulfillment out of an empty life.	In the coldhearted variation, hero is afraid to love and/or be loved; in the brokenhearted variation, hero and/or heroine either cannot find or cannot hold on to a lover.	In the coldhearted variation, heroine's love changes hero into a loving male; in the brokenhearted variation, hero and/or heroine either find the perfect mate, or patch up their broken relationship.	In both variations, narrative supports the traditional gender role of the deferential female while downplaying, and occasionally challenging, the traditional gender role of the dominant male.	In both variations, narrative supports the traditional family while requiring that the husband/father assume more responsibility for the emotional labor in the family than he did previously.	In both variations, narrative supports patriarchal ideology while allowing for "readings of resistance" in its depictions of a "softer" male.
Foil Plots (Four variations: the *prick*, *dweeb*, *bitch*, and *temptress* foil plot)	Hero and/or heroine seek to find the perfect mate.	Hero and/or heroine need to overcome or reject a romantic foil.	Hero and/or heroine overcome or reject a romantic foil and recognize they are meant for each other.	In all four variations, narrative supports traditional gender roles.	In all four variations, narrative supports the traditional family.	In all four variations, narrative supports patriarchal ideology.
Permission Plots (Two variations: the *acceptance* and *separation* permission plot)	Hero and/or heroine seek sanction, approval, and/or permission to love one another.	A parent or parent figure disapproves of the relationship; hero and/or heroine are afraid of hurting parent or parent figure and/or of losing their inheritance.	Hero and/or heroine win parent or parent figures' approval and are accepted into the disapproving family, or hero and/or heroine separate from the disapproving family.	In both variations, narrative supports traditional gender roles.	In both variations, narrative supports the traditional family: hero bonds with the parent or parent figure in the acceptance variation and replaces "him" in the separation variation.	In both variations, narrative supports patriarchal ideology, while occasionally appearing to challenge it.

have an equal chance of arbitrarily being selected to be the driving force of any given narrative.[13] Or at least theoretically they do. For in practice, as the next chapter demonstrates, the numbers do suggest a different story.

Chapter 10

Constructing Inequality: By Point of View

Much earlier in this book, I argued that when it comes to the Hollywood romantic comedy, the hero all too often is the story while the heroine is the vehicle that makes the story possible. Table 3 documents the extent to which this is indeed the case by detailing the percentage of pursuit plots, coldhearted redemption plots, and brokenhearted redemption plots in the sample that are depicted from the male point of view, from the female point of view, and equally from both the male and the female point of view.[1]

In considering the information contained in Table 3, a couple of cautions are in order. The point of view that is being examined should not be confused with the different types of point of view that are often associated with prose narrative (e.g., subjective, objective, omniscient, first person, third person). To the degree that the movie camera is able to freely cut from person to person and place to place, the cinematic point of view is almost always omniscient. The audience—seeing through the lens of the movie camera—sees everything except the movie camera. This absence of seeing, in turn, is precisely what makes Hollywood cinema such a powerful ideological medium. For the "invisible" movie camera hides the fact that what appears to be really happening on screen is always ideologically mediated: it is a construction, a work of art, a story.[2] As noted previously, the key question is: "whose story?" By point of view, therefore, I am less interested in who, if anybody, is telling the story as I am in who is

Table 3
Percentage of Pursuit Plots, Coldhearted Redemption Plots, and Brokenhearted
Redemption Plots Depicted from the Male Point of View, the Female Point of
View, and Equally from Both the Male and the Female Point of View*

	Depicted from the Male Point of View	Depicted from the Female Point of View	Depicted Equally from Both the Male and the Female Point of View
PURSUIT PLOTS (67 movies)	97.0% (65)	3.0% (2)	0% (0)
COLDHEARTED REDEMPTION PLOTS (62 movies)	85.5% (53)	14.5% (9)	0% (0)
BROKENHEARTED REDEMPTION PLOTS (90 movies)	48.9% (44)	20.0% (18)	31.1% (28)

*The percentages and frequencies appearing in Tables 3–10 are calculated from the data
    contained in Tables 11 and 12.

the defining character in the story—that is, the individual who most affects
and is affected by the narrative action. For the particular plot to play out or fail
to play out, who has to change or fail to change? Who does the narrative position viewers to most identify with? Whose wants and/or needs most tug at
viewer's hearts? The key word in all of this is "most." There are a number of
pursuit plots, for example, in which the heroine may do a bit of pursuing herself for a short period of time before backing off and letting the hero take
charge. Likewise, there are a number of coldhearted redemption plots and brokenhearted redemption plots in which the heroine may express some needs of
her own in a couple of scenes; she, too, may harbor bitterness from past
wounds and/or suffer great loneliness. But the key factor in determining point
of view is, ultimately, who is the more substantive character. Who are viewers
positioned into caring more about? Whose wants and/or needs mostly take
precedent and whose wants and/or needs are mostly subsumed?

As noted earlier, the pursuit plot and the redemption plot (both variations)
are the most ideologically significant of the four Hollywood romantic comedy
plots; in essence, these plots key all our love stories. Therefore, it is significant
to note just how often these plots are depicted primarily from the male point of

In a rare reversal of gender roles, Barbra Streisand woos, wows, and wins
Ryan O'Neill in *What's Up, Doc?* Courtesy of Photofest.

view versus how often they are depicted primarily from the female point of
view. Certainly, there is nothing that prohibits a screenwriter from telling his or
her story from the female perspective: presenting a pursuit plot, for example, in
which the female is the pursuer. And yet if we look at the row percentages in Table 3, the pursuit plot is depicted almost exclusively from the male point of
view. Out of the sixty-seven Hollywood romantic comedies in the sample that
include a pursuit plot, *only two* of these movies (3.0 percent) are depicted from
the female point of view, that is, picture a heroine who pursues a hero, encounters resistance from him, persists despite his resistance, and forces him to
change his mind about his feelings for her. The first of these movies is the 1972
Hollywood romantic comedy *What's Up, Doc?* in which an unflappable heroine is absolutely unstoppable in her pursuit of a reluctant hero: wooing him,
wowing him, and winning him. After *What's Up, Doc?*, however, it takes Hollywood another twenty-five years, until the summer of 1997, to release another

Hollywood romantic comedy that includes a pursuit plot from the female point of view. And in that movie, *My Best Friend's Wedding*, the pursuing heroine *doesn't* win the hero. To the contrary, in order to become the heroine, the pursuing heroine is forced to give up her pursuit—to graciously "let the hero go."

Despite these two exceptions, the fact remains that in the overwhelming majority of movies in the sample that include a pursuit plot, it is the hero who pursues the heroine, encounters resistance from her, persists despite her resistance, and eventually forces her to give in. Or to put this another way, the Hollywood romantic comedy pursuit plot almost exclusively structures masculinity and femininity along the following lines: real men know that "no" means "yes." Romantic courtship is a game. Females are game to the game (although part of the game is to pretend that they want no part of the game). The object of the game, for males, is to win the female, and the object of the game, for females (who are the object in the game), is to be won.[3]

At first glance, the row percentages in Table 3 suggest that females fare slightly better in the coldhearted redemption plot than they do in the pursuit plot. Out of the sixty-two Hollywood romantic comedies in the sample that include a coldhearted redemption plot, nine of these movies (14.5 percent) picture the heroine, not the hero, as the coldhearted character who needs saving and is in the end saved by the love of a redemptive lover. However, a closer look at these nine Hollywood romantic comedies—*Butterflies Are Free, The Goodbye Girl, All of Me, Baby Boom, Overboard, Prelude to a Kiss, Addicted to Love, My Best Friend's Wedding*, and *10 Things I Hate About You*—reveals that the heroine's transformation from coldhearted to kindhearted in every one of these movies primarily serves to fulfill the needs of someone other than the heroine. In two of these nine movies, that someone is a baby. And in the remaining seven movies, in varying degrees, that someone is the hero.

In other words, even the exceptions often turn out to be ideologically unexceptional. For example, in both *Baby Boom* (1987) and *Prelude to a Kiss* (1992), a coldhearted heroine declares early in the narrative that she does not want to have a baby. Her declaration, of course, is precisely what makes her a coldhearted heroine. Keying on her declaration, the coldhearted redemption plot from the female point of view then functions in both these movies to show the heroine—and viewers—that a woman who does not want to have a baby is at best, tragically misguided, and at worst, dangerously deviant. To save the heroine, both movies have to make her want, in spite of her wants, to have a baby. After all, as *Prelude to a Kiss* points out in its final scene: "Women make a life inside their body, and that life comes out and holds on to them—that baby is theirs for life." And after all, as *Prelude to a Kiss* then adds in its final lines: "Never to be squandered, the miracle of another human being."[4]

Celebrating the miracle of babies, and of women who make babies inside their bodies, both *Baby Boom* and *Prelude to a Kiss* utilize the coldhearted redemption plot from the female point of view to transform their reluctant heroines into good mothers. The remaining seven Hollywood romantic comedies that also include a coldhearted redemption plot depicted from the female point of view utilize it to transform their reluctant heroines into good wives so eventually they can become good mothers. Significantly, five of these movies—*Butterflies Are Free* (1972), *The Goodbye Girl* (1977), *All of Me* (1984), *Overboard* (1987), and *Addicted to Love* (1997)—combine the coldhearted redemption plot from the female point of view with a brokenhearted redemption plot from the male point of view.[5] This means that instead of a baby in the picture who needs a mother, there is a brokenhearted hero in the picture who needs a good wife. To the degree that the heroine initially resists becoming that good wife, she is pictured as an unsympathetic character. In order to become a sympathetic character, she has to change what she wants—or doesn't want—to comply with the hero's needs.

Consider, for example, how the coldhearted heroine's transformation from a ball-busting bitch who hates men in general and the hero in particular to a good wife who adores men in general and the hero in particular in the following four movies—*The Goodbye Girl, All of Me, Overboard,* and *10 Things I Hate About You* (1999)—is paralleled by the narrative's own transformation from condemning female frigidity in the first half of the picture to celebrating female devotion in the second half. And consider, too, how the underlying message in all four movies manages to reinforce traditional notions of what it means and takes to be a good wife.

By the end of *The Goodbye Girl,* for example, the transformed heroine is so in love with her supporting role in the narrative that she will do anything to keep the part. She whines; she cries. To get her to stop whining and crying, the hero finally has to promise her that he will never leave her side. The heroine's beaming smile in the film's final shots says it all: a female who sniffles is more desirable than a female who bristles.

Similarly, the final scenes in *All of Me* depict its transformed heroine as chaste and chastened—grateful at a second chance at life—while the most sexually dangerous female in the narrative, in comparison, is transmigrated into a horse. In other words, if you can't bridle the bride, turn the minx into a mare.

Not to be outdone, the final scenes in *Overboard* depict its transformed heroine—after the hero, earlier in the narrative, abducts her from a hospital where she is suffering from amnesia; cons her into taking care of him, his four boys, and their pigsty of a house by convincing her that she is his long-lost wife (she isn't); and falls in love with her because she is so good at housekeeping and child-rearing—profusely thanking the hero for changing her life; promising him and his four boys her eternal/maternal love; and asking him to give her what she most wants: "a baby girl." The lesson here: if an uppity woman tosses you off her yacht and into the ocean for calling her a "bored, rich bitch," be sure to go overboard in getting even; she'll love you for it.

Finally, the final scenes in *10 Things I Hate About You* depict its transformed heroine as a superpopular prom queen. To shed her high school image as a "bitter self-righteous hag who has no friends," or, as her guidance counselor calls her, "a heinous bitch," the heroine loses her baggy clothes, loosens her hair, and trades in her copy of *The Feminist Mystique* for a pair of sexy black panties. To cap off her transformation, she reads a poem to her class detailing the ten things that she hates most about the hero, while tearfully acknowledging in the poem's final line that what "I hate most of all is the way I don't hate you." The message this time: behind every man-hating feminist is a sexually repressed female looking for a hunk to turn her into a babe.[6]

To be sure, these underlying messages are not the only messages in these four movies, nor, necessarily, are they the overriding messages in these four movies. But in all four narratives, the coldhearted heroine's transformation from a ball-busting bitch to a good wife *does* fully reinforce traditional notions of femininity by affirming that a woman must be soft, not strident, if she ever hopes to get a man, and that a woman must get a man if she ever hopes to be happy.

This last point, so key to the Hollywood romantic comedy, is fully underscored in the 1997 Hollywood romantic comedy hit *My Best Friend's Wedding*, which, as discussed earlier, is only one of two movies in the sample to include a pursuit plot from the female point of view. It also happens to be the only movie in the sample to combine the pursuit plot from the female point of view with a coldhearted redemption plot from the female point of view. Significantly, the heroine of *My Best Friend's Wedding* is pictured as coldhearted because she has the "audacity" to wait too long (heck, she is almost twenty-eight years old!) to commit to a relationship. So turning twenty-eight, she decides that she is finally ready to marry the hero who, tired of waiting, has chosen to marry someone else: a sweetheart of a woman who is more than ready to be the "good wife." As the heroine plots up different ways to sabotage the hero's wedding, her best friend advises her to just tell the hero the truth. "Just tell him you love him . . . tell him you loved him for nine years but you're afraid of love . . . afraid of needing . . . of belonging to someone."

Like every coldhearted hero in every coldhearted redemption plot from the male point of view, what the heroine of *My Best Friend's Wedding* most needs, of course, is a redemptive lover. The pursuit plot is not a game for her—it is her life. Her salvation depends on a happy ending, which depends, in turn, on winning the hero. But unlike most of the coldhearted heroes, there is no happy ending for the heroine of *My Best Friend's Wedding*. After all, since the man she desperately wants is now happily coupled with another woman, his continued happiness—as well as the heroine's ultimate redemption—depends on her losing the hero. So, in the end, the heroine of *My Best Friend's Wedding* does what most Hollywood romantic comedy heroines do: she defers her needs to the hero's needs. And in so doing, she also affirms the message that women better not wait too long to commit to a man or they will end up, as she does, all alone.[7]

If we look closely, then, at all nine Hollywood romantic comedies in the sample that include a coldhearted redemption plot depicted from the female point of view, we see that the heroine's transformation in nearly every one of these movies completes the hero's happiness, which, in turn, completes the heroine's happiness (or as in the case of *My Best Friend's Wedding*, the heroine's redemption).[8] So while it may appear that females may fare slightly better in the coldhearted redemption plot than they do in the pursuit plot, this is not necessarily the case. As the exceptions demonstrate, simply shifting the point of view from male to female doesn't automatically change the ideological implications of the narrative. In eight out of the nine Hollywood romantic comedies that include a coldhearted redemption plot from the female point of view, the resolution of the love story manages, nevertheless, to thematically reaffirm traditional gender roles and sexual hierarchies.[9]

To a lesser degree, these numerical and narrative gender imbalances also apply to the brokenhearted redemption plot. As the row percentages in Table 3 indicate, out of the ninety Hollywood romantic comedies that include a brokenhearted redemption plot, forty-four of these movies (48.9 percent) depict the brokenhearted redemption plot from the male point of view. As detailed earlier, these films picture a brokenhearted hero who longs for the perfect woman to come along and complete his life. This necessitates, in turn, that the heroine must be, or must become, that perfect woman; and that the heroine can't say "no."

In contrast, only eighteen of the ninety Hollywood romantic comedies that include a brokenhearted redemption plot (20.0 percent) reverse the gender roles: keying on the needs and desires of a brokenhearted heroine. As we will see in Chapter 14, a few of these movies are ideologically challenging: picturing women as fully subjective human beings with needs and desires that extend beyond husbands and homes. But nearly every one of these movies was made back in the 1970s.[10] Since then, it seems that all plots lead to the altar. Keying on traditional themes of female insecurity, the more recent Hollywood romantic comedies in the sample that utilize the brokenhearted redemption plot from the female point of view picture their heroines as helpless without husbands, desperate to get married, and worried that they may either be too poor or too ugly to be loved. So in Hollywood romantic comedies such as *Pretty in Pink* (1986), *While You Were Sleeping* (1995), and *The Object of My Affection*

(1998), it is left up to the hero, and the narrative, to assure a poor heroine that as long as she is attractive, it doesn't really matter if she is rich. Similarly, in Hollywood romantic comedies such as *The Truth About Cats and Dogs* (1996), *The Mirror Has Two Faces* (1996), and *Never Been Kissed* (1999), it is left up to the hero, and the narrative, to assure a "homely" heroine that a good man, and some better makeup, will transform her into a beautiful bride. In other words, females can occasionally "matter more" in Hollywood romantic comedies as long as they recognize that what matters most is being pretty, getting married, and having a baby.

This then leaves another twenty-eight Hollywood romantic comedies (31.1 percent) in the sample that include a brokenhearted redemption plot depicted equally from both the male and the female point of view. Out of these twenty-eight Hollywood romantic comedies, fifteen focus on romantic courtship. To their credit, these fifteen films—*Lovers and Other Strangers* (1970), *The Owl and the Pussycat* (1970), *A Touch of Class* (1973), *Same Time, Next Year* (1978), *It's My Turn* (1980), *Murphy's Romance* (1985), *Broadcast News* (1987), *Frankie & Johnny* (1991), *It Could Happen to You* (1994), *Milk Money* (1994), *One Fine Day* (1996), *Fools Rush In* (1997), *The Other Sister* (1999), *Notting Hill* (1999), and *Drive Me Crazy* (1999)—position their viewers into identifying equally with both the hero and the heroine instead of, as in most Hollywood romantic comedies, mostly the hero. Because these movies do present their heroines as subjective human beings with needs and hurts; and because they give their viewers the chance to identify and empathize with those needs and hurts; and finally, because there are so few Hollywood romantic comedies in the sample that even give this much to their heroines, these movies do represent an improvement over the vast majority of Hollywood romantic comedies in the sample that focus primarily on the male point of view. Nevertheless, twelve of these fifteen films are thematically conventional, once again reinforcing the traditional female desire for men, marriage, and motherhood without ever questioning—as the more ideologically challenging Hollywood romantic comedies in the sample do—the often overtaxed role of women in the familial equation.[11]

The final thirteen movies in the sample that also include a brokenhearted redemption plot depicted equally from both the male and the female point of view pick up where most Hollywood romantic comedies leave off. Bypassing romantic courtship to focus, instead, on the institution of marriage, these thirteen movies—*Pete 'n' Tillie* (1972), *Up the Sandbox* (1972), *For Pete's Sake* (1974), *The Last Married Couple in America* (1980), *Irreconcilable Differences* (1984), *Funny Farm* (1988), *The War of the Roses* (1989), *Forget Paris* (1995), *Something to Talk About* (1995), *For Richer or Poorer* (1997), *The Parent Trap* (1998), *The Out-of-Towners* (1999), and *The Story of Us* (1999)—begin with a hero and a heroine who are already coupled with, or married to, each other.[12]

But their marriage is on the rocks, or, in some cases, the couple have already broken up. The job of the narrative is, of course, to save the marriage. To the degree that the marital rifts are mended in most of these movies, the ideological implications are rather obvious: love conquers all, and all marriages are salvable. Less obvious is what is left untouched: whether all marriages are, indeed, salvable; and why it is left up to the heroine in most of these movies to do most of the emotional labor of saving the marriage.[13]

That these narrative and numerical gender imbalances are left unexplored in most Hollywood romantic comedies is, of course, not all that surprising. After all, there are a total of 219 plots pictured in Table 3. Out of these 219 plots, 162 are depicted from the male point of view (74.0 percent), 29 are depicted from the female point of view (13.2 percent), and 28 are depicted equally from both the male and the female point of view (12.8 percent). So although we may like to think of Hollywood romantic comedies as the epitome of equality—two sorry halves that, meeting on common ground, merge into a happy whole—the numbers paint a different picture. First, there is the obvious: in most Hollywood romantic comedies, the male matters and the female matters less. Second, there is the invidious: in at least 97.0 percent of pursuit plots, 85.5 percent of coldhearted redemption plots, and 48.9 percent of broken-hearted redemption plots, the heroine is primarily responsible for the hero's happiness. Finally, there is the insidious: by implication, if a man is unhappy, then somewhere—somehow—some woman is partly or mostly responsible.

Chapter 11

Constructing Inequality: By Plots

In addition to point of view, another interesting area especially ripe for data analysis surrounds a critical question that has confounded Hollywood, well, ever since there has been a Hollywood. And that is what makes a particular Hollywood movie a blockbuster or, for that matter, a bomb. Leaving gender significations aside for the moment, which plots or plot combinations are going to sell the most tickets? What perfect mix of narrative ingredients will make the most money? Which particular stories are in the "can't miss" categories and which are in the "sure loser" categories?

Of course, there are no categorical answers to these questions; if there were, no movie would ever bomb. Nevertheless, this does not stop studios from paying "experts" exorbitant fees to track, poll, advise, and/or guide their production decisions. After all, with such big bucks at stake—an average $75 million to produce and promote a major Hollywood picture—Hollywood producers have to try, at least, to figure out which screenplays will make money and which will lose money.[1] Toward this end, the numbers in Tables 4 and 5 *attempt* to address which plots have the best and worst probabilities of commercial success. These numbers, however, must be viewed with a degree of caution. First off, nearly all the Hollywood romantic comedies in the sample combine multiple plots. So it is difficult to say which specific plot may most account for a particular movie's success or lack of success. For example, did moviegoers love *Pretty*

Table 4
Percentage Popularity Distribution of Plots

	Block-busters: Rankings 1-15	Hits: Rankings 16-50	Marginally Successful: Rankings 51-105	Disap-pointments: Rankings 106-140	Bombs: Rankings 141-155
PURSUIT PLOTS (67 movies)	11.9% (8)	34.3% (23)	23.9% (16)	19.4% (13)	10.4% (7)
male point of view (65)	10.8% (7)	33.8% (22)	24.6% (16)	20.0% (13)	10.8% (7)
female point of view (2)	50.0% (1)	50.0% (1)	0.0% (0)	0.0% (0)	0.0% (0)
REDEMPTION PLOTS (138 movies)	10.9% (15)	22.5% (31)	38.4% (53)	19.6% (27)	8.7 % (12)
coldhearted (62)	12.9% (8)	22.6% (14)	30.6% (19)	21.0% (13)	12.9% (8)
male point of view (53)	13.2% (7)	24.5% (13)	28.3% (15)	18.9% (10)	15.1% (8)
female point of view (9)	11.1% (1)	11.1% (1)	44.4% (4)	33.3% (3)	0.0% (0)
brokenhearted (90)	8.9% (8)	21.1% (19)	44.4% (40)	17.8% (16)	7.8% (7)
male point of view (44)	18.2% (8)	25.0% (11)	38.6% (17)	11.4% (5)	6.8% (3)
female point of view (18)	0.0% (0)	22.2% (4)	61.1% (11)	11.1% (2)	5.6% (1)
both the male and the female point of view (28)	0.0% (0)	14.3% (4)	42.9% (12)	32.1% (9)	10.7% (3)
FOIL PLOTS (79 movies)	13.9% (11)	24.1% (19)	35.4% (28)	17.7% (14)	8.9% (7)
prick (34)	11.8% (4)	23.5% (8)	35.3% (12)	20.6% (7)	8.8% (3)
dweeb (24)	12.5% (3)	29.2% (7)	33.3% (8)	16.7% (4)	8.3% (2)
bitch (26)	11.5% (3)	34.6% (9)	30.8% (8)	7.7% (2)	15.4% (4)
temptress (10)	10.0% (1)	0.0% (0)	60.0% (6)	30.0% (3)	0.0% (0)
PERMISSION PLOTS (10 movies)	20.0% (2)	20.0% (2)	20.0% (2)	40.0% (4)	0.0% (0)
acceptance (5)	40.0% (2)	0.0% (0)	20.0% (1)	40.0% (2)	0.0% (0)
separation (5)	0.0% (0)	40.0% (2)	20.0% (1)	40.0% (2)	0.0% (0)

Woman as much as they did back in 1990 because of its pursuit plot, which, after all, was quite subtle, or because of its coldhearted redemption plot? Did *"Crocodile" Dundee* smash box office records back in 1986 because of its brokenhearted redemption plot or its dweeb foil plot? Did *The Wedding Singer* captivate audiences in 1998 because of its pursuit plot, its brokenhearted redemption plot, or its foil plot; and if it was its foil plot, was it its prick foil plot or its bitch foil plot? For that matter, was it the plots at all that most attracted moviegoers to these movies, or was it the stars? Or the hype? Or the timing? Or something else?

Furthermore, even if some plots work better than others, not all plots are evenly distributed in every movie. In most movies, one plot plays a larger role than the other plots. While the pursuit plot, for example, threads its way through the entire 1987 Hollywood romantic comedy *The Pick-up Artist*, it is not even introduced into the 1986 Hollywood romantic comedy *About Last Night* until the last half hour of that movie. Likewise, the pursuit plot makes only a small cameo appearance late in the 1998 remake of *The Parent Trap*. For most of that movie, the pursuit plot takes a second billing to the brokenhearted redemption plot and the bitch foil plot.

Finally, there is the fact that content analysis, like all statistical analysis, can only suggest. It cannot prove. At best, statistics are indicators, never prognosticators. After all, if stories can distort facts, statistics can also distort facts, perhaps even more so than stories because they purport not to distort facts. On the other hand, no methodology is foolproof. The best any methodology can offer is a piece to a puzzle. The puzzling question here pertains to why some love stories are enormously popular and last a long time, and other love stories are either never told or, if told, fade over time from our storybooks. Along these lines, the statistics in Tables 4 and 5 provide, if not the answers, information that may get us closer to the answers.

In considering the numbers in Table 4, there are three ways to assess the popularity of the various Hollywood romantic comedy plots: first, by absolute frequency of appearances in the sample; second, by proportional frequency of appearances in the sample; and, third, by relative distribution of appearances across the five popularity categories.[2] As the totals in Table 4 indicate, the most frequently utilized plot in the sample is the redemption plot, which appears in 138 out of the "top" 155 Hollywood romantic comedies released from 1970–1999, or 89 percent of the movies in the sample. The redemption plot is then followed by the foil plot, which appears in 79 out of the 155 movies in the sample (51.0 percent); the pursuit plot, which appears in 67 out of the 155 movies in the sample (43.2 percent); and, finally, the permission plot, which appears in 10 out of the 155 movies in the sample (6.5 percent). By absolute frequency of appearances in the sample, then, the most popular Hollywood romantic comedy plot is, by far, the redemption plot, and the least popular Hollywood romantic comedy plot is, by far, the permission plot.

But these numbers may be a bit misleading if we consider that there are two variations of the redemption plot, which doubles its chances of appearing in the sample; four variations of the foil plot, which quadruples its chances of appearing in the sample; and two variations of the permission plot, which doubles its chances of appearing in the sample. On the other hand, there is only a single variation of the pursuit plot, which, relative to the other plots, severely limits its chances of being included in the sample. So if we control for these variational discrepancies by considering proportional frequency of appearances instead of absolute frequency of appearances, the popularity rankings change. By this new measure, the popularity of the pursuit plot dramatically increases, nearly equaling the popularity of the redemption plot, while the popularity of the foil plot drops to third, and the popularity of the permission plot remains on the bottom.

Although both of these particular measures are useful, the most detailed and perhaps best measure for assessing the popularity of the various Hollywood romantic comedy plots is to ignore their total appearances in the sample and focus instead on their relative distribution across the five popularity categories. This new focus changes the critical question from "how frequently do the different plots appear" to "when the different plots do appear, how likely are they to end up in movies that are blockbusters and hits as opposed to movies that are disappointments and bombs?"

By this measure, we see that the different plots depicted in Table 4 are, for the most part, relatively evenly distributed across the five popularity categories, indicating that when they do appear in a particular Hollywood romantic comedy, that movie is equally likely to end up in a commercially successful category (i.e., a blockbuster or a hit) as it is to end up in a commercially unsuccessful category (i.e., a disappointment or a bomb). Nevertheless, a number of statistically significant exceptions are contained in the data in Table 4 that do suggest that some Hollywood romantic comedy plots are, indeed, more popular than others.

Note, for example, the relative distribution of the sixty-seven pursuit plots across the five popularity categories pictured in Table 4. Out of the sixty-seven Hollywood romantic comedies in the sample that include a pursuit plot, thirty-one of these movies (46.2 percent) appear in the blockbuster/hits categories, while only 20 (29.9 percent) appear in the disappointment/bombs categories. Although this statistical skewing toward the more popular of the five popularity categories by no means demonstrates that utilizing a pursuit plot will guarantee a commercially successful film, it does suggest that including a pursuit plot in a Hollywood romantic comedy may improve its chances of being commercially successful. And this is despite the fact that, as detailed earlier, the pursuit plot is the plot most likely to be told from the male point of view, as well as the plot that most epitomizes the "genderization" in our culture of males and females into active subjects and passive objects.

As a matter of fact, of the four basic Hollywood romantic comedy plots, the pursuit plot is the one *most* heavily skewed toward the more commercially successful movies. Following closely behind the pursuit plot is the foil plot, which, like the pursuit plot, is also heavily skewed toward the more commercially successful movies. Out of the seventy-nine Hollywood romantic comedies in the sample that include a foil plot, thirty of these movies (38.0 percent) appear in the blockbuster/hits categories, while twenty-one (26.6 percent) appear in the disappointment/bombs categories. Again, while this by no means demonstrates that utilizing a foil plot will guarantee a commercially successful film, it similarly suggests that including one or more romantic foils in a Hollywood romantic comedy may also improve its chances of being commercially successful.

Furthermore, if we focus on the Hollywood romantic comedies in the sample that utilize *both* a pursuit plot and a foil plot, we find that these Hollywood romantic comedies are even more heavily skewed toward the blockbuster/hits categories. Excluding the two Hollywood romantic comedies in the sample that employ the pursuit plot from the female point of view, there are thirty-nine Hollywood romantic comedies in the sample that include both a pursuit plot and a foil plot.[3] Out of these thirty-nine movies, nineteen (48.7 percent) appear in the blockbusters/hits categories and only nine (23.1 percent) appear in the disappointment/bombs categories.[4] So yet again, although there are no guarantees, by a more than a 2-to-1 margin, moviegoers seem to like Hollywood romantic comedies that include both a pursuit plot and a foil plot.

If we dig deeper, examining all the different *plot variations* pictured in Table 4, we find that the three most popular plot variations are the brokenhearted redemption plot from the male point of view, the bitch foil plot, and the dweeb foil plot.[5] Out of the forty-four Hollywood romantic comedies in the sample that include a brokenhearted redemption plot from the male point of view, more than twice as many of these movies appear in the blockbuster/hits categories as the disappointment/bombs categories (nineteen movies versus eight). Out of the twenty-six Hollywood romantic comedies in the sample that include a bitch foil plot, exactly twice as many of these movies appear in the blockbuster/hits categories as the disappointment/bombs categories (twelve movies versus six). And out of the twenty-four Hollywood romantic comedies in the sample that include a dweeb foil plot, just under twice as many of these movies appear in the blockbuster/hits categories as the disappointment/bombs categories (ten movies versus six).

On the other hand, the least popular of the different plot variations pictured in Table 4 is, by far, the brokenhearted redemption plot depicted equally from both the male and the female point of view.[6] Out of the twenty-eight movies in the sample that include a brokenhearted redemption plot depicted equally from both the male and the female point of view, only four of these movies (14.3 percent) appear in the blockbuster/hits category, while twelve of these movies (42.8 percent) appear in the disappointment/bombs category. This may suggest one of two things. Moviegoers may be having a tough time identifying equally with the needs of both a hero and a heroine. Or, since thirteen of these twenty-eight movies focus on married couples trying to salvage their marriage, moviegoers may be more interested in love stories that deal with the joys and heartbreaks of romantic courtship than they are in love stories that deal with the joys and heartbreaks of married life. Once again, while these numbers do not guarantee that these particular movies will be box office failures, they do suggest that they may face tough odds. To the degree that moviegoers may be voting with their feet, as well as with their wallets, the main idea espoused in most of these thirteen movies—that all marriages are indeed salvable—may be, at least for now, a hard sell.[7]

Regardless of which of the three popularity measures one ultimately uses, the percentage distributions in Table 4 offer a number of interesting insights into the popularity, or lack of popularity, of the various plots. Again, however, we need to be careful about reading too much into these numbers because of the cautions noted earlier. Furthermore, while these numbers may indicate different degrees of popularity between the various plots, they provide no information about the relative persistency of the various plots. How have the various plots fared across time? Which of the four Hollywood love stories have begun to fade with time? On the other hand, which of the four Hollywood love stories are doing better now than ever? To address these questions, Table 5 examines the various Hollywood romantic comedy plots as they have appeared across the last thirty years of the twentieth century. For reasons that will become clear in the next couple of chapters, these thirty years are broken down into three critical time frames: *the 1970s Hollywood romantic comedies* (consisting of those movies in the sample released from 1970–1977), *the transitional Hollywood romantic comedies* (consisting of those movies in the sample released from 1978–1983), and *the 1980s and 1990s Hollywood romantic comedies* (consisting of those movies in the sample released from 1984–1999). In examining the percentage distributions in Table 5, we need to consider the fact that each of these three critical time frames emphasizes different social themes (in the genre) and different social climates (in the country) as they relate to gender roles and relationships.

Table 5
Percentage Distribution of Plots by Time Frames

	The 1970s Hollywood Romantic Comedies: 1970-1977 (21 movies)	The Transitional Hollywood Romantic Comedies: 1978-1983 (25 movies)	The 1980s and 1990s Hollywood Romantic Comedies: 1984-1999 (109 movies)
PURSUIT PLOTS	47.6% (10)	40.0% (10)	43.1% (47)
male point of view	42.9% (9)	40.0% (10)	42.2% (46)
female point of view	4.8% (1)	0.0% (0)	0.9% (1)
REDEMPTION PLOTS	85.7% (18)	88.0% (22)	89.9% (98)
coldhearted	42.9% (9)	36.0% (9)	40.4% (44)
male point of view	33.3% (7)	36.0% (9)	33.9% (37)
female point of view	9.5% (2)	0.0% (0)	6.4% (7)
brokenhearted	66.7% (14)	52.0% (13)	57.8% (63)
male point of view	28.6% (6)	32.0% (8)	27.5% (30)
female point of view	9.5% (2)	8.0% (2)	12.8% (14)
both the male and female point of view	28.6% (6)	12.0% (3)	17.4% (19)
FOIL PLOTS	42.9% (9)	48.0% (12)	53.2% (58)
prick	23.8% (5)	20.0% (5)	22.0% (24)
dweeb	4.8% (1)	12.0% (3)	18.3% (20)
bitch	14.3% (3)	16.0% (4)	17.4% (19)
temptress	4.8% (1)	4.0% (1)	7.3% (8)
PERMISSION PLOTS	9.5% (2)	4.0% (1)	6.4% (7)
acceptance	4.5% (1)	4.0% (1)	2.8% (3)
separation	4.5% (1)	0.0% (0)	3.7% (4)

What is perhaps most striking about the percentage distributions in Table 5 is how evenly distributed the various plots are across the three critical time frames. Except for a slight upward trend in the brokenhearted redemption plot from the female point of view, and a more pronounced upward trend in the foil plot including, in particular, the dweeb and temptress foil plot variations, all the other plots have been remarkably consistent in their appearances over the thirty-year time period.[8] There have been a few slight dips and recoveries but, overall, we cannot really conclude that any of the four Hollywood love stories are on the verge of extinction. The permission plot is still hanging on, barely, although its big fade-out occurred in the late 1960s. As for the three other Hollywood love stories, they are currently doing as well as they were in the 1970s. If anything, the percentage distributions in Table 5 are remarkable for being so unremarkable. As noted earlier, there are certainly more Hollywood romantic comedies being made today than there were in the past.[9] But not much has changed in the thirty years from 1970–1999 in the structural distributions of the four Hollywood love stories. Along these lines, what is perhaps most significant about the numbers in both Tables 4 and 5 is the one variable that is missing. And that is the absence of any other Hollywood love stories.

Can it be that there are *just* four Hollywood love stories? And, if not, shouldn't we really be asking the question: where are the *other* Hollywood love stories? After all, if cultural meaning is indeed constructed through oppositions, then there must be an alternative love story for every love story.[10] This, then, raises two key questions. First, can we identify these alternative love stories—imagine in our mind's eye what they might look like? And, second, can we find any examples of such alternative love stories in the history of the Hollywood romantic comedy—to locate a past that points to the possibility, at least, of a different future?

Chapter 12

Constructing Inequality: By Genre Types

If plot structures are all that mattered, then this book would be finished. We can conclude that the Hollywood romantic comedy is always classical in form and conservative in function. And we can also conclude that its texts have not changed very much, if at all, in the thirty years from 1970–1999. But plot structures, as it turns out, are not all that matter. Similar stories are not all told the same ways. This means we cannot make the giant leap, as many structural analysts tend to do, directly from the stories (plots) to what the stories are saying (themes). Any connection between plots and themes has to also take into account how plots are framed: both the familiar and not so familiar ways that genre movies often tell their stories. Building on the groundbreaking work in genre analysis of Thomas Sobchack, Will Wright, and John Cawelti, these "ways" can be divided into five basic Hollywood romantic comedy genre types: the conventional Hollywood romantic comedy, the screwball Hollywood romantic comedy, the parody Hollywood romantic comedy, the ironic Hollywood romantic comedy, and the unconventional Hollywood romantic comedy.[1] Like all classifications, these five genre types provide a means—a baseline in addition to plots—to identify and measure generic, as well as cultural, change.

The first of the five Hollywood romantic comedy genre types, the *conventional Hollywood romantic comedy*, is the predominant genre type. These films are, essentially, the "most familiar" films: what immediately comes to mind when we think about a Hollywood romantic comedy. From opening to closing credits, they are fixed in formula and mired in mimesis. Their characters are caricatures. Their plots are but preludes to endings. Their narratives contain no surprises; there can be no surprises. Classical in form and conservative in function, these films serve to comfort, not agitate. In these movies, the plots do solely determine the themes, which, in these movies, are always ideologically affirming. For purposes of this study, to be classified as a conventional Hollywood romantic comedy, a Hollywood romantic comedy has to satisfy four conditions: (1) its characters must be character types, (2) its plots must play out to their logical (anticipated) conclusions, (3) its themes must reinforce traditional gender roles, and (4) there must nothing in the Hollywood romantic comedy that calls into question the Hollywood romantic comedy. Furthermore, all these conditions must be linked in the conventional Hollywood romantic comedy to a happy ending depicting a wedding or a promise of a wedding, or, if the couple is already married, a reaffirmation of their wedding vows.

The second of the five Hollywood romantic comedy genre types, the *screwball Hollywood romantic comedy*, is both structurally and ideologically more complex than the conventional Hollywood romantic comedy. In the screwball Hollywood romantic comedy, the form of the love story is always ideologically challenging while the love story itself may or may not be ideologically challenging. The discrepancy between style and substance in the screwball Hollywood romantic comedy is significant. For just as the conventional Hollywood romantic comedy tends to be classical in nature, the screwball Hollywood romantic comedy tends to be modern in nature. And like modernity itself, its many ambiguities and contradictions afford its viewers greater opportunities to envision, and ride on, occasional currents of ideological resistance.[2]

For purposes of this study, to be classified as a screwball Hollywood romantic comedy, a Hollywood romantic comedy has to satisfy five conditions. These include: (1) frenetic action and pacing; (2) verbal sniping, or quick quips, between the hero and the heroine symbolizing the "war of the sexes"; (3) mistaken identities, including confused, and/or ambiguous sexual identities and/or gender roles; (4) a love story; and (5) a caper plot.[3] Simply put, the definition of a screwball Hollywood romantic comedy is any Hollywood romantic comedy that meets, and sustains, all five of these conditions.[4]

In rating the five genre types on a scale ranging from "most ideologically affirming" to "most ideologically challenging," the screwball Hollywood romantic comedy is always more ideologically challenging than the conventional Hollywood romantic comedy, which, as indicated earlier, is never ideologically challenging. Combining frenetic pacing, confused sexual identities, and multiple plot lines along with a playful self-consciousness, the screwball Hollywood romantic comedy tends to project a rebellious sense of humor. These are films that are, essentially, ass-backwards: where the unexpected, rather than the expected, is the norm. And this extends, as well, to gender roles since it is often the heroine in these movies who, at least initially, propels the romantic courtship. As in all conventional Hollywood romantic comedies, that romantic courtship eventually culminates in a wedding or a promise of a wedding. And it is at this point—the end of the romantic courtship—the start of the marriage—the end of the movie—that the screwball Hollywood romantic comedy can go either one of two ways. If the picture of the married (or soon to be married) couple at the end of the movie includes a strong heroine and a weak (or weaker) hero, then the screwball Hollywood romantic comedy manages to both affirm the institution of marriage while challenging the terms of that institution—envisioning a heterosexual partnership in which the female, not the male, is the more dominant partner. But if the picture of the married (or soon to be married) couple at the end of the movie includes a settled-down heroine and a revitalized hero, then the screwball Hollywood romantic comedy manages to contain the subversive potential of its own aesthetic form—using the end of its narrative to restore the natural order in which the male, not the female, always comes out on top. While the screwball Hollywood romantic comedy is always more ideologically challenging than the conventional Hollywood romantic comedy, depending on its ending, it may or may not be as ideologically challenging as the next two Hollywood romantic comedy genre types: the parody Hollywood romantic comedy and the ironic Hollywood romantic comedy.

The third of the five Hollywood romantic comedy genre types, the *parody Hollywood romantic comedy*, is a conventional Hollywood romantic comedy that, through its excesses, ridicules Hollywood romantic comedy conventions. Reversing the fourth condition of the conventional Hollywood romantic comedy, it ensures that everything in the movie—*including the kitchen sink*—calls into question the Hollywood romantic comedy. Like all film parodies, the parody Hollywood romantic comedy accomplishes its task through an overdose of conventions. Instead of acting, there is overacting. Instead of soft romantic music, there is a symphony of badly played violins. Instead of a watery eye, there is a torrent of tears. Instead of a key kiss, there is "sucking face."

In turning the familiar—through its extremes—into the absurd, the parody Hollywood romantic comedy serves to satirize both the love story and the audience watching the love story. For in getting the audience to laugh at what it so often takes *so* seriously, it gets the audience to laugh at itself. In both form and function, then, it is always more ideologically challenging than the conventional Hollywood romantic comedy, and it is equally, if not more, as ideologically challenging as the screwball Hollywood romantic comedy. Through its excesses, it transforms its narrative into a series of jokes. And through these jokes, it exposes the impression of reality that classical cinema so carefully crafts and conveys as, instead, an ideological practice and product.

While the parody Hollywood romantic comedy serves to satirize, the fourth of the five Hollywood romantic comedy genre types, the *ironic Hollywood romantic comedy*, dares to disturb. Like the parody Hollywood romantic comedy, the ironic Hollywood romantic comedy employs Hollywood romantic comedy conventions to challenge the conventional Hollywood romantic comedy. But instead of doing so through excesses, it relies on a surprise ending that sours everything that proceeds it. Simply put, an ironic Hollywood romantic comedy is a conventional Hollywood romantic comedy that, at the last possible moment, turning on itself, turns dark.

The bitter ending transforms the comedy into a tragedy: negating the narrative and denying narrative pleasure.[5] As genre analyst Thomas Sobchack puts it: "There is no release of tensions, since the inevitable conclusion for which the audience has come and which would send them back into the real world smiling has not taken place. Rather than stasis, such endings produce agitation, discomfort, a vague anxiety."[6] Although it may use a different tool—a hammer instead of a feather—the ironic Hollywood romantic comedy is equally, if not more, as ideologically challenging as the parody Hollywood romantic comedy. Instead of tickling its audience with excess, it conks them over the head with inversion in a way that, as genre analyst John Cawelti notes, "deliberately invokes the basic characteristics of a traditional genre in order to bring its audience to see that genre as the embodiment of an inadequate and destructive myth."[7]

The fifth and final genre type, the *unconventional Hollywood romantic comedy*, is a catchall category for nonconventional Hollywood romantic comedies that cannot be classified as screwball, parody, or ironic Hollywood romantic comedies. Being "nonconventional," these movies either fail to meet one or more of the four conditions that characterize conventional Hollywood romantic comedies and/or fail to include a happy ending depicting a wedding or promise of a wedding (or, if the couple is already married, a reaffirmation of their wedding vows). In terms of their ideological significance, these movies run the gamut, ranging from somewhat ideologically affirming to very ideologically challenging. Most of the unconventional Hollywood romantic comedies in the sample do ultimately question and/or challenge dominant gender conventions. But it is important to note that a few of them do not: finding ways, instead, to reinforce conventional themes through unconventional means.

Consider, for example, how the ambitious heroine of the unconventional Hollywood romantic comedy *Broadcast News* (1987) ends up paying dearly for her resistance—caught up in a cautionary tale that, affirming dominant gender conventions, warns women not to choose careers over families and, at the same time, not to be too choosy when it comes to men. Pursued by two heroes—one smart and the other charming—the heroine first analyzes, then agonizes, and finally says "no" to both of them. Throughout the movie, *Broadcast News* pictures all three of its major players obsessed with their careers, which, the narrative argues, cannot substitute for a healthy love life. But in the end, it is the heroine who gets singled out for the harshest criticism.

"Maybe the best part of your life is over," the smart hero bitterly warns the heroine after she romantically rejects him toward the end of the narrative. "Five, six years from now . . . I'll be walking along with my wife and my two lovely children and we'll bump into you, and my youngest son will say something and I will tell him it's not nice to make fun of single, fat ladies." The final shots of *Broadcast News* work to fulfill the smart hero's prophecy. For they depict, years later, the smart hero economically successful and happily married. And they depict the charming hero even more economically successful, with a beautiful young fiancée by his side. In both cases, the pictures suggest that men can, and should, balance families and careers. But the last picture of the heroine, on the other hand, depicts her still obsessed with her work. And while she ambivalently mentions, in passing, that there is "this guy" she is "sort of seeing," the final few shots picture her unattached and uncommitted, looking like a poster child for spinsterhood, babbling about transfers and promotions. The ideological message of the final few shots is anything but understated: men can have it all while women must choose between work and family. Furthermore, although women may occasionally resist the conventional Hollywood romantic comedy happy ending, to do so entails turning the love story, as well as their life story, into a tragedy.

An even more graphic example of a Hollywood romantic comedy that manages to reinforce conventional themes through unconventional means is the 1989 hit movie *The War of the Roses*. The film's opening scene serves to introduce the film's narrator, a divorce lawyer who, talking into the camera, addresses the audience. He has a story to tell about two former clients. And he wants the audience, as well as a prospective client sitting in his office, to "listen carefully." As the divorce lawyer begins to tell his story, *The War of the Roses* cuts to a series of flashbacks that picture his two former clients—the hero and the heroine—meeting in Nantucket, making love, getting married, having children, buying their "dream house" in the suburbs, and watching their children grow up and move on. Eventually, the heroine decides that she, too, wants to move on. "I don't really want to be married to you anymore," she tells the hero. "When I look at you lately, I just want to smash your face in." Then after smashing his face in, the heroine sues for divorce and demands ownership of the house. "You will never get that house!" the hero warns.

"There are two dilemmas that rattle the human skull," the divorce lawyer, as narrator, laments to viewers toward the end of the film. "How do you hold on to someone who won't stay? And how do you get rid of someone who won't go?" Playing out the divorce lawyer's lament, the final scenes of *The War of the Roses* picture the heroine struggling to get rid of the hero who, in turn, won't go. "You may find this hard to believe, but I still love you," he tells her. "What you can't believe is that I don't want you," she snaps back. Vowing to fight to the death, the hero and the heroine proceed to fight to the death with the very objects of their success, their material possessions, eventually serving as the instruments of their demise. In the movie's climactic scene, the two of them end up entangled in their chandelier which—snapping free—crashes to the floor and cuts them to pieces. The hero's final dying act is to reach out his hand and place it on the heroine's shoulder. The heroine's final dying act is to reach out her hand, grab his hand, and fling it off her shoulder.

It is important to note that the ending of the love story between the hero and the heroine in *The War of the Roses* is as dark and disturbing as any scene, in any movie, in the sample. And it raises all sorts of ideologically challenging questions. What is it about eighteen years of marriage, for example, that hardens love into hate? Why do so many wives feel trapped and suffocated in their supporting roles? What does it say about a society when men's sexual obsessions with women end, all too often, in the death of women? It goes without saying, perhaps, that these are not the sort of questions that would encourage an audience to leap up out of their seats and wildly cheer for family values. But *The War of the Roses* manages, nevertheless, to contain the subversive potential of its own love story by framing it as a story within a story. Instead of ending with the violent death of the hero and the heroine—killed in the sanctuary of their own home *by* their own home—the movie ends where it begins, with the divorce lawyer, sitting in the sanctuary of his office, talking to his prospective client and, at the same, talking through his prospective client in order to talk to the audience.

"Some story, huh!" the divorce lawyer observes. Then advising his prospective client that "a civilized divorce is a contradiction in terms," he offers him a choice. He will help him obtain "a quick and clean divorce," or, he tells him: "You can get up and go home and try to find some shred of what you once loved about the sweetheart of your youth . . . it's your life." The second to final shot in *The War of the Roses* pictures the prospective client slowly getting up, walking out the door, and heading home to his wife. The final shot in *The War of the Roses* pictures the divorce lawyer picking up the telephone, calling his wife, and telling her: "Hi, what are you doing? Coming home. Love you."

While the conclusion of the love story in *The War of the Roses* is uncompromisingly brutal, the "conclusion after the conclusion" is conventionally sweet. The narrative device of the story within a story—filtered through the lens of the divorce lawyer—turns *The War of the Roses* into a cautionary tale. And that cautionary tale, in turn, transforms the thematic message of the movie from

Kathleen Turner and Michael Douglas in *The War of the Roses*,
an unconventional Hollywood romantic comedy that first raises,
then dismisses, the question: What is it about eighteen years of marriage
that can harden love into hate? Courtesy of Photofest.

"this is what can happen in marriages" to "this is what can never be allowed to happen in marriages." Reaffirming the institution of marriage and, for that matter, challenging the option of divorce, the cautionary tale instructs husbands and wives to hug, hold, forgive, cling, and compromise. *Or else.*

It is interesting to note that out of the 109 Hollywood romantic comedies in the sample that were released from 1984–1999, there are a total of forty-six movies that include a pursuit plot from the male point of view. In only two of these movies, the heroine manages to successfully resist the hero's pursuit. These two movies are, not surprisingly, *Broadcast News* and *The War of the Roses*.[8] Although the form of the message may be unconventionally delivered in both movies, the substance of the message, nevertheless, reinforces the status quo. Female resistance is a mistake. In the first movie, the female pays for her mistake by losing her last two chances at happiness (pick: either the smart hero or the charming hero). In the second movie, she pays for it with her life. It goes without saying, perhaps, that neither of these two movies include a key kiss.

This said, it is important to note that "thematically conventional" unconventional Hollywood romantic comedies like *Broadcast News* and *The War of the Roses* are, despite their ideological reaffirmations, always more ideologically challenging than conventional Hollywood romantic comedies. By first exposing, and then containing, cracks in the love story rather than pretending that there are no cracks, these movies tend to be more ambiguous, which, in turn, provides greater opportunities for multiple readings. For example, viewers who are so inclined can overlook, or discount, the final scene in *The War of the Roses* and focus, instead, on the heroine's final dying act: viewing it, if they choose, as an act of liberation. Similarly, while some viewers may see the heroine as a "real bitch" for rejecting a sympathetic hero who seems to love her, other viewers may see through that sympathetic hero to see the heroine's defiance as heroic.

It is also important to note that while "thematically conventional" unconventional Hollywood romantic comedies like *Broadcast News* and *The War of the Roses* are always more ideologically challenging than conventional Hollywood romantic comedies, the overwhelming majority of the unconventional Hollywood romantic comedies in the sample are not thematically conventional, and thus even more ideologically challenging. To help visualize all this information, we can graphically present the ideological range of the five different genre types as shown in Figure 1.

As Figure 1 illustrates, in varying degrees, all four nonconventional Hollywood romantic comedy genre types (i.e., screwball, parody, ironic, and unconventional) manage to question and/or challenge some aspects of the Hollywood romantic comedy. By examining the balance between the four nonconventional Hollywood romantic comedy genre types (questioning and/or challenging the Hollywood romantic comedy) and the conventional Hollywood romantic

Figure 1
Ideological Range of the Five Hollywood Romantic Comedy Genre Types

```
Conventional----
            Screwball----------------------------
                    Parody------------------------------
                            Ironic------------------------------
            Unconventional--------------------------------------------------
```

**Affirming Dominant   Questioning Dominant   Challenging Dominant
Gender Conventions   Gender Conventions   Gender Conventions**

comedy genre type (fully affirming the Hollywood romantic comedy), we can assess the overall health of the genre. To that end, the percentage distributions of Hollywood romantic comedy genre types presented in Table 6 serve as a gauge, indicating how well the Hollywood romantic comedy is doing these days.

From the figures in Table 6, it would appear that, overall, the Hollywood romantic comedy is doing relatively well. As the totals indicate, the genre type that appears most frequently in the sample is, by far, the conventional genre type. Of the "top" 155 Hollywood romantic comedies in the sample, 116 of these movies (74.8 percent) are conventional Hollywood romantic comedies. As previously mentioned, the plots in these movies do solely determine the themes, which in these movies are always ideologically conventional. On the other hand, there are only three screwball Hollywood romantic comedies, one parody Hollywood romantic comedy, and three ironic Hollywood romantic comedies in the sample.[9] This leaves thirty-two unconventional Hollywood romantic comedies—rounding out the "top" 155—to do most of the work of questioning and/or challenging the Hollywood romantic comedy.

In absolute numbers, these thirty-two movies seem to represent a small dissenting voice in what amounts to a generic chorus of ideological affirmation. But it is important to note that on at least one indicator of popularity these films actually resonate better than the 116 conventional Hollywood romantic comedies in the sample. Although none of these thirty-two movies appear in the blockbuster category, overall, they are slightly *less* skewed toward the disappointment/bombs categories than the 116 conventional Hollywood romantic comedies. Indeed, if we add the screwball, parody, and ironic Hollywood romantic comedies into the calculations, we find that the four nonconventional generic types have an even better chance of appearing in the blockbuster/hits

Table 6
Percentage Popularity Distribution of Genre Types

	Block- busters: Rankings 1-15	Hits: Rankings 16-50	Marginally Successful: Rankings 51-105	Disappoint- ments: Rankings 106-140	Bombs: Rankings 141-155
Conventional (116 movies)	12.1% (14)	20.7% (24)	30.2% (35)	30.2% (35)	6.9% (8)
Screwball (3 movies)	33.3% (1)	0.0% (0)	66.7% (2)	0.0% (0)	0.0% (0)
Parody (1 movie)	0.0% (0)	100.0% (1)	0.0% (0)	0.0% (0)	0.0% (0)
Ironic (3 movies)	0.0% (0)	33.3% (1)	33.3% (1)	33.3% (1)	0.0% (0)
Unconven- tional (32 movies)	0.0% (0)	28.1% (9)	40.6% (13)	9.4% (3)	21.9% (7)

categories (with twelve of these movies in the blockbuster/hits categories and eleven in the disappointment/bombs categories) than the conventional Hollywood romantic comedies (with thirty-eight of these movies in the blockbuster/hits categories and forty-three in the disappointment/bombs categories). And although these numbers are by no means earthshaking, they do demonstrate that moviegoers do not automatically fall in love with conventional Hollywood romantic comedies nor do they automatically reject nonconventional Hollywood romantic comedies.[10]

This said, it also must be noted that in terms of absolute numbers, the conventional Hollywood romantic comedy has been, by far, the dominant genre type. But as the percentages in Table 7 also reveal, the dominant Hollywood romantic comedy genre type has not always dominated. And this raises all sorts of interesting questions, in turn, about the nature of genres and, by extension, the nature of culture.

As the column percentages for the 1970s Hollywood romantic comedies indicate, for an eight-year period from 1970–1977, the four nonconventional Hollywood romantic comedy genre types outperformed conventional Hollywood romantic comedies by a 6-1 margin. Out of the twenty-one Hollywood romantic comedies in the sample released from 1970–1977, only three of these movies—*The Owl and the Pussycat* (1970), *For Pete's Sake* (1974), and *The Goodbye Girl* (1977)—were conventional Hollywood romantic comedies. As we will see in the next chapter, the overwhelming majority of the

Table 7
Percentage Distribution of Genre Types by Time Frames

	The 1970s Hollywood Romantic Comedies: 1970-1977 (21 movies)	The Transitional Hollywood Romantic Comedies: 1978-1983 (25 movies)	The 1980s and 1990s Hollywood Romantic Comedies: 1984-1999 (109 movies)
Conventional	14.3% (3)	64.0% (16)	89.0% (97)
Screwball	4.8% (1)	0.0% (0)	1.8% (2)
Parody	0.0% (0)	4.0% (1)	0.0% (0)
Ironic	14.3% (3)	0.0% (0)	0.0% (0)
Unconventional	66.7% (14)	32.0% (8)	9.2% (10)

nonconventional 1970s Hollywood romantic comedies questioned, challenged, and/or redefined the terms of the institution of marriage. And as we will see in Chapter 14, they often did so through pursuit plots that ultimately failed and redemption plots in which redemption was, in the end, utterly impossible. In so doing, these movies ripped away the veneer of optimism that typically characterizes the Hollywood romantic comedy. And in so doing, these movies raised the intriguing question of whether the four Hollywood love stories, particularly as they relate to women, are really love stories at all.

In his classic essay on generic transformation, John Cawelti charts out a "life cycle characteristic of genres as they move from an initial period of articulation and discovery, through a phase of self-conscious awareness on the part of both creators and audiences, to a time when the generic patterns become so well-known that people become tired of their predictability."[11] He then links the proliferation of "nonconventional" films during the 1970s to a period of "generic exhaustion," which, he contends, "is a common phenomenon in the history of culture." Cawelti concludes by noting: "The present significance of generic transformation as a creative mode reflects the feeling that not only the traditional genres but the cultural myths they once embodied are no longer fully adequate to the imaginative needs of our time."[12]

Looking over the column percentages in Table 7 for the 1970s Hollywood romantic comedies, we can easily see how Cawelti, writing at the end of the 1970s, could have concluded that our major traditional genres had reached a point of generic exhaustion.[13] But as the column percentages for the transitional Hollywood romantic comedies and, even more strikingly, for the 1980s and

1990s Hollywood romantic comedies demonstrate, Cawelti's conclusions—at least as they pertain to the Hollywood romantic comedy—turned out to be premature. From 1978–1983, conventional Hollywood romantic comedies made a remarkable comeback. And from 1984–1999, they represented an overwhelming 89 percent of the Hollywood romantic comedy market share. Even more significantly, as we will see in the next chapter, out of the "top" 109 Hollywood romantic comedies released from 1984–1999, *only one* of these movies thematically dared to directly challenge the Hollywood romantic comedy.

In a final analysis, the percentages in Table 7 present us with somewhat of a contradiction. On the one hand, they demonstrate that the conventional genre type does not always dominate, suggesting that genres are, by "nature," both variable and vulnerable. On the other hand, they also demonstrate that the conventional genre type is remarkably resilient: suggesting that there are significant limitations to that variability and vulnerability. Knocked down in the 1970s, the conventional Hollywood romantic comedy was never knocked out. And since 1984, it has been doing better than just "relatively well." As a matter of fact, it has been doing better than ever.[14]

Chapter 13

Constructing Inequality:
By Themes

As just detailed, conventional Hollywood romantic comedies constitute nearly three-quarters of the "top" 155 Hollywood romantic comedies released from 1970–1999, and 89 percent of the "top" 109 Hollywood romantic comedies released from 1984–1999. And as noted earlier, the leap from plots to themes in conventional Hollywood romantic comedies isn't a leap at all: it is a direct connection. This means that all the symbolic messages detailed in Chapters 1–8 of this book apply in these movies. To briefly recap some of these messages: males win females and females are won. Men know more than women know what women really want. Male persistence, in the face of female resistance, is heroic. Female resistance is wrong, and sometimes can be dead wrong. Women are more than happy to serve as spectacle in a world where they must wait to be rescued by men . . . from men. Females can occasionally "matter more" as long as they recognize that what matters most is men, marriage, and motherhood. Males need females; females need to be needed. Females are happiest making other people happy. The good wife is always a forgiving wife. Women are not very bright. Women are, by nature, predatory rivals. Heroines need the benevolence of heroes, just as women need the benevolence of patriarchy, to protect them from themselves.

All these messages serve, of course, to reinforce the deferential female gender role while, at the same time, relegate the feminine to secondary status. And all these messages are either affirmed, questioned, or challenged in Hollywood romantic comedies by incorporating them into one of three major themes: social regeneration through coupling, self-actualization coupled with coupling, or self-actualization through uncoupling. These three major themes are, once again, ideal types that in addition to plots and genre types provide yet another means to identify and measure generic, as well as cultural, change.

Hollywood romantic comedies that key on the first of the three major Hollywood romantic comedy themes, *social regeneration through coupling*, channel all the messages detailed in the first eight chapters of this book into a single thematic imperative: marriage. To state the obvious, the goal of these Hollywood romantic comedies is to romantically bring the hero and the heroine together and, more specifically, to bring them to the altar. But the coupling between the hero and the heroine, of course, symbolizes more than just coupling. First, and most obvious, because the coupling is between a hero and a heroine, it represents heterosexual coupling and, through the absolute absence of any alternative types of coupling, rejects all alternative types of coupling. And, second, because the coupling is always officially sanctioned by either the church or the state, the wedding ritual represents a social action that regenerates communal values.[1]

Included in these communal values, however, are all the messages that, as detailed earlier, relegate the feminine to secondary status. At the same time, one very important message that is always left out of these movies is that what often gets subsumed in the wedding (or promise of a wedding) is female identity and female autonomy.[2] Instead, heterosexual romantic coupling, followed by marital coupling, is always pictured as natural and unproblematic while any female resistance to such coupling is always depicted as deviant. To the degree that these Hollywood romantic comedies affirm social regeneration through coupling without ever questioning the terms of that coupling, it can be argued that these Hollywood romantic comedies also affirm the social regeneration of patriarchy.

Hollywood romantic comedies that key on the second of the three major Hollywood romantic comedy themes, *self-actualization coupled with coupling*, question the terms of coupling without necessarily rejecting coupling. As with the first group of Hollywood romantic comedies, these movies tend to end with a wedding or a promise of a wedding (or, if the couple is already married, with a reaffirmation of their wedding vows). But unlike the first group of Hollywood romantic comedies, the "final coupling" occurs in these movies only after a crisis, or series of crises, that significantly questions, and then redefines, the terms of coupling.

Typically, there are two different ways that these movies manage to redefine the terms of coupling. The first way is by depicting the heroine, from beginning to end, as the stronger and more substantive individual in the partnership.

Reversing generic conventions, these Hollywood romantic comedies envision an alternative love story in which the "happy couple" consists of a dominant female and a deferential male who, finding one another without losing themselves, find redemption in coupling. The second way is by ensuring that the heroine, not the hero, defines the terms of coupling. In these Hollywood romantic comedies, the heroine agrees to marry the hero (or, if they are already married, to stay married to the hero) only after the hero agrees to her demands. These demands include the right to forge her own identity and, most important, the right to get out of the relationship without any grief when, or if, she wants to get out. While the heroine in these Hollywood romantic comedies desires the hero, she also desires *more than just the hero*. In deference to her desires, the hero (as well as the narrative) eventually gives in to her demands.

In terms of the ideological scale introduced in the last chapter, Hollywood romantic comedies that key on self-actualization coupled with coupling are always more ideologically challenging than Hollywood romantic comedies that key on social regeneration through coupling. On the other hand, they are typically not as ideologically challenging as those Hollywood romantic comedies in the sample that key on the third of the three major Hollywood romantic comedy themes: *self-actualization through uncoupling*. For these particular movies do more than just question and redefine the terms of coupling. They also challenge the relevance and benevolence of the institution of marriage.

Refuting Thomas Sobchack's classic claim that "genre films" always favor "the security of passive identification with the crowd [over] the anxiety and loneliness engendered by the freeing of the self," the heroine, in these movies, eventually opts out of the romantic relationship (or, if she is married, the marriage), in order to "find herself."[3] Sometime her separation is temporary—giving her the chance to prove herself . . . to herself. Once on her own, the heroine learns that she can make it on her own. And that knowledge provides her with enough self-confidence so that if she ever decides to couple again, she can do so on her terms—not because she has to, but because she wants to. Other times, however, her leaving is permanent. The heroine concludes, in the end, that coupling with a male eventually—inevitably—subsumes the female. And under those terms, she also concludes that rather than kissing the hero, she has to kiss off the hero.

In either case, Hollywood romantic comedies that key on self-actualization through uncoupling picture female separation as emancipation. And the communal values that they propagate and perpetuate are those of women's liberation. As we will see when we take a closer look at many of these films in the next chapter, they manage to challenge patriarchal ideology by challenging the preference in our culture for female deference. Simply put, these are love stories in which strong, determined heroines dare to defy the love story by loving themselves . . . first and most. In these movies, women "matter." And as the eight-year-old Alice in the opening shots of *Alice Doesn't Live Here Anymore* (1975) puts it: "If anybody doesn't like it, they can blow it out their ass!"

Just as we did with genre types, we can graphically present the ideological range of the three major Hollywood romantic comedy themes. But in doing so, we need to briefly take into account a fourth category. Simply put, there are a handful of movies in the sample that are thematically *ambiguous*—films that either cannot make up their minds or try to have it both ways. In the sense that these movies are more open to multiple readings than those Hollywood romantic comedies in the sample that key on social regeneration through coupling, they are a bit more ideologically challenging. But since they also hedge their bets, vacillating between ideological affirmation and ideological challenge, they are not as ideologically challenging as those Hollywood romantic comedies in the sample that key on either self-actualization coupled with coupling or self-actualization through uncoupling.

As Figure 2 illustrates, in varying degrees, Hollywood romantic comedies that key on self-actualization coupled with coupling and self-actualization through uncoupling question and/or challenge dominant gender conventions. But as the percentage distributions in Table 8 demonstrate, even together, and even if we add to their combined forces the "ambiguous" films, they pose a relatively weak challenge.

As the totals in Table 8 indicate, the Hollywood romantic comedy theme that appears most frequently in the sample—social regeneration through coupling—is also the most ideologically affirming of the three Hollywood romantic comedy thematic types. Out of the "top" 155 Hollywood romantic comedies released from 1970–1999, a total of 124 of these movies (eighty per-

Figure 2
Ideological Range of the Three Major Hollywood Romantic Comedy Themes

**Social Regeneration
through Coupling---**
          (Ambiguous)-----
                    **Self-actualization
                    Coupled with Coupling-----**
                              **Self-actualization
                              through Uncoupling---**

**Affirming Dominant   Questioning Dominant   Challenging Dominant
Gender Conventions   Gender Conventions   Gender Conventions**

Table 8
Percentage Popularity Distribution of Themes

	Block-busters: Rankings 1-15	Hits: Rankings 16-50	Marginally Successful: Rankings 51-105	Disap-point-ments: Rankings 106-140	Bombs: Rankings 141-155
Social Regeneration through coupling (124 movies)	11.3% (14)	21.8% (27)	31.5% (39)	29.0% (36)	6.5% (8)
Ambiguous (5 movies)	0.0% (0)	0.0% (0)	40.0% (2)	20.0% (1)	40.0% (2)
Self-actualization coupled with coupling (8 movies)	12.5% (1)	37.5% (3)	37.5% (3)	12.5% (1)	0.0% (0)
Self-actualization through uncoupling (18 movies)	0.0% (0)	27.8% (5)	38.9% (7)	5.6% (1)	27.8% (5)

cent) key on social regeneration through coupling. In so doing, these 124 movies affirm all the messages that, as outlined earlier, relegate the feminine to secondary status. This then leaves thirty-one Hollywood romantic comedies in the sample to thematically question and/or challenge the Hollywood romantic comedy. And while, overall, these thirty-one movies are relatively evenly distributed between the blockbuster/hits category and the disappointment/bombs category, in absolute numbers, they pale in comparison to the movies that key on social regeneration through coupling.[4]

Just as we saw with genre types, the most ideologically affirming Hollywood romantic comedy theme—social regeneration through coupling—is the dominant Hollywood romantic comedy thematic type. But also just as we saw with genre types, the dominant Hollywood romantic comedy thematic type has not always dominated. For as the percentage distributions in Table 9 clearly demonstrate, dominant cultural conventions can, and occasionally do, undergo sudden and significant transformations, even as the dominant culture continually works to reduce and then reverse such transformations.[5]

As the column percentages for the 1970s Hollywood romantic comedies in Table 9 clearly demonstrate, for an eight-year period from 1970–1977, the most ideologically challenging of the three Hollywood major romantic comedy thematic types—self-actualization through uncoupling—was the domi-

Table 9
Percentage Distribution of Themes by Time Frames

	The 1970s Hollywood Romantic Comedies: 1970-1977 (21 movies)	The Transitional Hollywood Romantic Comedies: 1978-1983 (25 movies)	The 1980s and 1990s Hollywood Romantic Comedies: 1984-1999 (109 movies)
Social Regeneration through Coupling	14.3% (3)	64.0% (16)	96.3% (105)
Ambiguous	14.3% (3)	0.0% (0)	1.8% (2)
Self-actualization Coupled with Coupling	14.3% (3)	16.0% (4)	0.9% (1)
Self-actualization through Uncoupling	57.1% (12)	20.0% (5)	0.9% (1)

nant thematic type. During these years, it outperformed the most ideologically affirming of the three major Hollywood romantic comedy thematic types—social regeneration through coupling—by a 4-to-1 margin. Furthermore, if we add in the ambiguous Hollywood romantic comedies and the Hollywood romantic comedies that keyed on self-actualization coupled with coupling, the three more ideologically challenging Hollywood romantic comedy thematic types outperformed the most ideologically affirming Hollywood romantic comedy thematic type during these years by a 6-to-1 margin. In other words, there *was* a time in the history of the Hollywood romantic comedy when the key kiss and the happy ending were not the rule, they were the exception.

Then in a very short period, the "rules" changed. As the column percentages for the transitional Hollywood romantic comedies in Table 9 clearly demonstrate, what was, was no more. Out of the "top" twenty-five Hollywood romantic comedies released from 1978–1983, only five of these movies (twenty percent) keyed on self-actualization through uncoupling, while sixteen (sixty-four percent) keyed on social regeneration through coupling: a nearly complete reversal of the 4-to-1 margin that characterized the ideological preferences of the previous time frame.

In other words, the key kiss and the happy ending were back. And as the column percentages for the 1980s and 1990s Hollywood romantic comedies in Table 9 clearly show, by the end of the 1990s, the key kiss and the happy ending—securely wrapped in the ideologically affirming theme of social regeneration through coupling—were firmly entrenched and virtually unchallenged. Furthermore, as the frequency distributions in Table 10 also clearly demonstrate, the textual war over the social meanings of the key kiss and the happy ending—played out through the three major Hollywood romantic comedy themes—was all but over as far back as 1984.

What Tables 9 and 10 both clearly depict is the same pattern of generic variance detailed at the end of the last chapter. During the 1970s and, to a lesser degree, in the early 1980s, the women's movement infiltrated the Hollywood romantic comedy. And as we will see in the next chapter, the Hollywood romantic comedy responded to this infiltration through a series of texts that questioned, challenged, and/or rejected the four Hollywood love stories. In stark contrast, however, out of the "top" 109 Hollywood romantic comedies released from 1984–1999, only one (0.9 percent) dared to thematically challenge the terms of coupling, and only one other (0.9 percent) dared to thematically question the terms of coupling.[6]

In December 1989, the heroine of the movie *She-Devil* refused to re-embrace her coldhearted ex-husband in the film's final scenes. Instead of a happy ending, *She-Devil* gave audiences a triumphant heroine. In return, audiences gave *She-Devil* the cold shoulder; the movie bombed at the box office. Ten years—and seventy-four Hollywood romantic comedies later—the millennium would end without another Hollywood romantic comedy keying on self-actualization through uncoupling. Similarly, there was only one Hollywood romantic comedy with more than 3.398 million admissions released from 1982–1999 that keyed on self-actualization coupled with coupling. And the "big" concession that the hero/husband eventually made in that one movie—*Something to Talk About* (1995)—was to "allow" the heroine to enroll in veterinary school so that she could "find herself" and he, in turn, could save their marriage. In other words, by the summer of 1995, the Hollywood romantic comedy had slid so far backward in its depictions of gender roles and gender relationships that simply allowing a woman to go to work—to be more than just a housewife—had to be construed as a great stride forward.[7]

Table 10
Year-by-Year Frequency Distribution of Themes

YEAR	Social Regeneration through Coupling	Ambiguous	Self-actualization Coupled with Coupling	Self-actualization through Uncoupling
1970	1	0	0	3
1971	0	1	0	1
1972	0	2	2	2
1973	0	0	0	2
1974	1	0	0	1
1975	0	0	0	1
1976	0	0	0	0
1977	1	0	1	2
1978	2	0	1	1
1979	4	0	1	1
1980	3	0	0	1
1981	3	0	1	1
1982	3	0	1	0
1983	1	0	0	1
1984	7	1	0	0
1985	3	0	0	0
1986	3	0	0	0
1987	10	0	0	0
1988	6	0	0	0
1989	5	0	0	1
1990	3	0	0	0
1991	6	0	0	0
1992	5	0	0	0
1993	5	0	0	0
1994	6	1	0	0
1995	6	0	1	0
1996	8	0	0	0
1997	7	0	0	0
1998	10	0	0	0
1999	15	0	0	0

Part III

The Four Other Hollywood Love Stories

Chapter 14

Once Upon a Time, They Did Not Always Live Happily Ever After

Women have served all these centuries as looking glasses, possessing the magic and delicious power of reflecting the figure of man at twice its natural size.

Virginia Woolf[1]

I could live without a man.

Ellen Burstyn in *Alice Doesn't Live Here Anymore*

In categorizing and characterizing both genre types and themes, it must be pointed out that we are talking about propensities, not absolutes. Even the most ideologically affirming texts, after all, have moments, points, passages that are open to all sorts of ideologically challenging interpretations. And as recent works in cultural studies and poststructuralism have more than adequately demonstrated, the act of "reading against the grain" to exploit these moments, points, passages, can serve as an effective weapon of ideological resistance. But, like all weapons, "reading against the grain" has its limitations. Dig deep enough and we can read resistance into anything, which, of course, says almost nothing. In other words, if we dig too deep, we may completely miss the point. Although no text is ideologically absolute, there are some texts in which the ideological affirmations far outweigh the ideological challenges, and there are others in which the ideological challenges far outweigh the ideological affirmations. *And there are some time periods that favor the former over the latter, and other time periods that favor the latter over the former.*

The percentage distributions of genre types and themes presented in the last two chapters counter the conventional notion that genres—if they change at all—change only gradually and grudgingly over long periods of time. Indeed, old stories may never die, but this does not mean that they are always best sellers. A close examination of the Hollywood romantic comedy clearly demonstrates that for a short, but sustained, period of time in the 1970s and early 1980s, the old stories no longer worked—and the genre did change. Furthermore, a close examination of that generic change counters the prevailing view among many social critics that Hollywood, during the 1970s, was indifferent and impervious to the women's movement. As media scholar Susan J. Douglas puts it, reinforcing that prevailing view:

> Hollywood's solution [to the women's movement] was simple: Hey, let's just pretend women don't exist for a few years while all of this blows over. Good parts for women in films became scarcer than circle pins . . . mostly, in the early and mid-1970s, women were invisible in the movies. The medium that had responded most rapidly to changing sexual mores in the late 1950s and early 1960s was one of the slowest to respond to the changing status of women in the early 1970s. Women having sex they could deal with; women having aspirations, hey, that was something else.[2]

And as film scholar Molly Haskell puts it, echoing Douglas's observations: "Hollywood responded to the women's movement by ignoring it in the late '60s and early '70s, which is really when the movement was at its peak . . . women virtually disappeared from the cinema."[3] To be fair to both Douglas and Haskell, on one important level, their observations are quite accurate: women were largely left out of the major Hollywood productions in the 1970s. Consider, for example, the "top" twenty Hollywood movies, by admissions, released in the 1970s. These films include: *Star Wars* (144,394,619), *Jaws* (128,078,818), *The Exorcist* (94,285,714), *The Sting* (89,142,857), *The Godfather* (78,646,424), *Close Encounters of the Third Kind* (74,439,462), *Love Story* (69,998,145), *Airport* (66,111,284), *American Graffiti* (65,714,286), *Grease* (65,432,518), *Blazing Saddles* (63,227,513), *The Towering Inferno* (61,375,661), *National Lampoon's Animal House* (60,512,821), *Superman* (57,358,127), *Smokey and the Bandit* (56,832,927), *One Flew Over the Cuckoo's Nest* (55,172,414), *Rocky* (55,039,975), *The Poseidon Adventure* (54,901,961), *M*A*S*H* (53,684,211), and *Young Frankenstein* (45,647,266). And then consider that out of these twenty movies, women get to play a memorable role in only three of them.

In *The Exorcist*, Linda Blair gets to vomit. In *Love Story*, Ali MacGraw gets to die. And in *Grease*, Olivia Newton-John gets to dance alongside John Travolta.

Nevertheless, there are three major problems with the prevailing view that Hollywood, during the 1970s, was indifferent and impervious to the women's movement.[4] First, we cannot focus solely on blockbusters. The overwhelming majority of Hollywood movies, after all, are not blockbusters. And although blockbusters certainly get the most attention from critics and analysts, that attention flies in the face of the fact that blockbusters are often not the most representative movies of a genre.[5] Second, we cannot focus only on the size of the roles that women get to play in movies. In other words, we cannot draw all our inferences from simply counting the number of minutes that women appear on screen or the number of lines they get to deliver. The context of the appearances are, after all, often far more important than the appearances. Furthermore, as we will soon see, some of the most ideologically challenging Hollywood romantic comedies produced in the 1970s focus almost exclusively on males in order to depict the damage that patriarchy does, not only to women, but also to men. And, third, we cannot focus only on the most popular genres. If we want to explore how Hollywood cinema depicts gender relations, it doesn't make too much sense, after all, to spend most of our time focusing on genre films in which men and women barely interact (e.g., action-thrillers, adventures, space pictures, war movies, disaster films). Although these films certainly can tell us a great deal about how Hollywood often views men (strong, dominant, heroic) and about how Hollywood often views women (victims, cheerleaders, window dressing), they have much less to tell us about how Hollywood views the social relationships between men and women. For that information, what better place to turn to than our love stories?

Since 1970, the one Hollywood genre that has most embodied our love stories has been the Hollywood romantic comedy. And if we take a close look at the films produced by that genre from 1970–1977 and, to a lesser degree, from 1978–1983, we see that contrary to the prevailing view, the concerns of the women's movement, and of women, were front and center. Simply put, with just a few exceptions, the Hollywood romantic comedy spent most of the 1970s employing its texts in order to, essentially, attack itself.

What quickly becomes apparent in examining these texts is an undeniable pattern of ambiguity, ambivalence, innovation, reversal, and disruption threading its way through the various narratives. The very word "variance," of course, implies change. But it also implies the "five d's": difference, discrepancy, dissension, defiance, and discord. To the degree that the conventional Hollywood romantic comedy is largely fueled by the belief that men, marriage, and motherhood drive all feminine desires, and to the degree that most Hollywood romantic comedies released in the 1970s question and/or challenge these desires, we see, during the 1970s, a genre at variance with its own beliefs.

Consider, for example, how the very first of the 1970s Hollywood romantic comedies, *Lovers and Other Strangers* (1970), manages to question the institution of marriage while redefining the terms of marital coupling.[6] From its provocative title to its bittersweet ending, *Lovers and Other Strangers* is an unconventional Hollywood romantic comedy that suggests that lovers, in the end, become strangers. Ostensibly, the movie centers around Mike (Michael Brandon) and Susan (Bonnie Bedelia) who, after a year of going together, finally agree to get married. As part of that agreement, the hero, Mike, and the heroine, Susan, promise each other that when, and if, they want to get out, they can get out. But while Mike and Susan's wedding celebration serves as the focal point of *Lovers and Other Strangers*, the narrative circles around its hero and heroine in order to focus, instead, on all the other wedding guests.

The wedding celebration, in essence, provides the movie with its Hollywood romantic comedy backdrop. But it is the surprise announcement by Mike's brother and sister-in-law—Ritchie and Joan—that they are thinking about getting a divorce, and the reaction to that announcement by Mike's parents—Frank and Bea—that ultimately drives the drama. For the interaction between the parents and the children symbolically reflects the changing views from one generation to the next regarding the viability of marriage. As far as the parents—Frank and Bea—are concerned, marriage may not be perfect, but it sure beats the alternative. As far as the children—Ritchie and Joan—are concerned, there's *got* to be an alternative.

In the middle of the wedding celebration, Bea takes Joan aside to find out what is going on: why she wants a divorce. Fishing for information, Bea confides to Joan how her own husband, Frank, once strayed. "I left him for a few days," she tells Joan. "But I came back. Where was I going to go?" Joan assures Bea, however, that it is nothing like that: Ritchie has been faithful. "It's just that," Joan explains, "I loved Ritchie ever since I was fifteen. And the whole time I was going with him, I floated on air. So I really thought we'd get married and live happily ever after. I loved the way he moved. I loved the way his hair smelled like raisins when he kissed me. And the best part of being in his arms," Joan continues, "was that I could get a good whiff of his hair. Well, I don't know if it's me or Ritchie that's changed but it's just no big deal anymore to feel him or smell him."

As Joan and Bea continue their conversation, *Lovers and Other Strangers* cuts to Frank and Ritchie engaged in their own discussion. Frank tells his son that Bea and him were incompatible from the start. "But we learned to compromise," he adds. Ritchie tries to explain to his father, however, that the times have changed; compromise isn't enough. "When we first got married, we cared. We're strangers, now," he sighs. "We're all strangers," Frank responds. "But after awhile, you get used to it. You become deeper strangers, which is sort of love."

"No, that's habit. I want more than that," Ritchie protests.

"There is no more," Frank fires back.

"There's got to be more," Ritchie concludes.

Through the use of its generational oppositions, *Lovers and Other Strangers* posits two visions of marriage in conflict with one another. As much as the parents try, they cannot comprehend the changing times. When Frank asks Bea, for example, why Joan wants a divorce, all Bea can do is shake her head and tell him: "Ritchie's hair stopped smelling like raisins." As *Lovers and Other Strangers* cuts from couple to couple, it reveals that nearly all the couples attending the wedding celebration are, like Ritchie and Joan, unhappily coupled. The wedding celebration winds down. The bride and groom leave. One by one, the other couples file out. The camera turns to Frank and Bea, sitting alone, contemplating the marriage of one son and the divorce of another. "I can understand her wanting to leave," Bea mutters, "but I can't understand her leaving." Frank nods.

The film's final scene, squeezed between its closing credits, is almost an afterthought. It pictures the hero and heroine on their honeymoon night bickering over the television. The heroine reminds the hero how he promised her that if she didn't like marriage, she could get out any time. "Well, I want out," she pouts. The hero clicks off the television so that they can kiss and make love: the sexual urge temporarily providing the impetus for a truce. It is, of course, a small compromise in a narrative that suggests that, for better or worse, women are free to leave and because of that freedom, sustained marriages and bigger compromises may no longer be possible.

While *Lovers and Other Strangers* suggests that women are free to leave, the second of the 1970s Hollywood romantic comedies, *Diary of a Mad Housewife* (1970), shows why women might want to go. From its opening shots picturing its heroine barraged by countless interruptions while racing through thankless chores, *Diary of a Mad Housewife* positions its viewers to identify and sympathize with a woman who is, literally, at the end of her rope. And to the degree that *Diary of a Mad Housewife* shoots most of its action through the perspective of its harried housewife so that nearly everything viewers see and hear is filtered through her eyes and ears, the movie manages, in essence, to substitute the "male gaze" for a female lens.

What that lens reveals, in the end, is a woman who is trapped by marriage, gender, and role. "You're Mrs. Jonathan Balsa, my wife! My wife is a reflection of me," Jonathan (Richard Benjamin) announces to Tina (Carrie Snodgress) in the movie's opening scene. Disgusted by what he sees, he orders his wife to shape up: to change her clothes, fix her hair, stop smoking, and get cracking on the housework. A few moments later, when Tina accidentally serves Jonathan an undercooked hard-boiled egg, Jonathan gently taps it, then giggles to his daughters: "Your mother made Phi Beta Kappa at Smith, but I don't think she can make a four-minute egg!" The girls stare ahead. Tina says nothing. After breakfast, however, as she watches her husband step into a cab on his way to work, she wonders whatever happened to the prince she married. "Who is the man in all those clothes?" she whispers to herself. "Are you in there, Jonathan? Come out, come out, wherever you are."

Bullied and battered—living with a man who loves his wing tip shoes more than he loves his wife—Tina begins to have an affair. Defying the conventions of the prick foil plot, however, *Diary of a Mad Housewife* depicts the "new man" in her life, not as a hero who can rescue the heroine from her coldhearted husband, but as a lover who turns out to be even more hateful than her husband. That depiction, in turn, serves to expose the conventional narrative as a trap. Forced to choose between two prick foils, Tina chooses, instead, to question the narrative. And her questioning ultimately serves in *Diary of a Mad Housewife* as a metaphor for an emerging feminist consciousness. By the time that Jonathan tries to come clean toward the end of the movie, confessing that he lost all their money, is about to get fired, and has been cheating on her all along, Tina is wary of acts and roles. "Do you want a divorce?" Jonathan asks, begging for a second chance. "Or do you think we can pick up the pieces and work out a better marriage than we've ever had?" As Jonathan cries his crocodile tears, Tina silently listens. And by not allowing her to answer, the film denies its viewers the conventional closure in which the good wife always forgives and, in so doing, redeems the "repentant" hero.

Instead, *Diary of a Mad Housewife* cuts to an ending that pictures Tina in group therapy finishing her "story," which, it turns out, is the narrative. "So that's my story," she tells the group. "What should I do?" All the group members begin screaming out different answers. "Keep him!" "Split!" "Keep both of them!" "Get a good lawyer!" As the screaming escalates, the camera slowly begins to zoom in on Tina's face until, in the film's final shot, all that is seen are Tina's eyes. In the end, *Diary of a Mad Housewife* is a movie without an ending. For while it includes a prick foil plot and a coldhearted redemption plot, it provides no narrative closure for either plot. And instead of reinforcing pleasure, that absence of closure serves to question pleasure, which, in turn, serves to question the status quo.[7]

Like the heroine in *Diary of a Mad Housewife*, the heroine in *Up the Sandbox* (1972) also feels trapped by marriage, gender, and role. And like the heroine in *Diary of a Mad Housewife*, the heroine in *Up the Sandbox* also spends most of the movie desperately groping for an answer or an alternative. Reversing the

Carrie Snodgress and Richard Benjamin in *Diary of a Mad Housewife*, one of the first of the 1970s Hollywood romantic comedies to question women's assigned roles in the familial economy. Courtesy of Photofest.

conventions of the brokenhearted redemption plot, *Up the Sandbox* positions its viewers to identify and sympathize with a heroine who is brokenhearted *not* because she is alone, but because she is never left alone. The film's opening shots picture the heroine, Margaret (Barbra Streisand), bathing her baby boy and singing nursery rhymes to her little girl. When she asks her husband, Paul (David Selby), to watch the children for a few hours, he tells her that he is too busy. Like all "good wives," Margaret defers. Her husband, after all, is a college professor who, as her doctor puts it, "is involved with important ideas." It is important to note that throughout the entire movie, the narrative never questions the heroine's love for her husband or children. But when the heroine learns from her doctor that she is pregnant with a third child, the narrative does question whether love is enough.

Yearning for more than "just" being a housewife, Margaret begins to withdraw into a series of fantasies. She dreams that she is seduced by Fidel Castro who, in turn, rips off his beard, strips open his shirt, exposes his breasts, and reveals to her that he is secretly a woman. She envisions blowing up the Statue of Liberty with a cohort of black activists. She imagines smashing her mother's face into an anniversary cake for trying to turn her into a submissive, suburban housewife. The fantasies are woven in and out of the narrative in such a way as to make it difficult, viewing the movie, to separate "what is going on in the heroine's life" from "what is going on in the heroine's head." Each fantasy is rich in symbolism. But it is the need to fantasize, signifying the heroine's need to escape, as much as it is the symbolism embedded in the individual fantasies, that powers the movie's ideological challenge. For just as in *Diary of a Mad Housewife*, the heroine's slow withdrawal from reality turns out to be the only sane response to an insane scenario. And that insane scenario, in both films, is linked to the traditional demands placed on women that they take care of the home, the husband, and the children while finding the time, somehow, to also take care of themselves.

"I don't have the time to be an interesting woman!" Margaret fumes at Paul toward the end of the narrative. "I get one hour to see a doctor and he tells me how wonderful your work is while he has his hand on my tit and he gets paid for that because that's his work! You got one job, I got ninety-seven!" Eventually, Margaret collapses from exhaustion. When she finally recovers, her mother urges her to patch things up with her husband, reminding her: "Marriage is a seventy-five–twenty-five proposition, the woman gives seventy-five." Partially heeding her mother's advice, Margaret tells Paul that she feels "trapped, held back, suffocated." Paul asks what he can do to help. "You can't even take care of your own shirts," Margaret snickers. "Whose fault is that?" Paul fires back. "You take care of me as if I were a child and then you're surprised when I act like one." The last line is not insignificant. For in the context of the narrative, it exposes how much men resent women for playing the one role that, time and time again, the patriarchal narrative most encourages them to play.

"If you really want to help," Margaret urges Paul, "you can take the children for the day." Paul defers. Left alone, Margaret fantasizes about getting an abortion only to be stopped, at the last second, by her husband. At the conclusion of the fantasy, she finds herself sitting alone in the sandbox. In the film's final scene, Margaret catches up with Paul in the park. While her husband and children spin in circles on the merry-go-round, she finally announces that she is pregnant. Before Paul can say anything, she imagines asking him how he feels about "bringing another child into a world as crazy as this." She envisions him replying: "It'll be wonderful." And she hears herself whispering: "Okay, we'll give it a try." As she continues to picture the exchange, the sounds of the calliope suddenly stop—snapping her back to reality. "I want to talk to you!" Paul shouts. But Margaret isn't ready to talk. Instead, she steps into a cab, remarks that it is a beautiful day, tells her husband that she will see him later, adds that she loves him, and rides off for an afternoon by herself. The film's final shots picture Paul, temporarily abandoned, hoisting his two children up into his arms and carrying them through the park.

So much, then, for the prevailing view that Hollywood's solution to the women's movement during the 1970s was to ignore it. To the contrary, the Hollywood romantic comedy was obsessed with, and transformed by, the women's movement during the 1970s. Anticipating the mantra "the personal is political," the Hollywood romantic comedy attacked through the most personal of modes: the story. And through its stories, it sought to make problematic the most personal of stories: the love story.

Admittedly, the ending of *Up the Sandbox*, like the ending of *Diary of a Mad Housewife*, is riddled with ambiguity and ambivalence. But it would be inaccurate to read that ambiguity and ambivalence, like some feminist critics did at the time, as "a clumsy reaffirmation of the notion that staying at home and having babies is the best thing for a woman to do."[8] For while it is true that the heroine does not permanently break free from her marital and maternal responsibilities, the narrative enables her to begin redefining those responsibilities from a twenty-five–seventy-five proposition to a fifty–fifty partnership. It is not insignificant, after all, that *Up the Sandbox* begins with a father who is too busy to look after his children and ends with a father looking after his children. Nor is it insignificant that the narrative opens with a mother stuck with her children and closes with a mother leaving her children. Nor, for that matter, is it insignificant that while the heroine eventually rejects abortion and divorce, her words "Okay, we'll give it a try" are not the most ringing endorsement for marriage and motherhood. On the other hand, what is, perhaps, most significant, is that such a love story—crying out as it does for a more equal distribution of housework and child-rearing—could be written off by some feminist critics in the early 1970s as a cop-out for questioning, rather than radically rejecting, marriage and motherhood. For it only goes to show just how high the expectations were for the genre, and the movement, in the early 1970s when ambitious narratives, as well as ambitious heroines, were the norm rather than the exception.

While *Lovers and Other Strangers* questions the viability of marriage, and *Diary of a Mad Housewife* and *Up the Sandbox* question the viability of women after marriage, a number of other 1970s Hollywood romantic comedies aim their guns/lens in a different direction: questioning men's inability to emotionally and/or sexually relate to women. Perhaps the most memorable and disturbing of these movies is the 1971 Hollywood hit *Carnal Knowledge*. Whether one chooses to classify *Carnal Knowledge* as a satirical drama, a dramatic black comedy, or a tragic romantic comedy, it is, unquestionably, an unconventional love story in which love is doomed, in the end, by hate. "If you had a choice," the hero, Jonathan (Jack Nicholson), asks his best friend, Sandy (Art Garfunkel), in the film's opening shot, "would you rather love a girl or have her love you?" Sandy replies that he'd rather *be in love* than be the one who loves or is loved. "Me, too," Jonathan declares. "But I wouldn't want to get hurt, though."

It is the fear of getting hurt that motivates all of Jonathan's and Sandy's actions in *Carnal Knowledge*. For throughout the movie, they are pictured as men who are so afraid of getting hurt, they strike before they can be struck. Pursuing the one perfect female that can save them, they push all the real women who can, and want, to help them out of their lives. Obsessed with sexual conquest, they end up as sexual failures. And those sexual failures serve in *Carnal Knowledge* as a metaphor for the social failures of patriarchy.

Essentially a three-act play, *Carnal Knowledge* is divided into three separate segments that focus on three key time frames in Jonathan's and Sandy's lives: first, picturing them as Amherst College roommates; second, as young men in their thirties; and third, as adult men in their early forties. In the first segment, both Sandy and Jonathan sexually pursue and "conquer" Susan (Candice Bergen) who eventually decides to settle down with Sandy because, as she puts it, "he is the more vulnerable one." In the second segment, ten years later, Sandy begs Jonathan to help him "get laid" because he is bored to death with Susan, marriage, and monogamy. Meanwhile, Jonathan moves in with Bobbie (Ann-Margret) because, as he tells Sandy, he cannot resist her "extraordinary breasts." But when Bobbie begins to demand marriage, Jonathan starts calling her a bitch. And when Bobbie tries to kill herself with sleeping pills in the final shots of the second segment, Jonathan screams at her semicomatose body: "Very slick! Very clever! But it's not going to work!"

The final segment of *Carnal Knowledge*, fast-forwarding another ten years, is only thirteen minutes long. But those thirteen minutes contain some of the most chilling footage in Hollywood history. The segment opens, innocently enough, with a home slide show. As Sandy and his new girlfriend (a teenager) look on, Jonathan clicks from slide to slide. Each slide, filling the entire movie screen, is a slide of a woman that Jonathan has either slept with, or dreamed of sleeping with. When he gets to a slide of Bobbie, we finally learn what happened to her. As Jonathan describes it: "And heeeeeere's Bobbie! King of the ball busters who conned me into marrying her and is now killing me with alimony!" Moving from slide to slide, Jonathan proceeds to describe each and every woman in his life as either "a ball buster," "a man-eater," "a castrator," or "a bitch." The only female who escapes his wrath is his daughter. "I don't know how this one got in here. This is my little girl Wendy . . . isn't she a dreamboat?" Jonathan mutters as we see, on screen, a happy-faced young girl. He pauses for just a second, then clicks on to the "next bitch." The slide show is presented in *Carnal Knowledge* as a "show within a show" and by the end of both shows, Sandy is left shaking his head and his girlfriend is left shaking in tears. Confronting Jonathan outside, Sandy begs him to "stop playing games." Jonathan, in turn, calls Sandy "a schmuck," and then feeling "a little schmucky" himself, leaves Sandy to visit the only woman that can still sexually turn him on.

As it turns out, she is a prostitute who is willing to tell Jonathan, for a hundred dollars, the "kind of man" that he really is. In the film's final scene, the two of them play out a tragic act that, like the slide show, Jonathan scripts. "You're a real man, a kind man," the prostitute tells Jonathan, stroking his loins. "I'm not kind," Jonathan snaps back, ordering her to get it right. "I don't mean that kind of 'kind,'" the prostitute whispers, finally getting it right:

> But the kindness that comes from enormous strength. From an inner power so strong that every act, no matter what, is more proof of that power. That's what all women want. That's why they try to put you down. Because your knowledge of yourself and them is so right—so true—that it exposes the lies, which they—every scheming one of them— live by. It takes a true woman to understand that the purest form of love is to love a man who denies himself to her. A man who inspires worship because he has no need for any woman because he has himself. And who is better, more beautiful—more powerful—more perfect—more strong— more masculine—more extraordinary—more robust—it's rising— more virile—more domineering—more irresistible—it's up—in the air!

As Jonathan sexually gets off on listening to the prostitute tell him how worthless all women are, he closes his eyes to conjure up the one perfect female that, throughout the movie, eludes him. The final shot in *Carnal Knowledge* fades to white to reveal, at last, his sexual fantasy. She is a female

Jack Nicholson and Art Garfunkel as two damaged men searching for the one perfect female in *Carnal Knowledge*. Courtesy of Photofest.

figure skater dressed in bridal white who, gliding across his dreams, spins in perfect circles across the ice. As we see her, through Jonathan's eyes, the ice goddess is unfathomable. Virginal and inviolable.

In its dark tone and resolution, *Carnal Knowledge* may appear, at first, to be the antithesis of a Hollywood romantic comedy. However, in its narrative structure, *Carnal Knowledge* is very much a Hollywood romantic comedy that, at every turn, defies conventions. The first segment of the film, after all, features a coldhearted hero in pursuit of a heroine. That heroine is forced to choose between the coldhearted hero or his best friend. Defying conventions, she chooses the "best friend": ensuring that the coldhearted hero's pursuit ends in failure. The second segment, also defying conventions, replaces the original heroine with a new heroine who wants, and needs, to save the coldhearted hero. But the coldhearted hero, it turns out, is beyond redemption. The third and final segment sums up the tragic price that we all pay for the roles and the games embedded in the plots. In the end, heroines end up being hated by coldhearted heroes who, hating themselves, despise anybody who can love them.[9]

Critically acclaimed and politically controversial at the time of its release, *Carnal Knowledge* serves, in the end, as an indictment. An indictment, certainly, of its coldhearted hero who is anything but heroic. But an indictment, as well, of the social construction of sexuality under patriarchy that ensures that everyone in the movie gets hurt. Attacking patriarchy by attacking men, it exposes men as impotent potentates. Victims of their own act, they cannot see that they are acting even as they admit to one another, and to themselves, that all their social interactions are an act. By the end of the movie, all that "acting" leads to an ideologically chilling revelation: Yes, the social construction of sexuality under patriarchy damages women. But it destroys men, too.[10]

While the one perfect female tragically eludes the hero throughout *Carnal Knowledge*, in *The Heartbreak Kid* (1972), yet another counterconventional 1970s Hollywood romantic comedy, that "dream girl" is eventually caught. But, as it turns out, there is a catch to the capture. Beginning with a wedding that leads to a sexual conquest and ending with a sexual conquest that leads to a wedding, *The Heartbreak Kid* positions its viewers to identify with the pleasures of the pursuit plot only to reposition its viewers, in its final shots, to question those pleasures.

In the film's opening scenes, the hero, Lenny (Charles Grodin), picks up a woman in a bar, dates her a couple of times, and then tries to make it with her. But the woman, Lila, insists that he marry her first. So instead of taking a cold shower, Lenny decides to take the plunge: he marries Lila. After the wedding, they head to Miami Beach for their honeymoon. On the drive down, Lenny and Lila sing love songs. But Lila has a lousy singing voice. And she can't eat an egg salad sandwich without smearing egg salad all over her chin. And she announces that she has to "make pee-pee" every time she finishes making love. And halfway down to Miami Beach, Lenny begins to wonder whether a cold shower would have been a better idea.

Lenny's love for Lila is further tested when in Miami Beach—lying on the beach—he spots a beautiful blond. As seen through his eyes, the beautiful blond, Kelly (Cybill Shepherd), is, literally, a sexual vision. Immediately, Lenny wants her more than he wants anything. But there is, of course, just one small problem. "I'm on my honeymoon!" Lenny shouts to Kelly as they play together on the beach. "So what else is new!" Kelly yells back. "The marriage is off," Lenny declares. "I had my doubts in Virginia. I was pretty sure in Georgia. But you settled things for me in Florida. I've been waiting for a girl like you all my life!"

As Lenny courts Kelly, *The Heartbreak Kid* pictures her as a sexual tease who is able to manipulate Lenny, her father, and every other man in the movie by simply batting her eyes. And this sexual power, in turn, creates a dilemma for the narrative. For as detailed earlier, the patriarchal narrative depends, in large part, on men being able to control their erections so they can control their women. To complete the pleasures of the love story, Lenny has to marry Kelly. But before the narrative can allow Lenny to marry Kelly, it has to strip her of her sexual power. In other words, to "make a man out of the man," the narrative has to deflate the woman. To that end, *The Heartbreak Kid* turns to—and then turns on—the conventions of the pursuit plot, the temptress foil plot, and the permission plot.

When Kelly's father learns that Lenny is after his "precious little girl," he whisks Kelly back to their home in Minnesota to get her as far away from Lenny as he can. In response, Lenny dumps Lila, finalizes his divorce, flies out to Minnesota, tracks Kelly to her college campus, and proposes marriage. "I'm very flattered," Kelly remarks, "but I got political science." Lenny refuses, however, to accept Kelly's brush-off. Instead, he persists. And in the face of that persistence, Kelly eventually weakens, yields, strips, sexually submits, and falls in love. "You're so positive about everything," she whispers to Lenny as they lie in bed together. "Daddy's the same way."

By the end of *The Heartbreak Kid*, Lenny is invincible while his "beautiful blond" is reduced, once again, to the sexually unattainable that, in patriarchy, is ultimately all too attainable. Determined to marry his "beautiful blond," Lenny quickly overcomes Kelly's father's determination not to let him marry his "beautiful blond." All that is left, then, is the wedding. But in an ironic twist that exposes, and explodes, the love story for just what it is, *The Heartbreak Kid* depicts the wedding as heartbreaking. After the ceremony, the camera zeroes in on Lenny, at the reception, sitting by himself. As Kelly searches for him, Kelly's father sees his daughter searching for Lenny—sees Lenny—and sees right through Lenny. What he sees—what the final shots of *The Heartbreak Kid* show—is the tragedy of the "male gaze." For once conquered, the object of its

Charles Grodin marries Cybill Shepherd, the girl of his dreams, in the final scene
of *The Heartbreak Kid*. Courtesy of Photofest.

desire is no longer desirable. Every sexual vision; every bride; every wife; every
woman; every precious little girl; and most especially, every beautiful blond—
is ultimately a commodity. By the end of the movie (and *by* the end of the
movie), Lenny is exposed as nothing but a pitchman, still pitching. Significantly, the final shots in *The Heartbreak Kid* picture its hero as a victim of his
own victory, appearing out of place at his own wedding, sadly humming a love
song to himself: bored and depleted.

While *Carnal Knowledge* attacks its hero through excess and *The Heartbreak
Kid* attacks its hero through irony, the 1975 Hollywood hit movie *Shampoo*
goes a step further—employing both excess and irony to similarly attack its
hero. Covering a twenty-four-hour period just before and after the 1968 presidential election of Richard M. Nixon, the movie details the sexual triumphs
and social failures of its hero: a Beverly Hills hairdresser who, more than anything else, wants to be taken seriously. But how seriously can you take a hero,
the narrative suggests, who asks a wealthy financial benefactor for a business
loan and then, while waiting twenty-four hours for his answer, proceeds to
have sex with the benefactor's wife (three times), his daughter (once), and his
mistress (three times)?

As it turns out, the hero's sexual prowess in *Shampoo* is driven more by impotence than virility. Powerless to say "no" to any woman who says "yes," the hero, George (Warren Beatty), is constantly jerked from bed to bed in a narrative that, reversing gender roles, reduces its hero to a sex object. "Grow up!" the hero's steady girlfriend begs him. "I'm trying, honey," George cries. "But I can't get out of my own way." Unwilling—unable—to change, George eventually rejects his steady girlfriend, the only woman who can save him, in order to pursue Jackie (Julie Christie), an ex-unsteady girlfriend, who is far more interested in saving herself.

Like the Nixon presidency that it satirizes, *Shampoo* is ultimately a comedy of manners that is driven by errors. Those errors include a pursuit plot that ends in a failed pursuit, a coldhearted redemption plot that ends without any redemption, and a foil plot in which both the hero and the heroine eventually choose the wrong foils. In the film's final scene, George desperately begs Jackie to marry him. "Please, please," he sobs. "I don't trust anybody but you." But Jackie spurns him, desiring a bigger role than being a housewife and a nursemaid to a hairdresser. The final shot in *Shampoo* pictures George all alone on top of a hill watching Jackie drive up to the financial benefactor's mansion; get out of her car; hug the wealthy foil; accept his ring; step into his Rolls Royce; and never once looking back, ride away. Much like the ending of *Carnal Knowledge* and *The Heartbreak Kid*, and much like the ending of the Nixon presidency, it is a tragic, final shot that pictures the hero as a zero; a dud of a superstud that is, in a final analysis, more pathetic than sympathetic.

Still, in addition to its depiction of an uppity hero who, in the end, gets his comeuppance, there is something else that is quite noteworthy about *Shampoo*'s ironic ending. And that is its picture of a heroine who, in the end, has the balls to say "no." For female defiance is very much at the heart of many of the counterconventional 1970s Hollywood romantic comedies. Instead of burning their bras, the heroines, in these movies, discard their men. Time and time again during the 1970s, we see women who say "no," and narratives that sympathize with women who say "no." Consider, for example, the narrative's sympathetic treatment of its heroine in the critically acclaimed, 1977 Hollywood romantic comedy hit *Annie Hall*.[11] And consider, too, how that sympathetic treatment suggests that for women, love isn't always the answer. Often it is the problem.

As a love story, *Annie Hall* is full of problems. To begin with, its hero, Alvy (Woody Allen), is anything but heroic. A hopeless romantic, his idea of romance is getting a good running start, leaping on top of his girlfriend, and playing "hide the salami" in the warm glow of a red light bulb. Alvy is possessive, insecure, and self-indulgent—more similar, in a final analysis, to a prick foil than a hero. When Annie (Diane Keaton) enters the picture, brightening Alvy's life with her goofy optimism and even goofier clothes, everything is set for a conventional, feel-good, Hollywood romantic comedy in which a cold-hearted hero is transformed, by a redemptive heroine's love, into a suitable marital partner. But, as it turns out, Alvy is beyond redemption. What seems like love on his part is self-love. Like so many other 1970s Hollywood romantic comedy heroes, Alvy is so full of himself that he cannot see that he is full of himself.

From Alvy and Annie's first awkward meeting in which they blabber about "the aesthetic qualities of merging art forms" while subtitles reveal Alvy wondering, to himself, what Annie "looks like naked" and Annie wondering, to herself, whether she is "smart enough for Alvy," *Annie Hall* exposes the hero's desire, in love stories, to *take* the heroine, and the heroine's desire, in turn, to be *taken seriously*. Perhaps even more significant, the movie also reveals that while these two desires may complement one another in our love stories, they are often incompatible in real life. It is a fact that Alvy himself recognizes when he comments in one of the film's final lines that that's why we are "always trying to get things perfect in art, because it's real difficult in life."

Throughout *Annie Hall*, the hero's need for the heroine is linked to the hero's need to control the heroine. From the moment Alvy meets Annie, he attempts to recreate her in his image—that is, to turn her into a morose neurotic. Among other things, Alvy picks out the books she should read, chooses the movies she should see, criticizes her for smoking grass, ridicules her for using black soap, and makes her feel guilty whenever she talks to other men. Unhappy with the way things are going, Annie explores with her female psychiatrist whether Alvy is suffocating her. She signs up for college courses. She jumps at an offer to start getting her songs recorded. And finally, she breaks up with Alvy who cannot understand how in the world she could ever break up with someone so wonderful.

"What went wrong?" Alvy mutters to himself after Annie leaves him. "Love fades," a passerby remarks. But the passerby could have just as easily replied: "Control grows tiresome." For the hero's tragedy in *Annie Hall* is that the heroine, in the end, chooses to resist the script. The climactic scene in *Annie Hall* pictures Alvy's desperate attempt to get Annie back. He proposes marriage. She turns him down. And when Alvy continues to push—still unable to *hear* her—Annie angrily walks out on him. It is a bitter ending for a Hollywood romantic comedy that is only slightly sweetened by an epilogue that depicts Alvy running into Annie, years later, and reminiscing about "old times."

In the final line of *Annie Hall*, Alvy suggests that romantic relationships are indispensable despite all their problems. "We need the eggs," he tells viewers. It is, of course, a nice line. But it is also a nice line that is out of place in a narrative that ultimately celebrates the female's right to reject laying, or sitting, on the eggs. Simply put, by short-circuiting its pursuit plot and its coldhearted redemption plot, *Annie Hall* enables its heroine to put her needs before the hero's

Woody Allen and Diane Keaton share happier times in *Annie Hall*.
Courtesy of Photofest.

needs without depicting her as a heartless bitch for doing so. And by denying the happy ending that defines men, marriage, and motherhood as the foundation of all *desirable* women's desires, *Annie Hall* positions its viewers to challenge that foundation and question those desires.[12]

Throughout the 1970s, Hollywood romantic comedy narrative after narrative similarly questions and/or challenges the established generic conventions and social traditions. In the final scenes of *There's a Girl in My Soup* (1970), *Shampoo* (1975), *Annie Hall* (1977), *An Unmarried Woman* (1978), *Manhattan* (1979), *Private Benjamin* (1980), and *Educating Rita* (1983), for example, the heroine rejects the hero: realizing that separating from the hero is the best thing that she can do for herself.[13] In the final scenes of *Blume in Love* (1973), *House Calls* (1978), and *Same Time, Next Year* (1978), the heroine agrees to continue to date, or live with, the hero while rejecting his marital proposal: realizing that not getting married is the best thing she can do for herself. In the final scenes of *Play it Again, Sam* (1972) and *A Touch of Class* (1973), it is the hero who lets the heroine go: realizing that the best thing he can do for the heroine is to let her go. In the final scene of *Semi-Tough* (1977), it is the hero who vows not to marry the heroine: realizing that the worst thing he can do for the heroine is to marry her. In the final scene of *Continental Divide* (1981), the hero and the heroine marry only to immediately split up for six months: realizing that being able to continue their separate careers, in different habitats, is the best thing they can do for their marriage.

During the 1970s, then, it is the love story and, by implication, the institution of marriage, that is under attack. Affirming the rights of the individual over the needs of the couple, we see a celebration of self-expression: movie after movie that emphasizes the freedom to uncouple or, at the very least, the freedom to envision, and experiment with, different kinds of coupling that allow for more freedom. In essence, what we have in the 1970s is the very narrative that, arguably, most impedes women—the love story—working to free women.[14] And in two of the most influential Hollywood romantic comedies of the decade—*Alice Doesn't Live Here Anymore* and *An Unmarried Woman*—it even manages to do so in a way that includes and incorporates men.

Only the last hour of Martin Scorsese's *Alice Doesn't Live Here Anymore* (1974) is a Hollywood romantic comedy and, even then, only in the broadest sense as it shifts from "road picture" to "love story." But like most of the other 1970s Hollywood romantic comedies, the love story in *Alice Doesn't Live Here Anymore* defies generic conventions to challenge traditional notions of coupling and marriage. From the movie's opening shots, picturing the heroine as a young child, to the movie's closing shots, picturing the heroine as a grown woman with a young child, the heroine is always at the center of *Alice Doesn't Live Here Anymore*. And when the hero finally arrives in the second half of the movie, *Alice Doesn't Live Here Anymore* rejects the central tenet of the love story by picturing the hero—and the act of coupling with the hero—as purely peripheral.

The movie's opening shots depict Alice as a determined, eight-year-old girl muttering, to herself, that she can sing better than Alice Faye. Then cutting ahead twenty-seven years, *Alice Doesn't Live Here Anymore* pictures Alice (Ellen Burstyn) as a depressed thirty-five-year-old woman trapped, like the heroine in *Diary of a Mad Housewife* and *Up the Sandbox*, by marriage, gender, and role. Married to a coldhearted husband whose idea of communication is ordering Alice to "Cook dinner!" and "Shut the kid up!," Alice cries herself to sleep at night. "He's not mean," she tries to explain to her girlfriend. "He's just loud, sometimes." Then in the next breath, Alice mutters to herself: "I'd be just as happy if I never saw one again. I could live without a man."

In a sense, *Alice Doesn't Live Here Anymore* is a test of whether Alice can, indeed, live without a man. For no sooner than she utters those words, the narrative "kills off" her husband in a truck accident. Suddenly, with no man in her life, Alice is forced to make it on her own. On the road—on her own—she struggles, persists, survives, and grows. By the time that Alice meets David (Kris Kristofferson) in the second half of the movie, she has gained enough self-confidence that she can fall in love with a man without having to have to count on a man. And it is that journey—from dependency to self-reliance—that ultimately defines the movie's thematic thrust: falling in love, like living with a man, is nice but not essential. Or, to put it another way, heroes may enter the picture as long as they don't steal the show.

"My idea of a man was strong and dominating," Alice tells David, explaining what first attracted her to her late husband. Turning her words around, the narrative goes out of its way to depict David as strong because he is not dominating. Alice's final act in *Alice Doesn't Live Here Anymore* is to declare, in no uncertain terms, that she is going to be a singer. Beyond that, the ending of the movie is open-ended, refusing to hint, one way or the other, whether Alice's future also involves marrying David except to suggest that if it happens, it will be nice but not essential. The final shot of the movie pictures Alice with her son, ready to meet the world and the future head-on. Conspicuously absent in that final shot is the hero: an absence that serves all the more to reinforce the heroine's newfound independence.

Paul Mazursky's *An Unmarried Woman* (1978) is so thematically similar to Martin Scorsese's *Alice Doesn't Live Here Anymore* that one can't help wondering if they collaborated on the two projects (they didn't). Like *Alice Doesn't Live Here Anymore*, *An Unmarried Woman* celebrates a heroine's journey from dependency to self-reliance. For the heroine, Erica (Jill Clayburgh), as well as for viewers identifying with the heroine, that journey is both heartbreaking and heartwarming: serving as a metaphor for every woman's struggle toward self-awareness and self-actualization. All of Erica's actions in the first twenty minutes of *An Unmarried Woman* suggest a woman who is absolutely in love with being married. Safely coupled, Erica views her life as bliss. She happily cooks dinner, spends time with her daughter, shares drinks with her girlfriends, fights with her husband, makes up with her husband, and makes love to her husband. In short, Erica makes do with what she's got, and what she's got is pictured as all she desires. Then out of the blue, one afternoon, Erica's husband blurts out: "I'm in love with somebody else." And before Erica knows what hit her, she is an unmarried woman, in her thirties, bitter and scared to death.

Erica tries to date. She's not ready. Instead she cries, lashes out, and cries some more. Eventually, she sees a female psychiatrist who urges her to go out, enjoy sex, and "get back into the stream of life." Following that advice, she ventures to a pickup bar and picks up an oversexed co-worker. The sex scene that follows is significant: depicting sex as desirable from a woman's point of view without depicting the woman as a slut for desiring it. And in that scene, Erica uses her sexual power to use a man who thinks that he is using her.

As Erica continues to experiment with her body and with her feelings, she slowly begins to rebuild her self-esteem. In a series of tender scenes that serve to show there is power in sisterhood and not all women, as many Hollywood movies suggest, live to scratch each other's eyes out, *An Unmarried Woman* pictures Erica bonding with her girlfriends and her daughter who, together, help her gain control over her future. That control is tested, however, when Erica meets Saul (Alan Bates). He is successful, confident, and gentle. They have sex. And *then* they fall in love.

As Erica draws closer to Saul, *An Unmarried Woman* pictures her, at the same time, fighting against drawing closer to Saul. "The problem was that I didn't do things with myself," she explains to Saul. "It was always Martin and Erica." Saul assures her that "Saul and Erica will be different from Martin and Erica." But when he invites her to spend the summer with him in Vermont, Erica turns him down. While promising to visit on weekends, she explains she is not quite ready for "Saul and Erica." In a tender and telling exchange late in the narrative, a dejected Saul suggests that perhaps he will "find a moose to keep him company."

"Am I only a sexual object to you?" Erica inquires.

"No," Saul answers. "You're a bright, willful, curious woman . . . who is also a sexual object." He begs her again to spend the summer with him in Vermont.

"I can't," Erica reiterates.

"Independent . . ." Saul mutters.

"Trying to be," Erica whispers.

"Woman." Saul concludes.

The final scene in *An Unmarried Woman* strikes a perfect balance between independence and coupling while positioning viewers to re-envision the terms of coupling. Departing for Vermont, Saul leaves Erica one of his huge paintings. Recognizing that struggle is a form of power, Saul also leaves Erica, by herself, to struggle with the painting. The final shots in *An Unmarried Woman* follow Erica as she lugs the painting up and down New York City streets; weaving in and out of people; getting blown in circles by the wind; and somehow, on her own, navigating.

In many ways, *An Unmarried Woman* serves as the crowning achievement of the counterconventional 1970s Hollywood romantic comedies. By showing

Jill Clayburgh struggles to balance her desire for Alan Bates with her desire
for independence in the climactic scene of *An Unmarried Woman.*
Courtesy of Photofest.

women as substantive characters rather than decorous objects. By depicting,
and by celebrating, the joys of sisterhood. By neither desexing nor
disempowering the sexual female. By identifying, and forcing its viewers to
identify, with the heroine. By emphasizing the many complexities of women
and depicting women as all the more human, and interesting, for those complexities. By ensuring that while Erica is ultimately complemented by Saul, she
is never completed by Saul. For all these reasons, *An Unmarried Woman* stands
out as one of the most significant movies in this study and, arguably, one of the
most significant Hollywood movies ever made.[15]

But apart from the substance of its text, *An Unmarried Woman* also stands
out for the way that it was immediately embraced by both film critics and social
critics on its release. Social critic Joan Mellen, for example, notes: "For the first
time since the 1940's, screen heroines are the equals of those strong characters
played by Rosalind Russell, Bette Davis, Joan Crawford, and Katharine Hep-
burn. . . . Today, audiences are being offered films with women characters

whose stories emphasize that regardless of career or marriage, a woman must first accept, respect, and take care of herself."[16] And sociologist Paul Starr sees in both *An Unmarried Woman* and *Alice Doesn't Live Here Anymore* evidence of a "rethinking of the male personality" and an "implicit critique of masculinity."[17] These "two movies," Starr argues, point to "changes in women's consciousness . . . [as well as] changing ideals of male character, represented by the contrast between the first husband and the new man and dramatized by the passage that the women in the films make between them."[18]

The strong sense of optimism in these observations is, of course, noteworthy. But what may be even more noteworthy is to compare that strong sense of optimism back in the spring of 1978 with this study's finding that by the spring of 1978 the generic transformation from counterconventional Hollywood romantic comedies—celebrating feminism—to conventional Hollywood romantic comedies—attacking feminism—was already well under way even as critics, at the time, marveled about the generic transformation in the opposite direction. After *An Unmarried Woman*, only one Hollywood romantic comedy, *Continental Divide* (1981), even comes close to achieving a similar "perfect balance" between independence and coupling. And after *Continental Divide*, only two Hollywood romantic comedies—*Educating Rita* (1983) and *She-Devil* (1989)—dare to thematically challenge the Hollywood romantic comedy by celebrating a heroine who—knowing that she is free to go—actually goes.

As a generic movement signifying social transformation, the counterconventional Hollywood romantic comedy is a significant but relatively short-lived phenomenon. By 1978, it is mostly over, and by 1984, it is over. To be sure, there are nine Hollywood romantic comedies in the sample that, released from 1978–1983, question and/or challenge traditional gender roles and expectations. But these movies are, by 1978, the exceptions. In their place, blockbusters like *Heaven Can Wait* (1978), *"10"* (1979), and *Arthur* (1981) are as thematically conventional in their resolutions as vanilla ice cream on top of apple pie. The last commercially successful Hollywood romantic comedy in the sample that opts for self-actualization through uncoupling is the 1980 hit movie *Private Benjamin*.[19] Even the most popular Hollywood romantic comedy in the sample, *Tootsie* (1982), for all its feminist intentions and proclamations, manages to ultimately affirm traditional gender roles and expectations. When the heroine walks off with the hero in *Tootsie*'s touching final shot—closing out the pleasures of the coldhearted redemption plot from the male point of view, as well as reinforcing the female's role in patriarchy to forgive—the gesture underscores the generic tilt away from the counterconventional 1970s Hollywood romantic comedies.

So from blockbusters to bombs, the early 1980s would mark the return of the Hollywood romantic comedy key kiss and happy ending. It would also signal the start of a generic backlash—a mean streak against women that, while not infiltrating all 1980s and 1990s Hollywood romantic comedies, runs through all too many of them. It turns out to be a backlash so successful that, by 1980, George Segal is able to blame his marital problems with Natalie Wood in *The Last Married Couple in America* on "police strikes, women's lib, gay lib, and condominiums." And it turns out to be a backlash so successful that, by 1984, Nastassja Kinski is able to forgive Dudley Moore, her husband in *Unfaithfully Yours*, for plotting to kill her when he erroneously suspects that she is cheating on him in a love story that argues: "Any man who does less is less than a man." And finally, it turns out to be a backlash so successful that, by 1999, the last Hollywood romantic comedy of the twentieth century, *The Bachelor*, is able to squeeze laughs out of its premise that just about every woman in America—including Brooke Shields and Mariah Carey who both appear in demeaning cameos—is a mentally unstable, foulmouthed, two-faced, gold-digging bitch foil.

In contrast to the strong sense of optimism back in the spring of 1978 with the release of *An Unmarried Woman*, we might want to consider film critic Jay Carr's reaction to the success of *Pretty Woman* in the spring of 1990: "Go to the movies these days and you'll mutter, 'You've regressed a long way, baby!'"[20] To

Capping off the 1990s with a "perfect picture" of generic backlash, Chris O'Donnell fights off an angry horde of prospective brides that are after his money in *The Bachelor*. Courtesy of Photofest.

see just how much the Hollywood romantic comedy has, indeed, regressed in recent years, all we need to do is consider this: after *Educating Rita* in the late fall of 1983, it would take another six years, until the late fall of 1989 when the heroine of *She-Devil* gets to exact her revenge on her cheating husband—and then, after that, still another six years, until the summer of 1995 when the heroine in *Something to Talk About* gets to go to veterinary school—for any Hollywood romantic comedy with more than 3.398 million admissions to thematically suggest that there may be something more for women to aspire to than men, marriage, and motherhood.

Conclusion

There are more movies now than ever . . . in theaters, on television, on cable, on tape, on discs, they're everywhere, you can't escape them, they are creatures, movies, incredibly astute, complex creatures who persuade us that they are manipulations of our culture. . . . But it's possible, I mean you just ought to consider [the] possibility that movies are a malign life form that came to earth a hundred or so years ago and have gradually come to dominate not only our feelings but our thoughts, our intellects.

E.L. Doctorow[1]

Karl Marx and Joseph Schumpeter both seem to have been wrong; it is not any ism but entertainment that is arguably the most pervasive, powerful and ineluctable force of our time—a force so overwhelming that it has finally metastasized into life.

Neal Gabler[2]

The year 2000 turned out to be yet another good year for the Hollywood romantic comedy. Early in the year, *Me, Myself, & Irene* (2000) grossed over $90 million with a manic Jim Carrey, torn by a split personality, playing both the movie's hero and prick foil. Later in the year, *Meet the Parents* (2000) grossed over $160 million with Robert De Niro as the "father-in-law from hell" breathing new life into the moribund permission plot. And at the end of the year,

What Women Want (2000) began a $180 million box office run that would propel it, in early 2001, past *Pretty Woman* as the highest grossing Hollywood romantic comedy of all time. Featuring a cocky Mel Gibson tamed by a forgiving Helen Hunt, the movie's happy ending suggested, once again, that what women *really* want is a good, old-fashioned, coldhearted redemption plot from the male point of view. As a sign of the times, these three movies—along with all the other Hollywood romantic comedies released in the year 2000—extended the streak of Hollywood romantic comedies that, throughout the 1980s and 1990s, thematically keyed on social regeneration through coupling.

As for this book's sample of Hollywood romantic comedies, it ends with the beginning of the year 2000. But this does not mean that this study of the Hollywood romantic comedy has to end with the beginning of the year 2000 or, for that matter, the year 2001. After all, the Hollywood romantic comedy will be around for a long time—perhaps for as long as there continues to be a Hollywood and there continue to be love stories. The typologies and classifications presented in this book provide all the necessary tools for continuing this study of the Hollywood romantic comedy. Now that the four Hollywood love stories have been identified, it doesn't take an expert to track the basic Hollywood romantic comedy plots, and their variations, across time. Most viewers will be able to identify which plots are being employed, or are about to be employed, within the first ten to twenty minutes of the movie. By the end of the Hollywood romantic comedy, most viewers will further be able to identify the genre type and the theme and, from there, to decipher the ideological significance of the Hollywood romantic comedy. As mentioned earlier, this does not mean that these viewers have to leave the movie hating it, especially if it is pleasing. But it does mean that they can leave the movie with a broader understanding of why its story(s) may be so pleasing, and what these pleasures may say about contemporary gender relations and genre constructions.

As this study demonstrates, the Hollywood romantic comedy is more prevalent today than it was in the 1970s, and it is more thematically conventional. But it would be wrong to conclude from this that there has been no progress in either gender relations or Hollywood romantic comedy genre constructions since the 1970s. Indeed, in many important ways, America has come to grips with how it has historically treated and mistreated its women. There have been significant changes in laws and there have been significant changes in attitudes. Not long ago, after all, in many parts of this country, women were routinely excluded from the best schools and the best jobs because they were "not men." Not long ago, in many parts of this country, women could not secure credit cards, obtain mortgages, or sign contracts without a man signing off for them. Not long ago, in many parts of this country, women could not obtain divorces on any grounds except adultery, and a divorced woman was considered unmarriageable, at least to any "decent" man, since, obviously, she was not a "lady." Not long ago, in many parts of this country, women could not legally charge their husbands with rape since sexual relations on demand were considered part of the marital contract. Not long ago, in many parts of this country, women had no legal access to birth control pills or abortions. Not long ago, in many parts of this country, women who had illegitimate children were branded for life as lowlifes. Not long ago, in many parts of this country, women had only two choices if they were victimized by sexual harassment—to agree to sexual relations or quit their job. And not long ago, in many parts of this country, women had only two choices if they were sexually assaulted—to keep it to themselves or be attacked a second time in court with their past sexual and mental histories, whether real, exaggerated, or imagined.[3]

Indeed, much has changed. Today, women make up just under one-half of the American labor force and, if current trends continue, may constitute the majority of the American labor force by the year 2050.[4] Today, two-thirds of all adult women, including married women with children, work outside the home.[5] Today, fifty-five percent of all undergraduate students in American colleges and universities are women with the imbalance, if anything, growing larger every year.[6] Today, there are legal protections against sexual harassment and marital rape; and there are rape shield laws, which, although not impenetrable, bolster existing legal protections against sexual assault. Today, while abortion remains a hotly contested issue in American political culture, most Americans don't look twice anymore if they come across a woman who is divorced, pregnant and unmarried, and/or sexually active before marriage. And yes, today, more than twenty years after *Private Benjamin*, women are not only in the army, they are flying fighter jets and piloting space shuttles.

Not surprisingly, many of these changes have spilled over into the Hollywood romantic comedy. While today's Hollywood romantic comedies are more thematically conventional than their 1970s predecessors, the heroines in these movies are, on average, more economically and sexually liberated than their predecessors. By and large, they have moved out of the kitchens and into the offices. They are typically better educated and wealthier than their 1970s counterparts. They know what they want and how to get what they want. They are not ashamed of their minds and they are not embarrassed about their bodies. They enjoy sex, talk about sex, and engage in sex, even if their sexual relations (with the hero) are usually framed quite discreetly, and, ultimately, their sexual desires are supplanted by their maternal desires.

Equally important, while today's Hollywood romantic comedy heroines are, on average, more liberated than their predecessors, today's Hollywood romantic comedy heroes are, on average, less dominant than their predecessors. As noted earlier, the most frequently utilized Hollywood romantic comedy plot—the redemption plot—points toward a modification in cultural attitudes about men. A strong man is not the same as a cruel man. A gentle man is not the same as a weak man. A loving man is a good man. And an unloving man who learns to love, no matter how late in life, is a better man for it. No muscle-bound brutes here. Any cowboys longing to ride alone into the sunset need not apply. God knows, we can only pray that some of this gentleness will spill over into the real world and result, someday, in a lot less angry and violent men.

And yet, despite these changes in both gender relations and Hollywood romantic comedy genre constructions, in a number of fundamental areas, not very much has changed. Women may make more money than ever before, but women still only make seventy-five cents to every dollar men make.[7] Women may have moved out of their homes and into the labor force in greater numbers than ever before, but women are still overwhelmingly socialized into traditionally female jobs and professions where they end up taking care of others, while still primarily responsible, after work, for taking care of their homes, husbands, and children.[8] Women may be more sexually liberated than ever before, but women are also increasingly prisoners of their own bodies—working more hours than ever before to keep their bodies in shape, and spending more money than ever before to show off that shape in the best possible light. Women may be better educated than ever before, but, arguably, women aren't taken any more seriously—still primarily judged on how they look rather than on what they think. Women may have more legal protections than ever before, but women are just as likely as ever to be sexually harassed and/or sexually assaulted, with their violators still far too often getting away with it.[9]

Not surprisingly, just as with the changes in gender relations, many of these contradictions have spilled over into the Hollywood romantic comedy. While today's Hollywood romantic comedy heroines may be, on average, more economically self-sufficient than their 1970s counterparts, they are less independent—typically depicted as helpless and hopeless without a man. While they may be better educated, they are not as smart—typically depicted as foolish in their initial choice of mate, shallow in their obsessions over men, and spiteful in the way they relate to other women. While they may know more about what they want and how to get what they want, they are less ambitious—typically depicted as wanting nothing more than a husband. And while they may be more sexually liberated than their 1970s counterparts, they are also more tied to old traditions—traditions that, ironically, will eventually put them back into the home and ultimately result in a negation of their sexual power.[10]

So what, then, do we have? A popular form of entertainment that naturalizes gender inequality and often masks an undercurrent of hostility toward its female protagonist and mostly female audience. A popular form of entertainment that even as it tries to be nonviolent, both reflects and reinforces its parent society's best and worst impulses. And that society, at its worst, is still a society filled with both conscious and unconscious hostility toward women. From misogynous lyrics in popular music; to web pages that, in addition to more traditional forms of pornography, offer snuff sites where surfers can download photo manipulations of young women—including their favorite female celebrities—tortured, dismembered, and murdered; to the frequency, and the vehemence, in which the word "bitch" has become a part of so many people's everyday vocabulary; women remain the target of a great deal of subtle, and not so subtle, anger in America.

Indeed, on the very day that I saw the last Hollywood romantic comedy of the twentieth century, *The Bachelor*, in a movie theater just outside of New Orleans—a movie as contemptuous toward women as any movie in the sample—I found the following words scrawled in black magic marker on the theater's bathroom wall: *No matter how good looking she may be, there is someone, somewhere, who is sick of her shit.* And sure enough, less than a month later, while eating in a restaurant in Los Angeles, I found the same message scrawled on yet another bathroom wall. From coast to coast, then, it seems like there are a lot of angry men all over America. And it also seems like most of these men are angry at women—the very group of people who, collectively, serve as the object of so much of their attentions and needs.

Yet another cultural contradiction.

And still another. For it is not only men in America who are socialized into putting down women. Women, too, are socialized into putting down each other—typically in battles over men. Indeed, the graffiti in the men's rooms in New Orleans and Los Angeles pales in comparison with the graffiti in girls' rooms in junior high schools and high schools all over this country. For in addition to the ever-present hearts with initials and arrows drawn through them, there is also the ubiquitous "so-and-so is a slut" or "so-and-so is a bitch." So just like men, women also learn early what their culture teaches them: to channel their anger toward other women. And not unexpectedly, one way or another, most of that anger eventually gets channeled back to them.

Not that any of this should come as much of a surprise. For if art imitates life, which, in turn, imitates art, all we need to do is remember that this is still a country, after all, where the top news story of 1999 was the impeachment hearings of a president.[11] And this is still a country that ultimately framed those impeachment hearings and its major participants in the following terms. The intern was a slut. The best friend was a bitch. The president may have been a cad, but he also did a good job. Besides, his wife forgave him, so why shouldn't we? Heck, let's face it. This is a still a country, after all, where even "the feminists," when push came to shove, backed "their man."[12]

As yet another example of life imitating art, or, in this case, life imitating the movies, the "presidential scandal" could not have been scripted any better: a quintessential Hollywood romantic comedy—played out in the national spotlight—complete with a temptress, a bitch foil, a prick foil (if you want to throw in the prosecutor), and a forgiving heroine closing out the narrative pleasures of the coldhearted redemption plot from the male point of view.[13] And yet, lost in that Hollywood romantic comedy's "happy ending" is the fact that—once again—a number of real women got hurt and a number of other real women got vilified while network pundits and comics, mostly but not exclusively male, capitalized on their pain.

Of course, even in its most hostile connotations, nobody can hold the Hollywood romantic comedy responsible for all the real women who continue to get hurt and/or vilified in America. Popular culture forms do not have that much power. After all, stories are only make-believe and movies aren't real. Narratives can never dictate what people say and do; ultimately people decide which scripts to accept and which ones to reject. So to say, for example, that Hollywood romantic comedies are the cause of either sexual inequality or sexual violence in American society would be—as Ryan O'Neal tells Barbra Streisand in *What's Up, Doc?* when she informs him that love means never having to say you're sorry—"the dumbest thing I ever heard."

So why, then, should people care?

Because our narratives do matter. Because our narratives, if they don't cause, certainly do affect. Because all the efforts in recent years by women, and on behalf of women, to improve the economic, social, and political conditions for women in this country have done little, if anything, to fundamentally change our narratives. Because in our narratives, men win women and women are won. Because in our narratives, men matter and women matter less. Because in our narratives, if women resist, they pay a price for that resistance. Because in our narratives, women rarely resist. Because in our narratives, the selfless female is the only female we really care about. Because in our narratives, it is better to be a male than a female. Because in our narratives, the love that heals men, often hinders women.[14]

To be sure, all this needs to be qualified. *What narratives?* I've only looked at one narrative in this study: the Hollywood romantic comedy as it is conveyed through its four love stories. *How much do narratives affect?* I've not even tried to quantify it; instead, I'm presenting it as a given that, to some degree, our identities are shaped—not determined—by the stories we see, and by the accumulation of the stories we see. *Do these stories only work to crush, contain, or co-opt ideological resistance?* Of course not. As I've said before, we are talking about propensities, not absolutes. All cultural texts have within them challenges to the dominant culture. But in some cultural texts, in order to uncover those ideological challenges, all we need to do is to scoop them up with a spoon. In other cultural texts, we need to dig them out with a jackhammer.

Romantic courtship is supposed to be equal. The four Hollywood love stories, as they conventionally play out, are typically not equal. Occasionally, they are hurtful and harmful. And when they are hurtful and harmful, they may contribute to attitudes and beliefs that, in real life, may hurt and harm women. To say this, of course, is not to say that American women are weak and helpless. Certainly, there are tens of millions of women in this country who are proud and strong and daring and defiant, and do not need the tools of textual analysis to teach them how to be proud and strong and daring and defiant. Certainly, there are tens of millions of women in this country who do not see themselves as victims, and do not act as victims. Certainly, there are tens of millions of women in this country who are assertive and self-confident. Certainly, there are tens of millions of women in this country who know what they want and know how to get what they want. Certainly, there are tens of millions of women in this country who want more than just a man. And certainly, there are tens of millions of women in this country who are in warm and wonderful relationships with men who are as kind and as caring as any man, or woman, could ever hope to be.

But these tens of millions of women are the way that they are *in spite of*, not because of, the conventional Hollywood romantic comedy. And this, in turn, raises two key questions: how much more could these women be—and how many more tens of millions of women could there be like them—if conventional Hollywood romantic comedies, along with similar narratives, offered both women and men more choices?

In considering these questions, both women and men might also want to take a second look at some of the counterconventional 1970s Hollywood romantic comedies to see what, if anything, they can appropriate from them to broaden their choices, options, and horizons. After all, women and men do have a choice: they can work to change the narratives, or they can wait for the narratives to change them. Even though they did not last very long, the counterconventional 1970s Hollywood romantic comedies showed that Hollywood love stories are not cast in stone. Neither are our love stories.

Although *Private Benjamin* was the last commercially successful Hollywood romantic comedy in the sample to key on self-actualization through uncoupling, and *She-Devil*, the last uncommercially successful Hollywood romantic comedy in the sample to key on self-actualization through uncoupling, these certainly won't be the last counterconventional Hollywood romantic comedies. As certain as gender roles and relationships are not forever fixed; as certain as genres can—and do—change; and as certain as new generations replace old generations, there will be Hollywood romantic comedies in the future, as there were in the past, positing alternative love stories that defy dominant gender conventions. There will be strong heroines who pursue just as much as they are pursued. There will be sweet heroes who emotionally give just as much as they emotionally get. There will be heroes who love heroes. There will be heroines who love heroines. There will be heroes without heroines; and there will be heroines without heroes; and there will be heroes and heroines who, loving each other, decide they must go their separate ways. And they, too, will all live happily ever after.

Until that day arrives, however, a critical rereading of the four Hollywood love stories can reveal, once again, all the subtle and not so subtle ways that social inequality is often reinforced as much, if not more so, by stories as by force. And this, in turn, can remind us, once again, of the force of stories to make a difference for better or worse in the battle for social equality, which, itself, demands that all people *truly* believe and practice the most fundamental American premise—that all men *and* women are created equal.

Appendix

Data Collection Tables

Table 11
The "Top" 155 Hollywood Romantic Comedies: Plots, Genre Types, and Themes*

RANK	TITLE OF MOVIE	PLOT	GENRE TYPE	THEME	YEAR
1	Tootsie	Redemption (coldhearted/m) Foil (prick)	Conventional	Social Regeneration through coupling	1982
2	"Crocodile" Dundee	Redemption (brokenhearted/m) Foil (dweeb)	Conventional	Social Regeneration through coupling	1986
3	Heaven Can Wait	Redemption (brokenhearted/m)	Conventional	Social Regeneration through coupling	1978
4	Pretty Woman	Pursuit/m Redemption (coldhearted/m)	Conventional	Social Regeneration through coupling	1990
5	The Goodbye Girl	Pursuit/m Redemption (coldhearted/f and brokenhearted/m)	Conventional	Social Regeneration through coupling	1977
6	There's Something About Mary	Pursuit/m Redemption (brokenhearted/m) Foil (prick)	Conventional	Social Regeneration through coupling	1998
7	Look Who's Talking	Pursuit/m Redemption (brokenhearted/m) Foil (prick)	Conventional	Social Regeneration through coupling	1989
8	Jerry Maguire	Redemption (coldhearted/m) Foil (bitch)	Conventional	Social Regeneration through coupling	1996
9	Arthur	Redemption (coldhearted/m) Foil (bitch) Permission (acceptance)	Conventional	Social Regeneration through coupling	1981
10	What's Up, Doc?	Pursuit/f Redemption (brokenhearted/m) Foil (bitch)	Screwball	Self-actualization coupled with coupling	1972
11	As Good As It Gets	Pursuit/m Redemption (coldhearted/m)	Conventional	Social Regeneration through coupling	1997
12	Coming to America	Pursuit/m Redemption (brokenhearted/m) Foil (prick) Permission (acceptance)	Conventional	Social Regeneration through coupling	1988

*The /m, /f, or /b after pursuit, coldhearted, or brokenhearted indicates "point of view" (male, female, or equally from both the male and the female point of view).

156

Table 11 (continued)

RANK	TITLE OF MOVIE	PLOT	GENRE TYPE	THEME	YEAR
13	"10"	Pursuit/m Redemption (coldhearted/m) Foil (temptress)	Conventional	Social Regeneration through coupling	1979
14	Sleepless in Seattle	Redemption (brokenhearted/m) Foil (dweeb)	Conventional	Social Regeneration through coupling	1993
15	Runaway Bride	Redemption (coldhearted/m) Foil (dweeb)	Conventional	Social Regeneration through coupling	1999
16	My Best Friend's Wedding	Pursuit/f Redemption (coldhearted/f)	Unconventional	Social Regeneration through coupling	1997
17	Shampoo	Pursuit/m Redemption (brokenhearted/m) Foil (prick and bitch)	Ironic	Self-actualization through uncoupling	1975
18	You've Got Mail	Pursuit/m Redemption (coldhearted/m) Foil (dweeb and bitch)	Conventional	Social Regeneration through coupling	1998
19	When Harry Met Sally	Pursuit/m Redemption (coldhearted/m)	Conventional	Social Regeneration through coupling	1989
20	Notting Hill	Redemption (brokenhearted/b)	Conventional	Social Regeneration through coupling	1999
21	Private Benjamin	Redemption (brokenhearted/f)	Unconventional	Self-actualization through uncoupling	1980
22	The Main Event	Pursuit/m Redemption (brokenhearted/m)	Conventional	Social Regeneration through coupling	1979
23	Michael	Redemption (coldhearted/m)	Conventional	Social Regeneration through coupling	1996
24	Shakespeare in Love	Pursuit/m Redemption (brokenhearted/m) Foil (prick) Permission (separation)	Unconventional	Social Regeneration through coupling	1998
25	The War of the Roses	Pursuit/m Redemption (coldhearted/m and brokenhearted/b)	Unconventional	Social Regeneration through coupling	1989
26	Semi-Tough	Pursuit/m Foil (prick)	Unconventional	Self-actualization through uncoupling	1977
27	Splash	Redemption (brokenhearted/m)	Conventional	Social Regeneration through coupling	1984

Table 11 (continued)

RANK	TITLE OF MOVIE	PLOT	GENRE TYPE	THEME	YEAR
28	Moonstruck	Pursuit/m Redemption (coldhearted/m and brokenhearted/f) Foil (dweeb)	Conventional	Social Regeneration through coupling	1987
29	Cocktail	Pursuit/m Redemption (coldhearted/m) Foil (bitch) Permission (separation)	Conventional	Social Regeneration through coupling	1988
30	While You Were Sleeping	Redemption (brokenhearted/f) Foil (prick)	Conventional	Social Regeneration through coupling	1995
31	Annie Hall	Pursuit/m Redemption (coldhearted/m)	Unconventional	Self-actualization through uncoupling	1977
32	The Wedding Singer	Pursuit/m Redemption (brokenhearted/m) Foil (prick and bitch)	Conventional	Social Regeneration through coupling	1998
33	Groundhog Day	Pursuit/m Redemption (coldhearted/m)	Conventional	Social Regeneration through coupling	1993
34	Love at First Bite	Pursuit/m Redemption (brokenhearted/m) Foil (dweeb)	Parody	Self-actualization coupled with coupling	1979
35	Boomerang	Pursuit/m Foil (dweeb and bitch)	Conventional	Social Regeneration through coupling	1992
36	Carnal Knowledge	Pursuit/m Redemption (coldhearted/m)	Unconventional	Self-actualization through uncoupling	1971
37	Seems Like Old Times	Pursuit/m Foil (dweeb)	Conventional	Social Regeneration through coupling	1980
38	Nine Months	Redemption (coldhearted/m)	Conventional	Social Regeneration through coupling	1995
39	Six Days, Seven Nights	Redemption (coldhearted/m) Foil (dweeb)	Conventional	Social Regeneration through coupling	1998
40	Starting Over	Pursuit/m Redemption (brokenhearted/m) Foil (bitch)	Conventional	Social Regeneration through coupling	1979
41	Working Girl	Foil (prick and bitch)	Conventional	Social Regeneration through coupling	1988
42	The Owl and the Pussycat	Redemption (brokenhearted/b)	Conventional	Social Regeneration through coupling	1970

Table 11 (continued)

RANK	TITLE OF MOVIE	PLOT	GENRE TYPE	THEME	YEAR
43	The Parent Trap	Pursuit/m Redemption (brokenhearted/b) Foil (bitch)	Conventional	Social Regeneration through coupling	1998
44	Housesitter	Pursuit/m Redemption (brokenhearted/m) Foil (bitch)	Conventional	Social Regeneration through coupling	1992
45	The American President	Redemption (brokenhearted/m)	Conventional	Social Regeneration through coupling	1995
46	Heroes	Redemption (brokenhearted/m)	Unconventional	Self-actualization coupled with coupling	1977
47	Bustin' Loose	Redemption (coldhearted/m) Foil (prick)	Conventional	Social Regeneration through coupling	1981
48	Best Friends	Pursuit/m Redemption (coldhearted/m)	Unconventional	Self-actualization coupled with coupling	1982
49	Doc Hollywood	Pursuit/m Redemption (brokenhearted/m) Foil (dweeb)	Conventional	Social Regeneration through coupling	1991
50	Hope Floats	Pursuit/m Redemption (brokenhearted/f) Foil (prick)	Conventional	Social Regeneration through coupling	1998
51	Four Weddings and a Funeral	Redemption (coldhearted/m)	Conventional	Social Regeneration through coupling	1994
52	Manhattan	Pursuit/m Redemption (brokenhearted/m) Foil (prick and bitch)	Unconventional	Self-actualization through uncoupling	1979
53	Broadcast News	Pursuit/m Redemption (brokenhearted/b) Foil (prick and dweeb)	Unconventional	Social Regeneration through coupling	1987
54	She's All That	Pursuit/m Redemption (coldhearted/m) Foil (prick and bitch)	Conventional	Social Regeneration through coupling	1999
55	House Calls	Redemption (coldhearted/m)	Conventional	Social Regeneration through coupling	1978
56	Sabrina	Redemption (coldhearted/m) Foil (dweeb)	Conventional	Social Regeneration through coupling	1995
57	Chapter Two	Redemption (brokenhearted/m)	Conventional	Social Regeneration through coupling	1979

Table 11 (continued)

RANK	TITLE OF MOVIE	PLOT	GENRE TYPE	THEME	YEAR
58	Bull Durham	Pursuit/m Redemption (brokenhearted/m) Foil (dweeb)	Conventional	Social Regeneration through coupling	1988
59	Tin Cup	Pursuit/m Redemption (brokenhearted/m) Foil (prick)	Conventional	Social Regeneration through coupling	1996
60	Something to Talk About	Redemption (coldhearted/m and brokenhearted/b)	Unconventional	Self-actualization coupled with coupling	1995
61	Never Been Kissed	Redemption (brokenhearted/f)	Conventional	Social Regeneration through coupling	1999
62	The Preacher's Wife	Redemption (coldhearted/m)	Conventional	Social Regeneration through coupling	1996
63	Pretty in Pink	Redemption (brokenhearted/f) Foil (dweeb)	Conventional	Social Regeneration through coupling	1986
64	Made in America	Redemption (coldhearted/m)	Conventional	Social Regeneration through coupling	1993
65	For Pete's Sake	Redemption (brokenhearted/b)	Conventional	Social Regeneration through coupling	1974
66	All of Me	Redemption (coldhearted/f and brokenhearted/m) Foil (bitch and temptress)	Screwball	Social Regeneration through coupling	1984
67	An Unmarried Woman	Redemption (brokenhearted/f)	Unconventional	Self-actualization through uncoupling	1978
68	One Fine Day	Redemption (brokenhearted/b)	Conventional	Social Regeneration through coupling	1996
69	About Last Night	Pursuit/m Redemption (coldhearted/m)	Conventional	Social Regeneration through coupling	1986
70	Force of Nature	Foil (temptress)	Conventional	Social Regeneration through coupling	1999
71	Blind Date	Redemption (brokenhearted/m) Foil (prick)	Conventional	Social Regeneration through coupling	1987
72	Roxanne	Redemption (brokenhearted/m) Foil (dweeb)	Conventional	Social Regeneration through coupling	1987
73	Practical Magic	Redemption (brokenhearted/f)	Conventional	Social Regeneration through coupling	1998

160

Table 11 (continued)

RANK	TITLE OF MOVIE	PLOT	GENRE TYPE	THEME	YEAR
74	A Touch of Class	Redemption (brokenhearted/b) Foil (bitch)	Unconventional	Self-actualization through uncoupling	1973
75	Mannequin	Redemption (brokenhearted/m) Foil (bitch)	Conventional	Social Regeneration through coupling	1987
76	Joe Versus the Volcano	Redemption (brokenhearted/m)	Unconventional	Social Regeneration through coupling	1990
77	Alice Doesn't Live Here Anymore	Redemption (brokenhearted/f)	Unconventional	Self-actualization through uncoupling	1974
78	The Mirror Has Two Faces	Redemption (brokenhearted/f) Foil (prick)	Conventional	Social Regeneration through coupling	1996
79	It Could Happen to You	Redemption (brokenhearted/b) Foil (bitch)	Conventional	Social Regeneration through coupling	1994
80	French Kiss	Pursuit/m Redemption (coldhearted/m) Foil (dweeb)	Conventional	Social Regeneration through coupling	1995
81	Pete 'n' Tillie	Redemption (coldhearted/m and brokenhearted/b)	Unconventional	Ambiguous	1972
82	Murphy's Romance	Redemption (brokenhearted/b) Foil (prick)	Conventional	Social Regeneration through coupling	1985
83	Lovers and Other Strangers	Redemption (brokenhearted/b)	Unconventional	Self-actualization through uncoupling	1970
84	Honeymoon in Vegas	Pursuit/m Redemption (brokenhearted/m) Foil (prick)	Conventional	Social Regeneration through coupling	1992
85	Same Time, Next Year	Redemption (brokenhearted/b)	Unconventional	Self-actualization coupled with coupling	1978
86	Can't Buy Me Love	Pursuit/m Redemption (brokenhearted/m)	Conventional	Social Regeneration through coupling	1987
87	How Stella Got Her Groove Back	Pursuit/m Redemption (brokenhearted/f)	Conventional	Social Regeneration through coupling	1998
88	Night Shift	Redemption (brokenhearted/m) Foil (bitch)	Conventional	Social Regeneration through coupling	1982

Table 11 (continued)

RANK	TITLE OF MOVIE	PLOT	GENRE TYPE	THEME	YEAR
89	The Truth About Cats and Dogs	Redemption (brokenhearted/f) Foil (temptress)	Conventional	Social Regeneration through coupling	1996
90	Micki and Maude	Redemption (brokenhearted/m)	Conventional	Social Regeneration through coupling	1984
91	Desperately Seeking Susan	Redemption (brokenhearted/f) Foil (prick)	Screwball	Social Regeneration through coupling	1985
92	Forget Paris	Redemption (brokenhearted/b)	Conventional	Social Regeneration through coupling	1995
93	Butterflies are Free	Redemption (coldhearted/f and brokenhearted/m) Permission (separation)	Unconventional	Self-actualization coupled with coupling	1972
94	The Woman in Red	Pursuit/m Redemption (coldhearted/m) Foil (temptress)	Conventional	Social Regeneration through coupling	1984
95	10 Things I Hate About You	Pursuit/m Redemption (coldhearted/f)	Conventional	Social Regeneration through coupling	1999
96	Diary of a Mad Housewife	Redemption (coldhearted/m and brokenhearted/f) Foil (prick)	Unconventional	Self-actualization through uncoupling	1970
97	Addicted to Love	Redemption (coldhearted/f and brokenhearted/m)	Conventional	Social Regeneration through coupling	1997
98	The Heartbreak Kid	Pursuit/m Foil (temptress) Permission (acceptance)	Ironic	Self-actualization through uncoupling	1972
99	Play it Again, Sam	Redemption (brokenhearted/m) Foil (prick)	Unconventional	Ambiguous	1972
100	For Love of the Game	Pursuit/m Redemption (coldhearted/m)	Conventional	Social Regeneration through coupling	1999
101	For Richer or Poorer	Redemption (brokenhearted/b)	Conventional	Social Regeneration through coupling	1997
102	L.A. Story	Pursuit/m Redemption (brokenhearted/m) Foil (dweeb, bitch, and temptress)	Conventional	Social Regeneration through coupling	1991
103	A New Leaf	Pursuit/m Redemption (coldhearted/m)	Unconventional	Ambiguous	1971
104	Green Card	Redemption (coldhearted/m) Foil (dweeb)	Conventional	Social Regeneration through coupling	1990

Table 11 (continued)

RANK	TITLE OF MOVIE	PLOT	GENRE TYPE	THEME	YEAR
105	Picture Perfect	Redemption (brokenhearted/f) Foil (prick)	Conventional	Social Regeneration through coupling	1997
106	The Best Man	Redemption (coldhearted/m) Foil (bitch)	Conventional	Social Regeneration through coupling	1999
107	Baby Boom	Redemption (coldhearted/f)	Conventional	Social Regeneration through coupling	1987
108	Fools Rush In	Redemption (brokenhearted/b) Permission (acceptance)	Conventional	Social Regeneration through coupling	1997
109	I.Q.	Pursuit/m Foil (prick)	Conventional	Social Regeneration through coupling	1994
110	Overboard	Redemption (coldhearted/f and brokenhearted/m) Foil (prick)	Conventional	Social Regeneration through coupling	1987
111	Paternity	Redemption (coldhearted/m)	Conventional	Social Regeneration through coupling	1981
112	The Object of My Affection	Redemption (brokenhearted/f)	Conventional	Social Regeneration through coupling	1998
113	Funny Farm	Redemption (coldhearted/m and brokenhearted/b)	Conventional	Social Regeneration through coupling	1988
114	Grosse Pointe Blank	Pursuit/m Redemption (coldhearted/m)	Conventional	Social Regeneration through coupling	1997
115	Sixteen Candles	Redemption (brokenhearted/f)	Conventional	Social Regeneration through coupling	1984
116	Continental Divide	Pursuit/m Redemption (coldhearted/m)	Unconventional	Self-actualization coupled with coupling	1981
117	Other People's Money	Pursuit/m Redemption (coldhearted/m)	Conventional	Social Regeneration through coupling	1991
118	Unfaithfully Yours	Redemption (coldhearted/m)	Conventional	Social Regeneration through coupling	1984
119	There's a Girl in My Soup	Pursuit/m Redemption (coldhearted/m) Foil (prick)	Ironic	Self-actualization through uncoupling	1970
120	The Out-of-Towners	Redemption (brokenhearted/b)	Conventional	Social Regeneration through coupling	1999

Table 11 (continued)

RANK	TITLE OF MOVIE	PLOT	GENRE TYPE	THEME	YEAR
121	Blame It On Rio	Redemption (coldhearted/m) Foil (temptress)	Conventional	Social Regeneration through coupling	1984
122	The Other Sister	Redemption (brokenhearted/b) Permission (acceptance)	Conventional	Social Regeneration through coupling	1999
123	Cousins	Foil (prick and bitch)	Conventional	Social Regeneration through coupling	1989
124	The Story of Us	Redemption (brokenhearted/b)	Conventional	Social Regeneration through coupling	1999
125	Valley Girl	Pursuit/m Foil (prick)	Conventional	Social Regeneration through coupling	1983
126	The Last Married Couple in America	Redemption (brokenhearted/b)	Conventional	Social Regeneration through coupling	1980
127	Kiss Me Goodbye	Foil (prick)	Conventional	Social Regeneration through coupling	1982
128	Frankie & Johnny	Pursuit/m Redemption (brokenhearted/b)	Conventional	Social Regeneration through coupling	1991
129	Blast From the Past	Pursuit/m Redemption (brokenhearted/m)	Conventional	Social Regeneration through coupling	1999
130	The Sure Thing	Pursuit/m Foil (dweeb and temptress)	Conventional	Social Regeneration through coupling	1985
131	Say Anything	Pursuit/m Redemption (brokenhearted/m) Permission (separation)	Conventional	Social Regeneration through coupling	1989
132	Speechless	Pursuit/m Foil (dweeb)	Conventional	Social Regeneration through coupling	1994
133	Only You	Pursuit/m Foil (dweeb)	Conventional	Social Regeneration through coupling	1994
134	Multiplicity	Redemption (coldhearted/m)	Conventional	Social Regeneration through coupling	1996
135	Prelude to a Kiss	Redemption (coldhearted/f)	Unconventional	Social Regeneration through coupling	1992

Table 11 (continued)

RANK	TITLE OF MOVIE	PLOT	GENRE TYPE	THEME	YEAR
136	Some Kind of Wonderful	Pursuit/m Redemption (brokenhearted/m) Foil (temptress)	Conventional	Social Regeneration through coupling	1987
137	Only the Lonely	Redemption (brokenhearted/m) Permission (separation)	Conventional	Social Regeneration through coupling	1991
138	It's My Turn	Redemption (brokenhearted/b) Foil (dweeb)	Conventional	Social Regeneration through coupling	1980
139	Milk Money	Redemption (brokenhearted/b)	Conventional	Social Regeneration through coupling	1994
140	Born Yesterday	Foil (prick)	Conventional	Social Regeneration through coupling	1993
141	First Monday in October	Redemption (coldhearted/m)	Unconventional	Self-actualization through uncoupling	1981
142	The Bachelor	Pursuit/m Redemption (coldhearted/m)	Conventional	Social Regeneration through coupling	1999
143	Up the Sandbox	Redemption (coldhearted/m and brokenhearted/b)	Unconventional	Self-actualization through uncoupling	1972
144	Used People	Pursuit/m	Conventional	Social Regeneration through coupling	1992
145	Heart and Souls	Redemption (coldhearted/m)	Conventional	Social Regeneration through coupling	1993
146	Defending Your Life	Redemption (brokenhearted/m)	Conventional	Social Regeneration through coupling	1991
147	Crossing Delancey	Pursuit/m Foil (prick)	Conventional	Social Regeneration through coupling	1988
148	She-Devil	Redemption (coldhearted/m and brokenhearted/f) Foil (bitch)	Unconventional	Self-actualization through uncoupling	1989
149	Irreconcilable Differences	Redemption (coldhearted/m and brokenhearted/b) Foil (bitch)	Unconventional	Ambiguous	1984
150	Educating Rita	Pursuit/m Redemption (brokenhearted/m)	Unconventional	Self-actualization through uncoupling	1983
151	An Ideal Husband	Redemption (coldhearted/m) Foil (bitch)	Conventional	Social Regeneration through coupling	1999

Table 11 (continued)

RANK	TITLE OF MOVIE	PLOT	GENRE TYPE	THEME	YEAR
152	Threesome	Pursuit/m Redemption (brokenhearted/m) Foil (prick and dweeb)	Unconventional	Ambiguous	1994
153	Drive Me Crazy	Redemption (brokenhearted/b) Foil (prick and bitch)	Conventional	Social Regeneration through coupling	1999
154	Blume in Love	Pursuit/m Foil (dweeb)	Unconventional	Self-actualization through uncoupling	1973
155	The Pick-up Artist	Pursuit/m Redemption (coldhearted/m)	Conventional	Social Regeneration through coupling	1987

Table 12
Year-by-Year Chronology of Hollywood Romantic Comedy Plots,
Genre Types, and Themes

YEAR	TITLE OF MOVIE	PLOT	GENRE TYPE	THEME
1970	Lovers and Other Strangers	Redemption (brokenhearted/b)	Unconventional	Self-actualization through uncoupling
1970	Diary of a Mad Housewife	Redemption (coldhearted/m and brokenhearted/f) Foil (prick)	Unconventional	Self-actualization through uncoupling
1970	The Owl and the Pussycat	Redemption (brokenhearted/b)	Conventional	Social Regeneration through coupling
1970	There's a Girl in My Soup	Pursuit/m Redemption (coldhearted/m) Foil (prick)	Ironic	Self-actualization through uncoupling
1971	A New Leaf	Pursuit/m Redemption (coldhearted/m)	Unconventional	Ambiguous
1971	Carnal Knowledge	Pursuit/m Redemption (coldhearted/m)	Unconventional	Self-actualization through uncoupling
1972	What's Up, Doc?	Pursuit/f Redemption (brokenhearted/m) Foil (bitch)	Screwball	Self-actualization coupled with coupling
1972	Play it Again, Sam	Redemption (brokenhearted/m) Foil (prick)	Unconventional	Ambiguous
1972	Butterflies are Free	Redemption (coldhearted/f and brokenhearted/m) Permission (separation)	Unconventional	Self-actualization coupled with coupling
1972	The Heartbreak Kid	Pursuit/m Foil (temptress) Permission (acceptance)	Ironic	Self-actualization through uncoupling
1972	Pete 'n' Tillie	Redemption (coldhearted/m and brokenhearted/b)	Unconventional	Ambiguous
1972	Up the Sandbox	Redemption (coldhearted/m and brokenhearted/b)	Unconventional	Self-actualization through uncoupling
1973	Blume in Love	Pursuit/m Foil (dweeb)	Unconventional	Self-actualization through uncoupling
1973	A Touch of Class	Redemption (brokenhearted/b) Foil (bitch)	Unconventional	Self-actualization through uncoupling
1974	For Pete's Sake	Redemption (brokenhearted/b)	Conventional	Social Regeneration through coupling
1974	Alice Doesn't Live Here Anymore	Redemption (brokenhearted/f)	Unconventional	Self-actualization through uncoupling

Table 12 (continued)

YEAR	TITLE OF MOVIE	PLOT	GENRE TYPE	THEME
1975	Shampoo	Pursuit/m Redemption (brokenhearted/m) Foil (prick and bitch)	Ironic	Self-actualization through uncoupling
1977	Annie Hall	Pursuit/m Redemption (coldhearted/m)	Unconventional	Self-actualization through uncoupling
1977	Heroes	Redemption (brokenhearted/m)	Unconventional	Self-actualization coupled with coupling
1977	Semi-Tough	Pursuit/m Foil (prick)	Unconventional	Self-actualization through uncoupling
1977	The Goodbye Girl	Pursuit/m Redemption (coldhearted/f and brokenhearted/m)	Conventional	Social Regeneration through coupling
1978	An Unmarried Woman	Redemption (brokenhearted/f)	Unconventional	Self-actualization through uncoupling
1978	House Calls	Redemption (coldhearted/m)	Conventional	Social Regeneration through coupling
1978	Heaven Can Wait	Redemption (brokenhearted/m)	Conventional	Social Regeneration through coupling
1978	Same Time, Next Year	Redemption (brokenhearted/b)	Unconventional	Self-actualization coupled with coupling
1979	Love at First Bite	Pursuit/m Redemption (brokenhearted/m) Foil (dweeb)	Parody	Self-actualization coupled with coupling
1979	Manhattan	Pursuit/m Redemption (brokenhearted/m) Foil (prick and bitch)	Unconventional	Self-actualization through uncoupling
1979	The Main Event	Pursuit/m Redemption (brokenhearted/m)	Conventional	Social Regeneration through coupling
1979	"10"	Pursuit/m Redemption (coldhearted/m) Foil (temptress)	Conventional	Social Regeneration through coupling
1979	Starting Over	Pursuit/m Redemption (brokenhearted/m) Foil (bitch)	Conventional	Social Regeneration through coupling
1979	Chapter Two	Redemption (brokenhearted/m)	Conventional	Social Regeneration through coupling
1980	It's My Turn	Redemption (brokenhearted/b) Foil (dweeb)	Conventional	Social Regeneration through coupling
1980	Seems Like Old Times	Pursuit/m Foil (dweeb)	Conventional	Social Regeneration through coupling
1980	Private Benjamin	Redemption (brokenhearted/f)	Unconventional	Self-actualization through uncoupling

Table 12 (continued)

YEAR	TITLE OF MOVIE	PLOT	GENRE TYPE	THEME
1980	The Last Married Couple in America	Redemption (brokenhearted/b)	Conventional	Social Regeneration through coupling
1981	Bustin' Loose	Redemption (coldhearted/m) Foil (prick)	Conventional	Social Regeneration through coupling
1981	Arthur	Redemption (coldhearted/m) Foil (bitch) Permission (acceptance)	Conventional	Social Regeneration through coupling
1981	Continental Divide	Pursuit/m Redemption (coldhearted/m)	Unconventional	Self-actualization coupled with coupling
1981	Paternity	Redemption (coldhearted/m)	Conventional	Social Regeneration through coupling
1981	First Monday in October	Redemption (coldhearted/m)	Unconventional	Self-actualization through uncoupling
1982	Night Shift	Redemption (brokenhearted/m) Foil (bitch)	Conventional	Social Regeneration through coupling
1982	Kiss Me Goodbye	Foil (prick)	Conventional	Social Regeneration through coupling
1982	Best Friends	Pursuit/m Redemption (coldhearted/m)	Unconventional	Self-actualization coupled with coupling
1982	Tootsie	Redemption (coldhearted/m) Foil (prick)	Conventional	Social Regeneration through coupling
1983	Valley Girl	Pursuit/m Foil (prick)	Conventional	Social Regeneration through coupling
1983	Educating Rita	Pursuit/m Redemption (brokenhearted/m)	Unconventional	Self-actualization through uncoupling
1984	Unfaithfully Yours	Redemption (coldhearted/m)	Conventional	Social Regeneration through coupling
1984	Blame It On Rio	Redemption (coldhearted/m) Foil (temptress)	Conventional	Social Regeneration through coupling
1984	Splash	Redemption (brokenhearted/m)	Conventional	Social Regeneration through coupling
1984	Sixteen Candles	Redemption (brokenhearted/f)	Conventional	Social Regeneration through coupling
1984	The Woman in Red	Pursuit/m Redemption (coldhearted/m) Foil (temptress)	Conventional	Social Regeneration through coupling
1984	All of Me	Redemption (coldhearted/f and brokenhearted/m) Foil (bitch and temptress)	Screwball	Social Regeneration through coupling

Table 12 (continued)

YEAR	TITLE OF MOVIE	PLOT	GENRE TYPE	THEME
1984	Irreconcilable Differences	Redemption (coldhearted/m and brokenhearted/b) Foil (bitch)	Unconventional	Ambiguous
1984	Micki and Maude	Redemption (brokenhearted/m)	Conventional	Social Regeneration through coupling
1985	The Sure Thing	Pursuit/m Foil (dweeb and temptress)	Conventional	Social Regeneration through coupling
1985	Desperately Seeking Susan	Redemption (brokenhearted/f) Foil (prick)	Screwball	Social Regeneration through coupling
1985	Murphy's Romance	Redemption (brokenhearted/b) Foil (prick)	Conventional	Social Regeneration through coupling
1986	Pretty in Pink	Redemption (brokenhearted/f) Foil (dweeb)	Conventional	Social Regeneration through coupling
1986	About Last Night	Pursuit/m Redemption (coldhearted/m)	Conventional	Social Regeneration through coupling
1986	"Crocodile" Dundee	Redemption (brokenhearted/m) Foil (dweeb)	Conventional	Social Regeneration through coupling
1987	Mannequin	Redemption (brokenhearted/m) Foil (bitch)	Conventional	Social Regeneration through coupling
1987	Some Kind of Wonderful	Pursuit/m Redemption (brokenhearted/m) Foil (temptress)	Conventional	Social Regeneration through coupling
1987	Blind Date	Redemption (brokenhearted/m) Foil (prick)	Conventional	Social Regeneration through coupling
1987	Roxanne	Redemption (brokenhearted/m) Foil (dweeb)	Conventional	Social Regeneration through coupling
1987	Can't Buy Me Love	Pursuit/m Redemption (brokenhearted/m)	Conventional	Social Regeneration through coupling
1987	The Pick-up Artist	Pursuit/m Redemption (coldhearted/m)	Conventional	Social Regeneration through coupling
1987	Baby Boom	Redemption (coldhearted/f)	Conventional	Social Regeneration through coupling
1987	Moonstruck	Pursuit/m Redemption (coldhearted/m and brokenhearted/f) Foil (dweeb)	Conventional	Social Regeneration through coupling
1987	Broadcast News	Pursuit/m Redemption (brokenhearted/b) Foil (prick and dweeb)	Unconventional	Social Regeneration through coupling
1987	Overboard	Redemption (coldhearted/f and brokenhearted/m) Foil (prick)	Conventional	Social Regeneration through coupling
1988	Funny Farm	Redemption (coldhearted/m and brokenhearted/b)	Conventional	Social Regeneration through coupling

Table 12 (continued)

YEAR	TITLE OF MOVIE	PLOT	GENRE TYPE	THEME
1988	Bull Durham	Pursuit/m Redemption (brokenhearted/m) Foil (dweeb)	Conventional	Social Regeneration through coupling
1988	Coming to America	Pursuit/m Redemption (brokenhearted/m) Foil (prick) Permission (acceptance)	Conventional	Social Regeneration through coupling
1988	Cocktail	Pursuit/m Redemption (coldhearted/m) Foil (bitch) Permission (separation)	Conventional	Social Regeneration through coupling
1988	Crossing Delancey	Pursuit/m Foil (prick)	Conventional	Social Regeneration through coupling
1988	Working Girl	Foil (prick and bitch)	Conventional	Social Regeneration through coupling
1989	Say Anything	Pursuit/m Redemption (brokenhearted/m) Permission (separation)	Conventional	Social Regeneration through coupling
1989	Cousins	Foil (prick and bitch)	Conventional	Social Regeneration through coupling
1989	When Harry Met Sally	Pursuit/m Redemption (coldhearted/m)	Conventional	Social Regeneration through coupling
1989	Look Who's Talking	Pursuit/m Redemption (brokenhearted/m) Foil (prick)	Conventional	Social Regeneration through coupling
1989	She-Devil	Redemption (coldhearted/m and brokenhearted/f) Foil (bitch)	Unconventional	Self-actualization through uncoupling
1989	The War of the Roses	Pursuit/m Redemption (coldhearted/m and brokenhearted/b)	Unconventional	Social Regeneration through coupling
1990	Joe Versus the Volcano	Redemption (brokenhearted/m)	Unconventional	Social Regeneration through coupling
1990	Pretty Woman	Pursuit/m Redemption (coldhearted/m)	Conventional	Social Regeneration through coupling
1990	Green Card	Redemption (coldhearted/m) Foil (dweeb)	Conventional	Social Regeneration through coupling
1991	L.A. Story	Pursuit/m Redemption (brokenhearted/m) Foil (dweeb, bitch, and temptress)	Conventional	Social Regeneration through coupling
1991	Defending Your Life	Redemption (brokenhearted/m)	Conventional	Social Regeneration through coupling
1991	Only the Lonely	Redemption (brokenhearted/m) Permission (separation)	Conventional	Social Regeneration through coupling

171

Table 12 (continued)

YEAR	TITLE OF MOVIE	PLOT	GENRE TYPE	THEME
1991	Doc Hollywood	Pursuit/m Redemption (brokenhearted/m) Foil (dweeb)	Conventional	Social Regeneration through coupling
1991	Frankie & Johnny	Pursuit/m Redemption (brokenhearted/b)	Conventional	Social Regeneration through coupling
1991	Other People's Money	Pursuit/m Redemption (coldhearted/m)	Conventional	Social Regeneration through coupling
1992	Housesitter	Pursuit/m Redemption (brokenhearted/m) Foil (bitch)	Conventional	Social Regeneration through coupling
1992	Boomerang	Pursuit/m Foil (dweeb and bitch)	Conventional	Social Regeneration through coupling
1992	Prelude to a Kiss	Redemption (coldhearted/f)	Unconventional	Social Regeneration through coupling
1992	Honeymoon in Vegas	Pursuit/m Redemption (brokenhearted/m) Foil (prick)	Conventional	Social Regeneration through coupling
1992	Used People	Pursuit/m	Conventional	Social Regeneration through coupling
1993	Groundhog Day	Pursuit/m Redemption (coldhearted/m)	Conventional	Social Regeneration through coupling
1993	Born Yesterday	Foil (prick)	Conventional	Social Regeneration through coupling
1993	Made in America	Redemption (coldhearted/m)	Conventional	Social Regeneration through coupling
1993	Sleepless in Seattle	Redemption (brokenhearted/m) Foil (dweeb)	Conventional	Social Regeneration through coupling
1993	Heart and Souls	Redemption (coldhearted/m)	Conventional	Social Regeneration through coupling
1994	Four Weddings and a Funeral	Redemption (coldhearted/m)	Conventional	Social Regeneration through coupling
1994	Threesome	Pursuit/m Redemption (brokenhearted/m) Foil (prick and dweeb)	Unconventional	Ambiguous
1994	It Could Happen to You	Redemption (brokenhearted/b) Foil (bitch)	Conventional	Social Regeneration through coupling
1994	Milk Money	Redemption (brokenhearted/b)	Conventional	Social Regeneration through coupling
1994	Only You	Pursuit/m Foil (dweeb)	Conventional	Social Regeneration through coupling
1994	Speechless	Pursuit/m Foil (dweeb)	Conventional	Social Regeneration through coupling

Table 12 (continued)

YEAR	TITLE OF MOVIE	PLOT	GENRE TYPE	THEME
1994	I.Q.	Pursuit/m Foil (prick)	Conventional	Social Regeneration through coupling
1995	While You Were Sleeping	Redemption (brokenhearted/f) Foil (prick)	Conventional	Social Regeneration through coupling
1995	French Kiss	Pursuit/m Redemption (coldhearted/m) Foil (dweeb)	Conventional	Social Regeneration through coupling
1995	Forget Paris	Redemption (brokenhearted/b)	Conventional	Social Regeneration through coupling
1995	Nine Months	Redemption (coldhearted/m)	Conventional	Social Regeneration through coupling
1995	Something to Talk About	Redemption (coldhearted/m and brokenhearted/b)	Unconventional	Self-actualization coupled with coupling
1995	The American President	Redemption (brokenhearted/m)	Conventional	Social Regeneration through coupling
1995	Sabrina	Redemption (coldhearted/m) Foil (dweeb)	Conventional	Social Regeneration through coupling
1996	The Truth About Cats and Dogs	Redemption (brokenhearted/f) Foil (temptress)	Conventional	Social Regeneration through coupling
1996	Multiplicity	Redemption (coldhearted/m)	Conventional	Social Regeneration through coupling
1996	Tin Cup	Pursuit/m Redemption (brokenhearted/m) Foil (prick)	Conventional	Social Regeneration through coupling
1996	The Mirror Has Two Faces	Redemption (brokenhearted/f) Foil (prick)	Conventional	Social Regeneration through coupling
1996	The Preacher's Wife	Redemption (coldhearted/m)	Conventional	Social Regeneration through coupling
1996	Jerry Maguire	Redemption (coldhearted/m) Foil (bitch)	Conventional	Social Regeneration through coupling
1996	One Fine Day	Redemption (brokenhearted/b)	Conventional	Social Regeneration through coupling
1996	Michael	Redemption (coldhearted/m)	Conventional	Social Regeneration through coupling
1997	Fools Rush In	Redemption (brokenhearted/b) Permission (acceptance)	Conventional	Social Regeneration through coupling
1997	Grosse Pointe Blank	Pursuit/m Redemption (coldhearted/m)	Conventional	Social Regeneration through coupling
1997	Addicted to Love	Redemption (coldhearted/f and brokenhearted/m)	Conventional	Social Regeneration through coupling

Table 12 (continued)

YEAR	TITLE OF MOVIE	PLOT	GENRE TYPE	THEME
1997	My Best Friend's Wedding	Pursuit/f Redemption (coldhearted/f)	Unconventional	Social Regeneration through coupling
1997	Picture Perfect	Redemption (brokenhearted/f) Foil (prick)	Conventional	Social Regeneration through coupling
1997	For Richer or Poorer	Redemption (brokenhearted/b)	Conventional	Social Regeneration through coupling
1997	As Good As It Gets	Pursuit/m Redemption (coldhearted/m)	Conventional	Social Regeneration through coupling
1998	The Wedding Singer	Pursuit/m Redemption (brokenhearted/m) Foil (prick and bitch)	Conventional	Social Regeneration through coupling
1998	The Object of My Affection	Redemption (brokenhearted/f)	Conventional	Social Regeneration through coupling
1998	Hope Floats	Pursuit/m Redemption (brokenhearted/f) Foil (prick)	Conventional	Social Regeneration through coupling
1998	Six Days, Seven Nights	Redemption (coldhearted/m) Foil (dweeb)	Conventional	Social Regeneration through coupling
1998	There's Something About Mary	Pursuit/m Redemption (brokenhearted/m) Foil (prick)	Conventional	Social Regeneration through coupling
1998	The Parent Trap	Pursuit/m Redemption (brokenhearted/b) Foil (bitch)	Conventional	Social Regeneration through coupling
1998	How Stella Got Her Groove Back	Pursuit/m Redemption (brokenhearted/f)	Conventional	Social Regeneration through coupling
1998	Practical Magic	Redemption (brokenhearted/f)	Conventional	Social Regeneration through coupling
1998	Shakespeare in Love	Pursuit/m Redemption (brokenhearted/m) Foil (prick) Permission (separation)	Unconventional	Social Regeneration through coupling
1998	You've Got Mail	Pursuit/m Redemption (coldhearted/m) Foil (dweeb and bitch)	Conventional	Social Regeneration through coupling
1999	She's All That	Pursuit/m Redemption (coldhearted/m) Foil (prick and bitch)	Conventional	Social Regeneration through coupling
1999	Blast From the Past	Pursuit/m Redemption (brokenhearted/m)	Conventional	Social Regeneration through coupling
1999	The Other Sister	Redemption (brokenhearted/b) Permission (acceptance)	Conventional	Social Regeneration through coupling
1999	Forces of Nature	Foil (temptress)	Conventional	Social Regeneration through coupling

Table 12 (continued)

YEAR	TITLE OF MOVIE	PLOT	GENRE TYPE	THEME
1999	10 Things I Hate About You	Pursuit/m Redemption (coldhearted/f)	Conventional	Social Regeneration through coupling
1999	The Out-of-Towners	Redemption (brokenhearted/b)	Conventional	Social Regeneration through coupling
1999	Never Been Kissed	Redemption (brokenhearted/f)	Conventional	Social Regeneration through coupling
1999	Notting Hill	Redemption (brokenhearted/b)	Conventional	Social Regeneration through coupling
1999	An Ideal Husband	Redemption (coldhearted/m) Foil (bitch)	Conventional	Social Regeneration through coupling
1999	Runaway Bride	Redemption (coldhearted/m) Foil (dweeb)	Conventional	Social Regeneration through coupling
1999	For Love of the Game	Pursuit/m Redemption (coldhearted/m)	Conventional	Social Regeneration through coupling
1999	Drive Me Crazy	Redemption (brokenhearted/b) Foil (prick and bitch)	Conventional	Social Regeneration through coupling
1999	The Story of Us	Redemption (brokenhearted/b)	Conventional	Social Regeneration through coupling
1999	The Best Man	Redemption (coldhearted/m) Foil (bitch)	Conventional	Social Regeneration through coupling
1999	The Bachelor	Pursuit/m Redemption (coldhearted/m)	Conventional	Social Regeneration through coupling

Notes

INTRODUCTION

1. Diane Raymond (1995), p. 122.

2. As detailed later in the book, the sample utilized for this genre study excludes Hollywood romantic comedies that sold less than 3.398 million tickets at the box office or, in other words, "movies that bombed so badly that they were in and out of the movie theaters quicker than their coming attractions." The 155 Hollywood romantic comedies that make up this genre study's sample represent a universal sample of all Hollywood romantic comedies released from 1970–1999 that sold more than 3.398 million tickets. Excluding those Hollywood romantic comedies that sold less than 3.398 million tickets allows the sample to be evenly proportioned between blockbusters, hits, marginally successful movies, disappointments, and bombs. Furthermore, the sample size, at 155 Hollywood romantic comedies (constituting the overwhelming majority of Hollywood romantic comedies released from 1970–1999), is certainly a representative sample of all the Hollywood romantic comedies released during that period.

3. These numbers are confined to the data set for this study, which include only those Hollywood romantic comedies with over 3.398 million admissions. There were forty-six Hollywood romantic comedies with over 3.398 million admissions released from 1970–1983, and forty-seven Hollywood romantic comedies with over 3.398 million admissions released from 1995–1999.

4. Although I occasionally use the terms "Hollywood love story" and "Hollywood romantic comedy" interchangeably throughout this book, these terms are not

completely synonymous. There are other Hollywood genres in addition to the Hollywood romantic comedy that interweave romantic courtship and romantic love into their narratives. However, with the demise of the romance and the musical in the early 1970s, the Hollywood romantic comedy is currently the only popular Hollywood genre that focuses *exclusively* on romantic courtship and romantic love.

5. See Bruno Bettleheim (1989) for the classical study of the fairy tale from a psychoanalytical perspective; see Jack Zipes (1989, 1997) for more contemporary critical readings of the fairy tale, and fairy tales, from a feminist perspective.

6. The major studios tend to be highly competitive and closely guard any information they have about audience demographics. However, the best estimates derived from Hollywood romantic comedies in which numbers have been made available indicate that the genre viewership is between fifty-five to sixty percent female (although, of course, the actual percentages will fluctuate from movie to movie).

7. This distinguishes the Hollywood romantic comedy, which typically employs little, if any, special effects and/or sweeping vistas, from many other Hollywood genres whose popular appeal rely, in large part, on the visual pleasures of spectacle (with their special effects and/or sweeping vistas overwhelming their stories).

8. See Stuart Hall (1980) and John Fiske (1992).

9. Of the "top" 155 Hollywood romantic comedies released from 1970–1999, only six of these movies, *Bustin' Loose* (1981), *Coming to America* (1988), *Boomerang* (1992), *The Preacher's Wife* (1996), *How Stella Got Her Groove Back* (1998), and *The Best Man* (1999) feature a black hero and heroine. Only one of these movies, *Made in America* (1993), features an interracial couple as a hero and a heroine. Significantly, all but one of these movies were "star vehicles" for already established black stars who had already been accepted and embraced by white audiences: Richard Pryor and Cicely Tyson (*Bustin' Loose*), Eddie Murphy (*Coming to America* and *Boomerang*), Denzel Washington and Whitney Houston (*The Preacher's Wife*), Angela Bassett (*How Stella Got Her Groove Back*), and Whoopi Goldberg (*Made in America*). The one remaining movie, *The Best Man,* cast an upcoming black star, Taye Diggs, in the hero role. Furthermore, none of the "top" 155 Hollywood romantic comedies features a Latino hero, or an Asian hero or heroine. Only one of the "top" 155 Hollywood romantic comedies, *Fools Rush In* (1997), features a Latino heroine (Salma Hayek). These facts limit the conclusions one can draw from any structural study. For example, since one of the four Hollywood love stories involves a pursuit plot in which one leading character romantically pursues another, it is critical to consider whether the norms of romantic courtship are evenly distributed between demographic groups. Are the norms the same for blacks as they are for whites? Do blacks in general bypass some of the "games" of romantic courtship in order to get to the sexual connection more quickly? Or, perhaps, do they draw out the games and, therefore, take longer to get to the sexual connection? How about Latinos? Or Asians? Does class play a role? Age? Sexual orientation? And if there are different norms of romantic courtship for different groups, then how, if at all, does that affect the way that the members of these groups perceive, and interpret, a Hollywood romantic comedy pursuit plot?

10. The concept of a white subject position can be equally problematic because whites also are not monolithic. Different ethnic, class, generational, regional, and religious backgrounds, for example, can also affect the way "different" whites perceive, and interpret, similar texts. Furthermore, in addition to the issue of race specificity, there is the issue of gender specificity. Focusing on female identification, film theorists have long raised questions as to whether there is, or can be, a female subject position in cinema. See Laura Mulvey (1975), Mary Ann Doane (1984), and Constance Penley (1988).

11. As Fiske (1992) notes: "The distribution of power in society is paralleled by the distribution of meanings in texts, and struggles for social power are paralleled by semiotic struggles for meaning" (Fiske, 1992, p. 305).

12. As the field of cultural studies correctly notes, there are also tens of millions of Americans who actively manipulate and/or appropriate popular culture texts in order to resist dominant ideologies. One does not automatically negate the other. Passive consumption and active engagement are both part of the American popular culture dynamic.

13. See Hall (1980).

14. Barry Keith Grant (1986), p. xii.

15. Arthur Asa Berger (1992), p. 73.

16. Gina Marchetti (1989), p. 187.

17. Roland Barthes (1973), p. 140; as cited in Dominic Strinati (1995), p. 110.

18. Barthes (1973), p. 56; as cited in Strinati (1995), p. 119.

19. In focusing on "the binary oppositions and sequences of actions from which the movie's thematic meanings are largely forged," I am building on the premise of film semiotics that textual meaning is constructed through the paradigmatic (oppositional) and syntagmatic (sequential) structures of shots, scenes, and/or stories.

20. Acting style, score, lighting, cinematography, casting, costume, setting, pacing, and mise en scene are all crucial components, among others, that make up a movie and can serve as ideological counterpoints to the stories.

21. See Virginia Wright Wexman (1993) for a study on the ideological implications of acting styles; see Raymond Bellour (1975) for an analysis of the signifying effects of shots, cuts, and sequences; and see James Monaco (1981) for a comprehensive analysis of different ways to critically read a film.

CHAPTER 1: THE PURSUIT PLOT

1. As quoted in Irving M. Zeitlan (1986) p. 36.

2. It should be noted that males are also often killed in slasher films, but not in great as numbers as females; not as graphically depicted; and not with the same sexual buildup that leads to, and culminates in, the slaughter. It also should be noted that as the slasher genre has become a bit more "campy" in recent years, the sexual intensity associated with such killings has been somewhat "lightened" by humor. Ethnographic studies of these more campy slasher films can help answer whether this generic transformation has, or has not, changed the visual and narrative pleasures of

the genre: both for female viewers, who constitute a significant segment of the audience for these campy slasher films, and for male viewers.

3. Carol J. Clover (1992) offers an interesting counterreading of slasher films and rape-revenge movies. While acknowledging, in line with Laura Mulvey's theory of the "male gaze" (Mulvey, 1975), that slasher films do offer male viewers some sadistic pleasures, Clover nevertheless maintains that "sadistic voyeurism" is not necessarily "the first cause of horror" (Clover, 1992, p. 19). Combining poststructuralism and psychoanalysis, Clover reads ideological resistance into the slasher film narrative noting, among other things, that in most slasher films, a strong heroine ultimately survives against incredible odds, even as, one by one, all her male and female friends are violently slaughtered. Although I am sympathetic to Clover's argument that sadistic voyeurism is not the *only* "pleasure" that the genre offers, I also think that sadistic voyeurism—at least as it relates to the more graphic, less campy, 1970s and 1980s slasher films—plays a much larger role with male viewers than her study suggests: both in movie theaters where male viewers can partially ignore the narrative while waiting for the "sexually exciting parts" and, especially, in videos where teenage males (and, for that matter, grown men) can bypass the narrative completely by fast forwarding to the torture and/or rape scenes—freeze the action—and sexually "get off" on the picture. Along these lines, it is significant to note that there are popular Internet sites devoted solely to just such pictures: still shots from slasher films—depicting the exact moment of female torture and death—that can then be viewed, downloaded, and printed out. This suggests, in turn, one of the reasons why the slasher genre may have toned down its graphic depictions of sexual violence in recent years: these depictions are now readily available in so many other forums. Why go to a movie theater, after all, when it is so much easier, and so much more private, to rent an "old" video of a sexually violent slasher movie, or to download pictures off the Internet of young women being raped, tortured, and/or killed, along with more "traditional" forms of pornography? It is in this sense—that many teenage boys (and, for that matter, grown men) use such pictures for their masturbatory "pleasures"—that I talk about "a generation of teenage boys learning early what their culture teaches them: to funnel their frustrations toward females, and to use sex as a purge and a sedative."

4. In addition to starring in the movie, Steve Martin also wrote the screenplay for *L.A. Story:* a screenplay that he affectionately referred to as a "valentine to romance" inspired, in large part, by his former wife and co-star: Victoria Tennant (Benenson, 1991; Martin, 1991).

5. These series of delays are not limited to the Hollywood romantic comedy; rather, the use of crisis and resolution is, as Judith Mayne (1993) points out, "the dominant pattern of classical film narrative" (Mayne, 1993, p. 25).

6. The device of parallel action crosscutting has been a Hollywood staple since the earliest days of Hollywood. By cutting back and forth between two series of simultaneously occurring events (e.g., a tied-up heroine about to be killed while, crosstown, a hero drives full speed to where she is being held), the director is able to prolong action, build suspense, and foreshadow an eventual coming together of the movie's central characters in a symbolically climactic scene.

7. A more detailed, shot-by-shot, textual analysis of the fifty parallel action crosscuts that constitute the climactic sequence in *L.A. Story* includes the following: (1) Sara at the airline counter confirming London as her final destination; (2) Harris sitting alone in his study; (3) Sara riding up the escalator to the departing gate; (4) the captain of Sara's jet switching on the jet's engines; (5) the engines revving up; (6) Harris slumping in his chair; (7) Sara buckling up her seat belt; (8) Harris breathing heavily; (9) the wheels of Sara's jet rolling down the runway; (10) Sara staring into space; (11) Sara's jet taxiing toward takeoff; (12) the electronic freeway sign blinking to life; (13) Harris leaning forward in his chair as the needle on his barometer turns from "very dry" to "cloudy"; (14) Sara sitting in her seat as, outside her window, fog rolls in; (15) Sara staring at the fog; (16) dark storm clouds; (17) lightning; (18) thunder; (19) rain; (20) the leaves in front of Harris's house whipped by wind; (21) the electronic freeway sign continuing to blink; (22) Harris's anemometer beginning to spin; (23) Sara's jet getting pelted by rain; (24) Sara staring into the rain; (25) more storm clouds; (26) more lightning; (27) Harris's anemometer continuing to spin; (28) the electronic freeway sign continuing to blink; (29) the compasses in the cockpit of Sara's jet spinning out of control; (30) the captain of Sara's jet reaching for the brake; (31) the wheels of Sara's jet rolling to a stop; (32) Harris staring out his window; (33) Sara staring out her window; (34) Harris's hand reaching up; (35) Sara's hand reaching up; (36) Harris's fingers touching his window; (37) Sara's fingers touching her window; (38) Sara's face lit by lightning; (39) Harris's face lit by lightning; (40) Sara's hand lit by lightning; (41) Harris's hand lit by lightning; (42) the electronic freeway sign showering the night sky with sparks; (43) cars speeding across the freeway; (44) storm clouds speeding across the sky; (45) Harris stepping out of his house into the pouring rain; (46) Sara's taxi pulling to a stop in front of Harris's house; (47) Harris staring at the taxi; (48) Sara running toward Harris, dropping her suitcases as she runs; (49) Sara and Harris embracing; (50) Sara and Harris kissing the *key kiss*.

8. In order to account for the gimmick of incorporating Albert Einstein into the narrative, the movie is set in Princeton, 1955; the look and feel of the picture is, nevertheless, contemporary.

9. While the context that the quote is placed in—a Hollywood romantic comedy—is purely fictional, the quote, itself, is not fictional. The real Albert Einstein did indeed profess: "I, for one, will never believe that God plays dice with the universe."

10. In addition to *Doc Hollywood,* both *She's All That* (1999) and *10 Things I Hate About You* (1999) also picture a hero betting that he can win the heart—and, implicitly, the panties off—of an unwilling heroine. In both movies, as in *Doc Hollywood,* the hero wins the bet and the heroine.

11. Although the hero's rape of the heroine in *Blume in Love* may seem incongruous with most people's idea of romantic pursuit, we shouldn't forget that *Blume in Love* is not alone in sympathetically linking rape with romantic pursuit. One of the most popular television soap opera story lines, after all, was Luke's rape of Laura on *General Hospital* in the early 1980s, leading to her forgiveness of his act, and their eventual marriage. Furthermore, as Janice Radway (1984) details in her study of ro-

mance novels, this exact same story line—romantic pursuit, followed by rape, followed by separation, followed by the resumption of romantic pursuit, followed by forgiveness, followed by a wedding—is structured into many of the most popular romance novels.

12. To its credit, *Blume in Love* tempers the hero's "winning of the heroine back" with an ideologically ambivalent ending that, while reaffirming the hero and heroine's recoupling, has the heroine, nevertheless, rejecting the hero's marital proposal.

CHAPTER 2: THE COLDHEARTED REDEMPTION PLOT

1. *Used People* (1992) is the only Hollywood romantic comedy in the sample that, utilizing a pursuit plot, does not combine it with any of the other Hollywood romantic comedy plots. All sixty-six other Hollywood romantic comedies in the sample that employ the pursuit plot combine it with one or more of the other Hollywood romantic comedy plots.

2. In its promotions for the movie, Touchstone Pictures never acknowledges that the heroine of *Pretty Woman* is a prostitute. Instead the heroine is variously described as "independent and carefree Vivian Ward" (as in the plot summary on the back cover of the video box for the movie) or "Vivian Ward, a young woman who lives by her wits on the streets of Hollywood" (as in the captions accompanying the publicity photos for the movie).

3. There is an Oedipal element in the movie's constant emphasis on Vivian's financial dependency on Edward inasmuch as Edward, early in the narrative, reveals how his late father left his mother penniless, which led to Edward's estrangement from his father. While Edward could not forgive his father, it never occurs to Edward—or the narrative—that he is putting Vivian in the same, precarious financial setting—and footing—that his mother was in; thus assuming, with his soon-to-be wife, the position of his dead father in the familial economy.

4. The opera scene in *Pretty Woman* is literally a repeat performance of the opera scene in *Moonstruck* with the camera, in both pictures, zeroing in on the heroine's tears.

5. The female journey from relative independence to near total dependency in Hollywood romantic comedies mirrors the female journey from independence (leaving home) to dependency (marrying the hero and reestablishing the home) in classic fairy tales; see Vladimir Propp (1968).

6. The "faith in God" metaphor, symbolizing "reuniting" with *the father,* also keys the heroic redemption in *Joe Versus the Volcano* (1990). After years of drifting aimlessly through his life—and days adrift on a raft at sea with little hope for survival—Joe (Tom Hanks) looks up to the heavens and whispers: "Dear God, thank you for my life." As in *Groundhog Day,* a hero who doesn't believe in anything is transformed, thanks to a heroine's love, into a hero who believes in God.

7. Janice Radway (1984) makes a similar observation about the appeal of romance novels: partly attributing their enormous popularity with female readers to their depiction of a softened, even feminized, male hero.

8. Significantly, in a number of Hollywood romantic comedies, the "natural" sexual hierarchy of the coldhearted redemption plot is reinforced through science fiction, as in *Groundhog Day*, and/or supernatural intervention, as in the 1996 Hollywood romantic comedy hit *Michael*, which enlists the help of the archangel Michael to, as the archangel puts it: "Give a man back his heart." Other Hollywood romantic comedies that employ science fiction and/or the supernatural in conjunction with the coldhearted redemption plot in order "to give a man back his heart" include *Heart and Souls* (1993), *Multiplicity* (1996), and *The Preacher's Wife* (1996). The last two movies represent a slight variation of the coldhearted redemption plot in that the hero in these movies is already married and, indeed, loves his wife and family. But he is coldhearted in the sense that he is more dedicated to his job than his marriage and, because of that, inadvertently neglects his wife and family. It takes science fiction (multiple clones in the case of *Multiplicity*) and the supernatural (a guardian angel in the case of *The Preacher's Wife*) to help the diverted hero get his priorities back in order: lighting his way back to the good wife and restorative family. Of course, there is nothing new in this formula with the most famous example, perhaps, dating back to the 1946 Hollywood romantic comedy Christmas classic *It's a Wonderful Life*. Furthermore, there are a number of Hollywood romantic comedies in the sample that employ science fiction and/or the supernatural in conjunction with the second variation of the redemption plot, the brokenhearted redemption plot, in order to help a brokenhearted man find, keep, or win the woman of his dreams. These movies include *Play it Again, Sam* (1972), *Heaven Can Wait* (1978), *Love at First Bite* (1979), *Splash* (1984), *All of Me* (1984), *Mannequin* (1987), *Look Who's Talking* (1989), *Joe Versus the Volcano* (1989), *L.A. Story* (1991), and *Defending Your Life* (1991). Significantly, there is only one Hollywood romantic comedy in the sample, *Prelude to a Kiss* (1992), that employs science fiction and/or the supernatural in conjunction with the coldhearted redemption plot in order "to give a woman back her heart." And there is only one Hollywood romantic comedy in the sample, *Practical Magic* (1998), that employs science fiction and/or the supernatural in conjunction with the brokenhearted redemption plot to help a brokenhearted woman find, keep, or win the man of her dreams.

CHAPTER 4: THE PRICK FOIL PLOT

1. In addition to the one ideological function, the prick foil plot accomplishes two other tasks: one commercial and one practical. First, as already mentioned, it broadens the text's polysemic appeal. Those who are so inclined can derive pleasure in watching the upper class roundly ridiculed without necessarily realizing that the ridiculing is a diversion. And, second, in addition to providing comic relief, it stretches out the narrative. To make a simple story (i.e., hero pursues and wins the heroine, and/or hero needs and gets the heroine) last for one-and-a-half to two hours per movie, movies often require other diversions to help fill up the time.

2. Isabelle's reluctance to couple with Sam, the kindhearted pickle vendor whom she views as someone beneath her, parallels the heroine's reluctance in the

1989 Hollywood romantic comedy blockbuster *Look Who's Talking* to couple with James (John Travolta), the good-natured cab driver whom she, likewise, views as someone beneath her. In both movies, the prick foil plot helps to boost the hero's stature until he equals, and then surpasses, the heroine's perceived worth.

3. If the husband is just a prick, rather than a *hopeless* prick, the narrative might discard the prick foil plot in favor of a coldhearted redemption plot: placing all the impetus on the heroine/wife, through her love, to save both the coldhearted hero/husband and the troubled marriage (e.g., *Pete 'n' Tillie*, *Funny Farm*, *The Preacher's Wife*).

4. A point that David R. Shumway (1991) argues in his reading of *Desperately Seeking Susan* (1985) as an ideological critique of the institution of marriage. However, Shumway's analysis that "one of *Desperately Seeking Susan*'s major reversals of genre conventions is that the film begins with a marriage and ends with a divorce" (ibid. p. 398) is incomplete. A more systematic analysis utilizing a larger sample (rather than choosing, and comparing, a few films as representative of an entire genre) would have revealed that there are actually two stories going on in *Desperately Seeking Susan*. As a screwball Hollywood romantic comedy, part of the movie involves a "caper plot" and, indeed, as Shumway argues, the two lead female characters are central to that caper plot: their relationship, and their actions in solving the caper, do challenge conventional notions of gender. If the caper plot were the only plot in *Desperately Seeking Susan*, Shumway's reading of the movie as "unconventional" would be accurate. However, *Desperately Seeking Susan*, like all Hollywood romantic comedies, also contains a love story. And the love story in *Desperately Seeking Susan* is quite conventional; it is, in essence, nothing more than a prick foil plot disguised as something more. Shumway's contention, then, that the movie critiques the institution of marriage because "it begins with a marriage and ends with a divorce," needs to be amended. As with *Cousins* (1989) and *Born Yesterday* (1993), both of which also begin with a heroine married to (or, in the case of *Born Yesterday*, living with) a prick foil, *Desperately Seeking Susan* begins with a marriage and ends—*after a divorce*—with a promise of a new marriage (signified by the key kiss at the end of its love story).

5. When a senator asks Billie, for example, if she thinks the United States should help the people in Europe now that the Eastern bloc has collapsed, she proffers: "We got enough problems with our streets before we start fixing the ones in Europe."

CHAPTER 6: THE BITCH FOIL PLOT

1. As Susan Faludi (1991, pp. 112–139) notes in her critical reading of *Working Girl*, the term "the bitch boss from hell" was purposely employed by 20th Century-Fox to characterize and promote Sigourney Weaver's role in the movie.

2. Faludi (1991), pp. 112–139. Faludi won a Pulitzer Prize in 1991 for "The Reckoning," a front-page article in *The Wall Street Journal* on the human costs of a corporate buyout; she also won the National Book Critics Award in 1991 for *Backlash: The Undeclared War on American Women*. In addition to her critical reading of

Working Girl in *Backlash*, Faludi also provides critical readings of other 1980s Hollywood movies in *Backlash* that, like *Working Girl*, co-opt feminism.

CHAPTER 7: THE TEMPTRESS FOIL PLOT

1. James Conlon (1989), p. 151.

2. To use a couple of Hollywood romantic comedy blockbusters as examples: the way the narrative, and the camera, pictures Annie (Meg Ryan) throughout *Sleepless in Seattle* epitomizes the first way that the Hollywood romantic comedy typically deals with the threat of female sexuality, and the way the narrative, and the camera, pictures Vivian (Julia Roberts) in the early scenes of *Pretty Woman*—and how that picture changes in the later scenes of that movie—epitomizes the second way.

3. There is also a fourth way that Hollywood romantic comedies may deal with the threat of female sexuality, but it only occurred in one Hollywood romantic comedy in the sample: *There's Something About Mary*. And that is emphasizing the heroine's sexuality, but containing the threat of that sexuality by depicting her, through the prick foil plot, as so pathetically stupid that there is no way she could ever use her sexual power against the hero, or against the male viewer.

4. In separating the sexually desirable female from the good wife, I do not mean to imply that Hollywood romantic comedy heroines are in no way sexually desirable. What is, or is not, sexually desirable will vary, of course, from viewer to viewer. I do mean to point out, however, that in depicting the heroine as the "good wife," the visual and narrative codes of the Hollywood romantic comedy significantly downplay her sexuality in order to emphasize, instead, her maternal characteristics, including her capacity, and willingness, to give and forgive.

5. Although most Hollywood romantic comedies that utilize the temptress foil plot find ways to humiliate their sexually desirable females to strip them of their sexual power, there are two Hollywood romantic comedies in the sample, *Some Kind of Wonderful* (1987) and *Forces of Nature* (1999), that, utilizing the temptress foil plot, treat their temptresses less harshly. To their credit, these two movies present their temptresses as fully subjective and sympathetic human beings. Nevertheless, both movies still manage to defuse their temptresses' sexual power by transforming them into tragic figures who, losing out to the less sexually desirable (and less sexually threatening) good wife, wind up heartbroken.

6. It should be noted that the lines of distinction between bitch foils and temptresses occasionally blur with female foils presented, in some Hollywood romantic comedies, as a combination of both bitches and temptresses. For example, the bitch foils in both *Working Girl* (1988) and *Boomerang* (1992) are also depicted as sexually desirable, and sexually aggressive, females. The decision, then, to code them as bitch foils rather than temptresses is one of weight. The narratives, in both movies, focus more on their economic power than their sexual power, although they eventually demean and dispense with them for both their economic power and their sexual power. Conversely, the temptress in *All of Me* (1984) is depicted as a "murderous" bitch as much as she is depicted as a temptress. Still, she is coded as a temptress rather than a

bitch foil because: (a) her sexual desirability, and her willingness to use that sexual desirability against the hero, are critical to her criminal behavior; and (b) the movie includes a second female foil who more "purely" fits the bitch foil profile. Although the coding, once again, may be a question of degree, both of the female foils in *All of Me* are, of course, appropriately dispensed with, although it is the temptress in the end who is the one that is most harshly humiliated and punished.

CHAPTER 8: THE PERMISSION PLOT

1. As early as 1934, the first Hollywood romantic comedy to win the Academy Award for Best Picture, *It Happened One Night*, included a permission plot.

2. See Ellen K. Rothman (1984) for more information on the history of courtship in America.

3. In addition to being the most popular Hollywood romantic comedy of all time, *The Graduate* also happens to be one of the most popular Hollywood movies of all time. For comparison purposes, its 85,571,393 tickets sold made it far more popular than the most popular Hollywood romantic comedy in the sample: *Tootsie* (56,253,968 tickets sold).

4. *West Side Story* sold 55,970,285 tickets, *Guess Who's Coming to Dinner* sold 43,589,744 tickets, and *Love Story* sold 69,998,145 tickets.

5. Interestingly enough, there is at least one contemporary media form that continues to heavily rely on the permission plot, and that is the television soap opera. However, in the television soap opera, it is almost always a woman (e.g., mother, sister, girlfriend) who disapproves of the romantic courtship. And that disapproval is depicted in such a way as to primarily emphasize female jealousy and rivalry. The women in these shows simply do not trust other women. And pictured with so much idle time on their hands that they do know what to do with themselves, they cannot help butting into everyone else's business. In other words, the heavy reliance on the permission plot in television soap operas is more a reflection of the culture's continued hostility toward women than any shift or lack of shift from dynastic to companionate models of marriage. In this sense, it has more in common with the bitch foil plot in Hollywood romantic comedies than it does with the permission plot in Hollywood romantic comedies.

6. Susan J. Douglas (1994), pp. 293–294.

CHAPTER 9: A SAMPLE AND A TYPOLOGY

1. This has left textual analysis open to one of its most stinging criticisms: is it scientific? This becomes an even more relevant question when sociological assertions are often made about narratives based on only a few textual examples. Even Roland Barthes's highly acclaimed contributions to the study of narratives, it turns out, are not immune to this criticism. As Dominic Strinati (1995) notes, Barthes's analysis of myth is vulnerable to "the problem of empirical validation." In making no "attempt to indicate why his interpretation is to be preferred to others," and in offering no

"systematic procedures" for testing his theories, Strinati raises—without directly answering—the question whether [Barthes's] semiology is "better viewed as a form of textual appreciation or literary criticism than as an objective social science?" (Strinati, 1995, pp. 123–124). Of course, one can argue that the division between literary criticism and social science is an artificial division. After all, if we are discussing empirical validity, it must be pointed out that statistics also distort and are distorted. What should be indisputable, however, is that textual analysis and content analysis can complement one another. By qualitatively characterizing and quantifiably categorizing, the two methodologies can, together, tackle the issue of "empirical validity."

2. The controversy over genre definitions is no small one. First off, genres can be, and often are, defined as commercial classifications. Because it takes fewer words, and less money, to persuade moviegoers into seeing a "classic western," a "thrilling action-adventure," or a "charming romantic comedy" than to articulate the aesthetic appeal of a particular film, Hollywood producers tend to classify movies into genres in order to mass market and mass distribute their product in the most cost-efficient manner. It is much easier, after all, to sell a genre that everyone knows about than to sell a movie that nobody has seen. But if genres are commercial classifications, they are also critical classifications that theorists can, and often do, employ to more precisely analyze the form and function of film. And while sometimes these commercial and critical classifications overlap, often they conflict. Meanwhile, to further complicate matters, there are some theorists who question whether it is analytically useful, or even possible, to classify films into genres at all. Consider, for example, the many differences of opinion between the authors of the following classic genre criticisms, all of which, with the exception of Harry M. Geduld and Ronald Gottesman, appear in Barry Keith Grant's *Film Genre Reader II* (1995). Andrew Tudor maintains that "genre notions" cannot be critically classified because, he argues, "they are sets of cultural conventions [and] genre is what we collectively believe it to be" (Tudor, 1973, p. 7). Geduld and Gottesman (1973) define genre as a "category, kind, or form of film distinguished by subject matter, theme, or techniques" while proceeding to critically classify more than seventy-five distinct genres (quoted in Thomas Sobchack, 1975, p. 102). Sobchack (1975), on the other hand, collapses all genres into a "single genre category": the "fictional genre film," which, he argues, "includes all that is commonly held to be genre film" (Sobchack, 1975, p. 102). Meanwhile, Judith Hess Wright (1974) argues that the only way to know what genre films are is to examine what genre films do. And what they do, she maintains, is to "serve the interests of the ruling class by assisting in the maintenance of the status quo, and [throwing] a sop to oppressed groups who, because they are unorganized and therefore afraid to act, eagerly accept the genre film's absurd solutions to economic and social conflicts" (J. Wright, 1974, p. 41). However, Barbara Klinger (1984), in contrast, identifies a "progressive genre" that stresses disequilibrium (excess and difference) over equilibrium (containment and repetition). And this progressive genre, she argues, challenges dominant ideologies through "themes [that] dramatize the demolitions of values positively propounded in dominant cinema's characterization of the role and nature of social institutions—such beliefs as the inviolability and/or ultimate benevolence of

the law, and the family as an institution of social and sexual 'salvation' for the individual members of a couple, especially women" (Klinger, 1984, p. 81).

3. There is, of course, the problem of "mixed genres" to consider since commonly used generic categories often overlap. As Gerald Mast, Marshall Cohen, and Leo Braudy (1992) note, one may either "rely on a judgement about what is important" in classifying a film as belonging to one genre or another, or one may "choose to decide to employ a compound category." But, as they also note, "this sort of judgement does not present genre criticism with an insoluble difficulty, for to be able to speak of a compound category at all implies that elemental genres exist in order to be compounded" (Mast, Cohen, and Braudy, 1992, pp. 429–430). Indeed, many of the movies in my sample do include mixed genre types, for example, *Tootsie* (romantic comedy and comedy), *Private Benjamin* (romantic comedy and army comedy), *Moonstruck* (romantic comedy and ethnic family drama), *Groundhog Day* (romantic comedy and fantasy), *Bull Durham* (romantic comedy and sports movie), *An Unmarried Woman* (romantic comedy and drama), and *Shampoo* (romantic comedy, drama, and political satire). The judgment I use to classify these, and other similar mixed genre films that appear in my sample as romantic comedies is fairly simple. They must be at least fifty percent or more romantic comedy (with a lesser plurality being acceptable in the case of a movie that combines more than two genres) while utilizing, or incorporating, one or more of the four basic Hollywood romantic comedy plots that were detailed in Part I of this book.

4. While most Hollywood movies tend to intertwine some degree of romance into their plots, a Hollywood romantic comedy must include more than a peripheral love interest. Rather, the interest in—and the outcome of—the love affair has to key most of the narrative action. For more information about the link between Hollywood cinema, Hollywood movies, and romance, see David Bordwell (1985); and David Bordwell, Janet Staiger, and Kristin Thompson (1985).

5. As discussed in Part I, there are some Hollywood romantic comedies in which a hero and a heroine are already romantically involved with—or married to—one another, thus bypassing the first step. Nevertheless, they are forced to face obstacles to the *continued* recognition, declaration, and legitimation of their love while moving toward a resolution that ultimately works out their relationship—or marital—crisis. The resolution of that crisis leads, in turn, to a happy ending that reaffirms their romantic commitment and/or wedding vows. On another note, there can also be, but there rarely are, Hollywood romantic comedies that depict a chance meeting between a hero and a hero—or between a heroine and a heroine—who together represent a potential gay couple. With the one exception of the ideologically ambiguous *Threesome* (1994), there are no Hollywood romantic comedies in the sample that depict either a gay hero or a gay heroine. There have been a few Hollywood romantic comedies made in recent years that have explored gay love (e.g., *Go Fish*, *Three of Hearts*, *Chasing Amy*), but none of them sold enough tickets at the box office to be included in the sample.

6. Other conventions that Hollywood romantic comedies typically employ include time (the present), location (the United States), characters (a hero and heroine,

eighteen to forty-five years of age, average-looking to very attractive, mostly middle-class, nearly always white), and the four basic Hollywood romantic comedy plots.

7. Grant (1995), pp. xvii–xviii.

8. Although I have conducted an exhaustive search to locate and to include in my sample all the Hollywood romantic comedies with over 3.398 million admissions that were released from 1970–1999, it is possible that I inadvertently ended up missing a few films, particularly in the disappointments and bombs categories, which include movies that are quickly in and out of the theaters, do not always appear in movie guides, and are not always tracked for gross by the studios. Furthermore, in addition to any inadvertent omissions, I have excluded all sequels from my sample. These include: *Arthur 2—On the Rocks* (1988), *"Crocodile" Dundee II* (1988), *Mannequin Two: On the Move* (1991), *Look Who's Talking Too* (1991), and *Look Who's Talking Now* (1993). Finally, I have also excluded from my sample any ensemble Hollywood love stories that focus on three or more heroes or heroines (e.g., *The Four Seasons*, *Mystic Pizza*, *Reality Bites*); as well as any "buddy movies" depicting, and bouncing back and forth between, each of the buddies' love interests (e.g., *Booty Call*, *Out-to-Sea*). I did, however, include *An Ideal Husband* (1999) because even though it involves two buddies and their love interests, one of the story lines—the redemption of the coldhearted best friend who, thanks to the love of a loving heroine, finally commits to love and marriage—is structurally more substantive and definitive along the lines of the Hollywood romantic comedy.

9. Although including all Hollywood romantic comedies with over 3.398 million admissions minimizes the issue of selectivity bias, it does not eliminate the issue of selectivity bias. My definition of a Hollywood romantic comedy, of course, involves an element of subjectivity. And including some Hollywood movies within that definition while excluding others also involves some element of subjectivity. Indeed, even though there is an overwhelming consensus among critics, producers, distributors, and consumers on most of the movies included in my sample that they constitute a Hollywood romantic comedy, a few of my inclusions—particularly concerning some of the counterconventional Hollywood romantic comedies in my sample—may be more debatable. When offering my critical readings of some of these movies, I have included either in my narrative, or in the endnotes, my justification for including them in the sample. Conversely, I may have left out some Hollywood movies released from 1970–1999 that some readers may think ought to have been included. This may be due to an unintentional oversight or it may be due to differing definitions of what constitutes a Hollywood romantic comedy.

10. Labels such as blockbusters, hits, disappointments, and bombs are commercial classifications based on the financial success or lack of success of individual films. As such, they should always be considered with caution since the labeling process is often quite subjective: based on both absolute factors (e.g., gross) and relative factors (e.g., the relationship between gross and production costs or the relationship between gross and advanced expectations of gross). Furthermore, the commercial success or lack of success of a particular film does not necessarily relate to its critical success or lack of success (i.e., how film critics view and review its aesthetic and/or so-

cial qualities). Finally, the labels do not necessarily indicate the possible social and/or historical significance of particular films. For example, the blockbuster *Heaven Can Wait* (1978) had little, if any, lasting social or historical significance after its theatrical run while bombs such as *Up the Sandbox* (1972) and *Educating Rita* (1983) became, years after their release, cult classics. For that matter, there are a number of films that did not make the "top" 155 list (e.g., *Girlfriends, She's Gotta Have It, Go Fish*) but were, nevertheless, enormously popular and influential among various marginalized groups of viewers.

11. The source for all the figures in Table 1 is Exhibitor Relations Company. Admissions are North American admissions based on the average ticket price in the year of the film's release divided by its gross. For most of the more recent films (1985–1999), the gross is an actual gross. For most of the "older" films (1970–1984), the gross is an estimated gross calculated from film rentals and studios' reported revenue when the movies were released.

12. See Ferdinand de Saussure (1916).

13. Females actually constitute slightly over half of the world's population so, theoretically at least, following the rules of linguistics, they ought to constitute slightly over half of the driving force of all narratives.

CHAPTER 10: CONSTRUCTING INEQUALITY. BY POINT OF VIEW

1. All the percentages and frequencies that appear in Tables 3 through 10 are calculated from the data contained in Tables 11 and 12. Table 11 codes each of the 155 Hollywood romantic comedies in terms of plot, point of view, genre type, and theme. Table 12 contains the same information, but instead of ranking the movies by admissions, lists them in chronological order. Furthermore, the foil plot and permission plot are not included in Table 3 because in the foil plot, it is the sex of the romantic foil that determines whether it is the hero or the heroine who acts to reject and/or overcome the romantic foil; and in the permission plot, the classic subject/object split between the hero and the heroine is less pronounced than in the other plots. Finally, because most of the movies in the sample combine two or more plots, the sum total of the number of movies that include a pursuit plot (67), a coldhearted redemption plot (62), and a brokenhearted redemption plot (90) exceeds the total number of movies in the sample (155).

2. Most moviegoers, of course, are consciously aware that a movie is "just a movie." But that awareness is primarily present before the movie starts or after the movie ends. What we are referring to here, however, is what viewers may unconsciously experience during the course of watching a movie: how the form, and medium, work to confuse "reel" with "real." See Jean-Louis Baudry (1970), André Bazin (1967), and Christian Metz (1975) for classic studies on this subject.

3. In actuality, although this occurs in the overwhelming majority of cases, the percentages are a bit less than the ninety-seven percent of Hollywood romantic comedies that, including a pursuit plot, present the pursuit plot from the male point of

view. This is because the pursuit plot is only fully successful in its structuring of masculinity and femininity along conventional lines when it is included in conventional Hollywood romantic comedies. Out of the sixty-five Hollywood romantic comedies in the sample that include a pursuit plot from the male point of view, seventeen are not conventional—leading to a tempering and, in some cases, reversing of the movie's more conventional ideological implications.

4. Although the line "women make a life inside their body, and that life comes out and holds on to them—that baby is theirs for life" and the line "never to be squandered, the miracle of another human being" are spoken by two different characters in *Prelude to a Kiss*'s final scene, both these characters aim their respective lines directly at the heroine, and both lines, together, thematically reinforce the movie's ultimate message to viewers: "Women are on the earth to give children to men."

5. Significantly, while five of the nine movies in the sample that include a coldhearted redemption plot from the female point of view also include a brokenhearted redemption plot from the male point of view, only three of the fifty-three movies in the sample that include a coldhearted redemption plot from the male point of view—*Diary of a Mad Housewife*, *Moonstruck*, and *She-Devil*—also include a brokenhearted redemption plot from the female point of view.

6. Although the Hollywood romantic comedy genre tends to downplay and/or denigrate female sexual desirability, there are a few "teen" Hollywood romantic comedies (e.g., *Can't Buy Me Love*, *She's All That*, *10 Things I Hate About You*) that tend to build up and/or emphasize their heroine's sexual desirability. These Hollywood romantic comedies, aimed at teenagers and starring teenagers (or actresses in their twenties playing teenagers), tend to have a different symbolic task—suggesting to teenage girls what they have to do to get a boyfriend (i.e., become sexually desirable); not what they have to do to get married and assume the role of the good wife (i.e., become less sexually desirable). Even in these teen Hollywood romantic comedies, however, the heroine's sexual desirability tends to be defused toward the end of the narrative with the emphasis shifting from her sexually arousing qualities to her emotionally nurturing qualities.

7. *My Best Friend's Wedding* attempts to temper its "tragic" ending by picturing, in its final shots, the heroine smiling, laughing, and dancing at the hero's wedding. It is a poignant last picture of the heroine—bittersweet—that fails to completely mask the ideological implications of the heroine's final actions: in addition to being a good dancer with a great smile, the heroine is also a good loser.

8. *My Best Friend's Wedding* is the one partial exception, featuring a coldhearted redemption plot from the female point of view in which the heroine's transformation, signified by "letting the hero go," completes her redemption. That redemption, while denying the heroine her happy ending, allows the hero to be happy with another woman.

9. The single exception is *Butterflies Are Free*. While the coldhearted heroine in *Butterflies Are Free* eventually returns to the brokenhearted hero in the film's final shots, the movie's ending also provides some degree of ideological resistance with the

heroine setting the terms of their final coupling ("I'll stay as long as I'm free to go when I choose to go"), and the hero agreeing to her terms.

10. The sole exceptions are *Educating Rita* (1983) and *She-Devil* (1989).

11. The three thematic exceptions are *Lovers and Other Strangers*, *A Touch of Class*, and *Same Time, Next Year*. See Arlie Hochschild's (1990) ethnographic study of married couples—focusing, particularly, on working wives and mothers—for more information on "the often overtaxed role of women in the familial equation."

12. In the case of *Lovers and Other Strangers*, the hero and the heroine are in the process of getting married after cohabitating with one another; their wedding serves as the focal point of the movie.

13. Four of the thirteen movies—*Pete 'n' Tillie*, *Up the Sandbox*, *Irreconcilable Differences*, and *Something to Talk About*—thematically question and/or challenge the institution of marriage; the remaining nine movies all ultimately reinforce the institution of marriage

CHAPTER 11: CONSTRUCTING INEQUALITY, BY PLOTS

1. The average $75 million figure is a 1999 figure; the numbers post-1999 will undoubtedly be higher, even controlling for inflation.

2. Because some movies in the sample include both the coldhearted variation of the redemption plot and the brokenhearted variation of the redemption plot, the sum total of movies that include a coldhearted redemption plot (62) and movies that include a brokenhearted redemption plot (90) exceeds the total of movies in the sample that include a redemption plot (138). Similarly, because some movies in the sample include one or more combinations of the four variations of the foil plot, the sum total of movies that include a prick foil plot (34), dweeb foil plot (24), bitch foil plot (26), and temptress foil plot (10) exceeds the total of movies in the sample that include a foil plot (79).

3. The total of thirty-nine movies, not delineated in Table 4, is derived from the data contained in Table 11. Of the two Hollywood romantic comedies that utilize a pursuit plot from the female point of view, one was a blockbuster (*What's Up, Doc?*) and the other was a hit (*My Best Friend's Wedding*). Of these, only *What's Up, Doc?* combines its pursuit plot with a foil plot. Including *What's Up, Doc?* in the calculations would skew these particular movies even more toward the blockbuster/hits categories.

4. Rounding out the thirty-nine movies in the sample that utilize both a pursuit plot and a foil plot, the remaining eleven movies (28.2 percent) appear in the marginally successful category.

5. This analysis excludes the pursuit plot from the female point of view. Although both the Hollywood romantic comedies in the sample that include a pursuit plot from the female point of view appear in the blockbuster/hits categories, the sample size (two movies) is too small to allow for conclusions.

6. This analysis excludes the temptress foil plot which, although equally unpopular, has a sample size that is too small (only four movies appearing in the pertinent popularity categories) to allow for conclusions.

7. Looking at the more recent Hollywood romantic comedies that, including a brokenhearted redemption plot depicted equally from the male and the female point of view, focus on mending the marital troubles of the hero and the heroine, only one of these movies, *The Parent Trap* (1998) managed to make it into the hits category. *Forget Paris* (1995) and *For Richer and Poorer* (1997), on the other hand, just barely managed to make it into the marginally successful category, while *The Out-of-Towners* (1999) and *The Story of Us* (1999) were both major disappointments.

8. This analysis excludes the pursuit plot from the female point of view since the sample size (two movies) is too small to allow for conclusions; it also excludes the permission plot and its variations since the overall sample size (ten movies) is also too small to allow for conclusions. Furthermore, there has been a significant dip and then moderate recovery in the brokenhearted redemption plot depicted equally from both the male and the female point of view.

9. Dividing the thirty years of the sample in half, we find that there were fifty-four Hollywood romantic comedies with over 3.398 million admissions released from 1970–1984, and 101 Hollywood romantic comedies with 3.398 million admissions released from 1985–1999.

10. The idea that all cultural meaning is constructing through oppositions is a core tenet of structuralism. See Ferdinand de Saussure (1916) and Claude Levi-Strauss (1963, 1977).

CHAPTER 12: CONSTRUCTING INEQUALITY. BY GENRE TYPES

1. While screwball has long been recognized and analyzed as a distinct generic type, Thomas Sobchack (1975), Will Wright (1975), and John Cawelti (1979) were among the first to identify and analyze the parody and ironic genre types.

2. Just how much of a "greater opportunity" to envision ideological resistance the screwball Hollywood romantic comedy affords its viewers is a matter of controversy among film scholars; see Brian Henderson (1978), Stanley Cavell (1981), Wes Gehring (1986), James Harvey (1987), and David R. Shumway (1991).

3. Many of the Hollywood romantic comedies in my sample include some of these conditions in a few of their scenes for comic purposes. To be classified as a *screwball* Hollywood romantic comedy, however, the movie has to meet, and sustain, all five conditions. The fifth condition, the caper plot, may not be absolutely necessary, but I am including it as one of the conditions because it plays a significant role in contributing to the confused sexual identities and/or gender roles. In depicting a wily heroine using her brains (and sometimes even her brawn) to outwit a villain or villains (usually, but not always, male), the screwball caper plot, often competes against the typically more conservative elements of the love story.

4. Definitions always tend to be a bit tricky and dangerous, and there are numerous definitions in the literature as to what *exactly* is a "screwball comedy" ranging from all Hollywood comedies, to all Hollywood romantic comedies, to only those Hollywood romantic comedies produced during Hollywood's "golden age of comedy" between 1934 and 1944. In a footnote at the end of his essay on screwball comedies, Shumway (1991), for example, first acknowledges the difficulty involved in defining screwball comedies; then cites a few examples of differing definitions; and finally, proffers his own definition: "For my purposes, it is only necessary to note that screwball comedy is a recognizable kind of Hollywood product" (Shumway, 1991, pp. 399–400) The classifications that I am using in this study to define "screwball comedy" are, admittedly, quite narrow but the alternative—offering definitions that are either "no definitions" or definitions so broad that, essentially, they define everything and nothing—seems to be equally, if not more, tricky and dangerous. For a more detailed analysis of the forms, functions, and effects of screwball comedies; see Cavell (1981), Gehring (1986), and Harvey (1987).

5. Turning a conventional Hollywood romantic comedy into an ironic Hollywood romantic comedy can be a relatively simple process: *just change the ending*. It has been widely reported, for example, that there was some debate over how to end the 1997 Hollywood romantic comedy *As Good As It Gets:* whether to have Helen Hunt take Jack Nicholson back, providing the conventional happy ending, or to reject Jack Nicholson, thus denying the conventional happy ending. The producers eventually decided on the former over the latter. Subsequently, *As Good As It Gets* went on to gross over $147 million, as well as to win the best actor and best actress Academy Awards for its two stars. We can only speculate whether the movie would have done better or worse if it chose irony over convention and denied the conventional happy ending.

6. Sobchack (1975), p. 112.

7. Cawelti (1979), p. 238.

8. It could be argued that the heroine of *Threesome* (1994) also manages to resist the pursuit plot, but the characters, roles, plots, themes, and messages in that movie are ambiguous. There are actually two heroes in *Threesome:* one hero who pursues the heroine, and another hero who pursues the first hero. The hero who pursues the heroine is actually pursuing sexual consummation with the heroine (which he eventually gets) as much as he is pursuing a more permanent union with her (which he is ultimately denied). The movie's final narration, however, informs viewers that both the pursuing hero and the denying heroine eventually "settle down" into happy, conventional, heterosexual, monogamous relationships, albeit with other lovers.

9. In addition to *Love at First Bite* (1979), an argument can be made that *There's Something About Mary* might also qualify as a parody Hollywood romantic comedy. However, while *There's Something About Mary* often borders on, and occasionally (as in its final scene) crosses into, the realm of parody, overall, its classical elements outweigh its parodic elements. True parodies such as *Love at First Bite, Blazing Saddles*, and *Airplane* parody their respective genres throughout the film, both telling a story while, at the same time, continuously satirizing the story.

10. Although these numbers do "demonstrate that movie-goers do not automatically fall in love with conventional Hollywood romantic comedies nor do they automatically reject non-conventional Hollywood romantic comedies," the slight advantage that the nonconventional Hollywood romantic comedies have over the conventional Hollywood romantic comedies has to be viewed with caution since the sample is limited to Hollywood romantic comedies released from 1970–1999 with over 3.398 million admissions. There have been many Hollywood romantic comedies released during these years with less than 3.398 million admissions and neither this study, nor any study, has examined how these movies have been distributed across the five popularity categories.

11. Cawelti (1979), p. 244.

12. Ibid.

13. Cawelti specifically cites the western, the detective story, the musical, and the domestic comedy as "our major traditional genres" (ibid.).

14. The remarkable resurgence of the conventional Hollywood romantic comedy in the 1980s and 1990s runs counter to the evolutionary view of genres posited in the 1970s by Cawelti (1979), and also by Wright (1975) in his structural study of the western. It suggests that generic transformation and, by extension, social transformation, may be more cyclical than evolutionary. In other words, rather than a straight line shooting us forward, we might want to envision, instead, a spiral in which each turn of the circle winds us back to a point just slightly ahead of where we first begin. The metaphor of that spiral, inching us forward, may help explain the apparent contradiction between the variability and vulnerability of genres and the stubborn resiliency of genres.

CHAPTER 13: CONSTRUCTING INEQUALITY. BY THEMES

1. As Northrop Frye (1970) notes, the wedding ritual serves as "the perfect example of a socially regenerative action." Cited in Thomas Sobchack (1975), p. 111.

2. The most obvious example of this is the still prevailing practice of wives assuming their husband's last names after marriage. Although this reflects traditional practices relating to lines of lineage and inheritance rights that have undergone some historical change, it also reflects ongoing socialization processes that "tell" women over and over that despite these changes, their self-esteem, status, and self-worth is still tied to whether or not they have husbands and, if they do, their husband's economic and social successes.

3. Sobchack (1975), p. 109. In his classic essay on the nature of genres, Sobchack argues that "the conflict between the individual and the group, between self-realization and communal conformity, between the anxiety and loneliness engendered by the freeing of the self and the security of passive identification with the crowd" is the central tension in genre films. Furthermore, Sobchack contends that "because of [their] classical nature," genre films always resolve their tension "in favor of the community." As a matter of fact, Sobchack concludes, "the only twentieth-century art that has consistently reenacted the ritual of reaffirmation of group values

has been the genre film" (ibid.). The fact that there have been Hollywood romantic comedies that key on self-actualization through uncoupling and that, for a period of time, these Hollywood romantic comedies were the dominant texts in the genre, questions the natural inevitability of the genre film's always siding with the "passive identification of the crowd."

4. As the percentage distributions in Table 8 demonstrate, the 124 Hollywood romantic comedies in the sample that key on social regeneration through coupling are relatively evenly distributed between the blockbuster/hits category (forty-one) and the disappointment/bombs category (forty-four), although these movies are more heavily skewed toward the blockbuster category (fourteen) than the bomb category (eight). The thirty-one remaining Hollywood romantic comedies in the sample are nearly evenly divided between the blockbuster/hits category (nine) and the disappointment/bombs category (ten). More specifically, the five ambiguous films in the sample are heavily skewed toward the disappointment/bombs category and the eight Hollywood romantic comedies in the sample that key on self-actualization coupled with coupling are heavily skewed toward the blockbuster/hits category. As for the eighteen Hollywood romantic comedies in the sample that key on self-actualization through uncoupling, these movies—like the Hollywood romantic comedies in the sample that key on social regeneration through coupling—are relatively evenly distributed between the blockbuster/hits category (five) and the disappointment/bombs (six) category. However, unlike the Hollywood romantic comedies in the sample that key on social regeneration through coupling, these movies are much more heavily skewed toward the bomb category (five) than the blockbuster category (zero). As a matter of fact, out of the fifteen blockbusters in the sample, only one movie, *What's Up, Doc?* (keying on self-actualization coupled with coupling), did not key on social regeneration through coupling.

5. See John Fiske (1989) for a good analysis of how the interplay between the forces of popular culture and the forces of dominant culture affects how—and how much—dominant ideologies may undergo significant transformations.

6. There have also been two Hollywood romantic comedies released during this time frame—*Irreconcilable Differences* (1984) and *Threesome* (1994)—that have been thematically ambiguous.

7. Although many Hollywood romantic comedy heroines have jobs, those jobs are typically pictured as secondary, and peripheral, to the "love story." In most recent Hollywood romantic comedies, as a matter of fact, viewers rarely get to see the "working" heroine working at anything except, of course, her love life. The difference in *Something to Talk About*, however, is that the heroine's desire to be "more than just a housewife" is the *primary* focus of the movie. While she eventually forgives her husband for his infidelity, she also makes it clear to him that she would never be able to forgive herself if she didn't, in her words, take the "chance to become someone that I can be proud of." Epitomizing "self-actualization coupled with coupling," the film's final scene pictures the heroine finishing her first day of veterinary school and then, to celebrate, meeting her estranged husband for a dinner date. The film's final shot—a freeze frame—pictures them locking wrists and smiling. Perfectly

centered in that freeze frame, visibly flashing on the fourth finger of the heroine's left hand, is her wedding ring.

CHAPTER 14: ONCE UPON A TIME, THEY DID NOT ALWAYS LIVE HAPPILY EVER AFTER

1. From Virginia Woolf (1929) *A Room of One's Own* as cited in Goodman (1999), p. B7.

2. Susan J. Douglas (1994), pp. 201–202.

3. Excerpted from Molly Haskell's commentary in the 1995 PBS presentation: "American Cinema: Romantic Comedy."

4. A view challenged by Susan Faludi, in her analysis of 1970s Hollywood movies (Faludi, 1991, pp. 112–139).

5. Because most Hollywood films do not end up as blockbusters, focusing only on blockbusters or, for that matter, only on blockbusters and hits, means excluding *most* Hollywood films. Nevertheless, many analysts continue to focus primarily on blockbusters and hits, in part, because they are the most publicized, and accessible, films (i.e., many older, less successful films were either never turned into videos or, if they were, those videos are often no longer in circulation).

6. By the term "1970s Hollywood romantic comedies," I am primarily focusing on the Hollywood romantic comedies released from 1970–1977. But I am also including some of the "transitional Hollywood romantic comedies" released from 1978–1983 to show that the generic shift from the ideologically challenging 1970s Hollywood romantic comedies to the ideologically affirming 1980s and 1990s Hollywood romantic comedies took some time to accomplish.

7. In this sense, *Diary of a Mad Housewife* meets two key conditions that Barbara Klinger (1984) uses to identify "progressive films." First, its depictions of the romantic couple and the family fit in with Klinger's remarks that "there is, in short, no longer any restful identity to be found in the family in these films; the center of hope in most narratives, the romantic couple, is shown as either cloyingly insipid or deranged, two spectral expressions of the same impulse to denaturalize and explode the myth of the happy, unproblematic founding unit of the family" (ibid., p. 81). And, second, its inconclusive ending satisfies Klinger's requirement that "the progressive film must escape the compromising forces inherent in the conventional procedure of closure. Whereas closure usually signals the ultimate containment of matters brought out in the narrative—the network of cause and effect is resolved, and the narrative returned to a final state of equilibrium—progressive films end in such a way as to 'refuse' closure" (ibid., pp. 82–83).

8. Rosalyn Drexler (1973), p. 13:6.

9. Certainly, some may question my classification of *Carnal Knowledge* and, for that matter, *Diary of a Mad Housewife* and *Up the Sandbox* as romantic comedies. Although these films may initially appear to be more dramatic than comedic, I have classified them as romantic comedies based on their plot structures, as well as their tone and tenor. Even though all three movies utilize dramatic conventions, their sa-

tiric excesses are, at the same time, poking fun at those conventions. Also, at least in the case of *Diary of a Mad Housewife* and *Up the Sandbox*, there is a hint of positive affirmation at the end of the narrative: a realization on the part of the heroine that the "problem" is not her; rather, it is the box that she has been placed in. Such a transformation—from a state of disorder at the start of the narrative (i.e., the heroine thinking that she may be crazy) to a state of order at the end of the narrative (i.e., the heroine realizing, and accepting, that she is not crazy)—is classically more character-istic of comedy than tragedy. I would argue, then, that all three films, like so many other counterconventional 1970s Hollywood romantic comedies, comply with John Cawelti's (1979) description of the "third and most powerful mode of generic trans-formation": the "use of traditional generic structures as a means of demythologiza-tion . . . invok[ing] the basic characteristics of a traditional genre in order to bring its audience to see that genre as the embodiment of an inadequate and destructive myth" (Cawelti, 1979, p. 238). In the case of the counterconventional 1970s Holly-wood romantic comedies, that "inadequate and destructive myth" is the unproblematic love story.

10. It is interesting to note that in terms of its plot resolution and its ideological considerations, *Carnal Knowledge* was remarkably similar to *Five Easy Pieces* (an ear-lier Jack Nicholson vehicle that was too heavily weighted toward drama to be in-cluded in this study's sample). Furthermore, both *Carnal Knowledge* and *Five Easy Pieces* were remarkably similar in their plot resolution and their ideological implica-tions to the 1997 black comedy *In the Company of Men*. All three movies were criti-cally acclaimed at the times of their releases; all three movies pictured a coldhearted hero who was beyond redemption; all three movies ensured that everyone in the film ended up paying for the roles, and the games, embedded in the plots; and all three films bitterly conveyed that the social construction of patriarchy destroys men just as much as it damages women. The key difference between the three movies, however, was that *Five Easy Pieces*, released in 1970, and *Carnal Knowledge*, released in 1972, were both commercial hits that had a tremendous social impact at the time of their releases. On the other hand, *In the Company of Men*, released in 1997, didn't even bomb well enough—with only 622,000 admissions—to come anywhere near being included in the "top" 155 Hollywood romantic comedies. It is also interesting to note that the most popular Hollywood romantic comedy of 1997, *As Good As It Gets*, featured a hero (played by an older Jack Nicholson in yet another award-winning performance) just as hateful as the heroes of *Carnal Knowledge* and *In the Company of Men*, but, unlike those two movies, *As Good As It Gets* conventionally used the key kiss and the happy ending to redeem its hateful hero, reaffirm its sacrificial heroine, and reverse the potential of its earlier ideological challenges.

11. *Annie Hall* is only one of three Hollywood romantic comedies that, in the twentieth century, won the Academy Award for Best Picture; the other two Holly-wood romantic comedies were *It Happened One Night* (1934) and *Shakespeare in Love* (1998).

12. For a detailed analysis of all of Woody Allen's creative works, including *An-nie Hall*, see Richard A. Schwartz (2000). Along the lines of so many 1970s

counterconventional Hollywood romantic comedies, Schwartz notes that Woody Allen films "such as *Annie Hall, Interiors, Hannah and Her Sisters, Another Woman, Alice, Husbands and Wives,* and *Celebrity* center around the personal growth of female protagonists as they come to know themselves better, reverse their character flaws, and alter their lives so they can live in greater harmony with their personal values" (ibid., p. xiv). To the degree that this focus on women, and women's needs, questions and/or challenges dominant gender conventions, it is significant to note that Woody Allen's films steadily declined in popularity after the 1970s. By 1985, for example, Woody Allen's *The Purple Rose of Cairo*—a wonderful example of a counterconventional 1970s Hollywood romantic comedy that, as much as *Annie Hall,* raises disturbing questions about traditional gender roles and relationships—bombed at the box office despite excellent reviews and, at less than 3 million tickets sold, did not make this study's sample. The last Woody Allen Hollywood romantic comedy to make this study's sample was *Manhattan,* released in 1979.

13. The heroine's rejection of the hero is less firm, and final, in *An Unmarried Woman* and *Manhattan* than in the other movies. The ending of *An Unmarried Woman* suggests that while the heroine is not ready to marry the hero, she still intends to continue seeing him. The final scene of *Manhattan* is even more open-ended; while the heroine rejects the hero's plea not to leave New York, she also implies that she will be back after six months in London. Still, despite her admonition to "have faith in people," it is left unclear how much she will change in the time away, and if those changes will end their relationship.

14. While challenging the love story and, by implication, the institution of marriage, the one major convention that is left relatively unchallenged in the counterconventional 1970s Hollywood romantic comedies is the fundamental gender opposition between a coherent masculinity and a coherent femininity. Even in the films that most question and/or challenge heterosexual romantic coupling, the films don't necessarily challenge the cultural specificity and boundedness of sex-gender categories. And to the degree that these categories often work in patriarchy against women, there are limits to the degree that the counterconventional 1970s Hollywood romantic comedies work to "free women." This does not negate, however, their significant social and historical challenge to the institution of marriage.

15. It was also a film that, ironically, almost didn't get made. As Joan Mellen (1978) notes, Paul Mazursky's script was rejected by four studios before it was finally accepted by 20th Century-Fox after Mazursky, on a second go-round, asked them to reconsider. To show how fixed popular perceptions of gender are—crossing gender lines—the script was first turned down by 20th Century-Fox because, according to Mazursky, "executives there weren't sure that sufficient audiences of newly aware women were awaiting positive female images on screen," and then turned down by a second studio because an "instrumental woman executive" there was "upset that the title character, Erica, does not go off to Vermont at the end with artist Saul Kaplan" (Mellen, 1978, p. 1.1).

16. Ibid.

17. Paul Starr (1978), p. 1.1.

18. Ibid.

19. After *Private Benjamin*, the only other movies in the sample that similarly keyed on self-actualization through uncoupling are *First Monday in October* (1981), *Educating Rita* (1983), and *She-Devil* (1989); unlike *Private Benjamin*, however, all three of these movies ranked in the bombs category.

20. Jay Carr (1990), p. B30.

CONCLUSION

1. Excerpted from E. L. Doctorow (2000), p. 109.

2. Neal Gabler (1998), p. 9.

3. Most occurred in the 1960s and 1970s, but a few, such as legal protections against sexual harassment and the introduction of rape shield laws, did not occur until the 1980s and 1990s.

4. U.S. Department of Labor Statistics, 1998.

5. Ibid.

6. U.S. Department of Education Statistics, 1998.

7. The seventy-five cents figure is a 1999 statistic derived from U.S. Census Bureau Statistics. Throughout the 1990s, the wage gap between men and women fluctuated between seventy-two and seventy-eight cents. These figures represent an increase from the fifty-nine-cent figure that was prevalent in the 1970s, although, as Susan Faludi (1991) reports, much of the narrowing of the wage gap in the 1980s was due to a decrease in men's wages, not an increase in women's wages. There continues to be debates over how much of the wage gap between men and women may be due to unequal pay for equal work versus how much may be due to differences in education, seniority, delayed careers, and/or occupational segregation. According to Alice Abel Kemp (1990), up to half of the wage gap is due to different career choices between men and women, while discrimination and other unaccounted factors contribute to the other half of the wage gap.

8. See Arlie Hochschild (1990). Also note Suzanne M. Bianchi and Daphne Spain's (1996) findings that "wives who put in an eight-hour day of working for wages average eleven hours more child care and housework each week than their husbands" (Bianchi and Daphne, 1996, pp. 1–47); cited in James M. Henslin (1999), p. 435. As Henslin further notes: "This is the equivalent of twenty-four 24-hour days a year" (ibid.). Although these imbalances are improving, a significant gap remains.

9. While U.S. Department of Justice statistics indicate that "somewhere in America, a woman is raped every two minutes," only one in five rapes is reported to the police (National Crime Victimization Survey; Bureau of Justice Statistics; U.S. Department of Justice, 1998). Furthermore, as much as fifty-four percent of all rape prosecutions result in either a dismissal or acquittal; nearly fifty percent of all convicted rapists are sentenced to less than one year behind bars; and only two percent of all rape victims ever get to see their attacker apprehended, convicted, and incarcerated (U.S. Senate Judiciary Report, *The Response to Rape: Detours on the Road to Equal Justice*, May 1993).

10. The negation of their sexual power is, of course, not an automatic conse-
quence of marriage—it stems from a culture that ties female sexual attractiveness to
youthful appearances; e.g., fresh and unblemished skin, and firm body shape and
tone that, after women age and/or have children, are "naturally" difficult to main-
tain. The shift from sexual to maternal is, at least in part, a psychological response to
a culture that primarily judges a woman's worth on a woman's appearance. As that
appearance "goes," women are forced to find new venues of self-worth.

11. For more information on to what degree, and with what effects, art imitates
life, which, in turn, imitates art, see Daniel J. Boorstin (1965); Marshall McCluhan
(1964); David Riesman et. al. (1969); Neil Postman (1985); Jean Baudrillard
(1988); and Gabler (1998).

12. In using the term "the feminists," I am specifically referring to most of the of-
ficers and leaders of the more established women's rights organizations in America
who, identifying themselves as feminists, muted their criticisms of the president's actions and behaviors in the "scandal" as well as unanimously supported him in the impeachment hearings. In offering this observation, I am not necessarily saying that the
president's actions and behaviors warranted impeachment; this involved interpretations of the Constitution, which, fought out in the political arena, ultimately resulted
in the president's acquittal.

13. The analogy of the bitch foil and prick foil is, technically, a bit of an extension here since neither vied for the romantic and/or sexual attentions, and affections,
of the hero or the heroine. On the other hand, the national drama ultimately played
out very much in line with the conventions of the coldhearted redemption plot from
the male point of view and the temptress foil plot.

14. In presenting this "list of because," I am following the lead of Carol J. Clover
(1992) who, at the end of her analysis of the Hollywood horror genre, also presents a
"list of because" as a narrative device to justify her study.

Bibliography

Adorno, Theodor. 1991. *The Culture Industry*. London: Routledge.

Allen, Robert C., editor. 1992. *Channels of Discourse, Reassembled: Television and Contemporary Criticism*. Second edition. Chapel Hill: University of North Carolina Press.

Althusser, Louis. 1971. Ideology and Ideological State Apparatuses. In *Lenin and Philosophy and Other Essays*. Translated by Ben Brewster. New York: Monthly Review Press, 127–186.

Barthes, Roland. 1967. *Writing Degrees Zero*. London: Cape.

———. 1968. *Elements of Semiology*. New York: Hill and Wang.

———. 1973. *Mythologies*. London: Paladin Books.

———. 1974. *S/Z*. Translated by Richard Miller. London: Jonathan Cape.

———. 1975. *The Pleasure of the Text*. Translated by Richard Miller. New York: Hill and Wang.

Baudrillard, Jean. 1988. *America*. Translated by Chris Turner. New York: Verso.

———. 1988. *Selected Writings*. Edited by Mark Poster. Stanford, Calif.: Stanford University Press.

Baudry, Jean-Louis. 1970, reprint 1986. Ideological Effects of the Basic Cinematographic Apparatus. In Philip Rosen, editor, *Narrative, Apparatus, Ideology*. New York: Columbia University Press, 286–298.

———. 1975, reprint 1986. The Apparatus: Metapsychological Approaches to the Impression of Reality in Cinema. In Philip Rosen, editor, *Narrative, Apparatus, Ideology*. New York: Columbia University Press, 299–318.

Baughman, Cynthia, editor. 1995. *Women on Ice: Feminist Essays on the Tonya Harding/ Nancy Kerrigan Spectacle*. New York: Routledge.

Bazin, André. 1967. *What Is Cinema?* Volume 1. Berkeley: University of California Press.

Bellour, Raymond. 1975. The Unattainable Text. *Screen* 16, 3 (Autumn): 19–27.

Benenson, Laurie Halpern. 1991. Steve Martin Targets L.A. *New York Times*. February 3: H13.

Berger, Arthur Asa. 1992. *Popular Culture Genres: Theories and Texts*. London: Sage.

Bettleheim, Bruno. 1989 (reissue). *The Uses of Enchantment: The Meaning and Importance of Fairy Tales*. New York: Vintage Books.

Bianchi, Suzanne M., and Daphne Spain. 1996. Women, Work, and Family in America. *Population Bulletin*, 51, 3, December 1996:1–47.

Blackman, Shane J. 1998. The School: "Poxy Cupid!": An Ethnographic and Feminist Account of a Resistant Female Youth Culture: The New Wave Girls. In Tracey Skelton and Gill Valentine, editors, *Cool Places: Geographies of Youth Culture*. London: Routledge, 207–228.

Boorstin, Daniel J. 1965, reprint 1987. *The Image: A Guide to Pseudo-Events in America*. New York: Atheneum.

Bordwell, David. 1985. *Narration in the Fiction Film*. Madison: University of Wisconsin Press.

Bordwell, David, Janet Staiger, and Kristin Thompson. 1985. *The Classical Hollywood Cinema: Style and Mode of Production to 1960*. New York: Columbia University Press.

Bourget, Jean-Loup. 1973. Social Implications in the Hollywood Genres. In Gerald Mast, Marshall Cohen, and Leo Braudy, editors, *Film Theory and Criticism: Introductory Readings*. Fourth edition. New York: Oxford University Press, 467–474.

Braudy, Leo. 1976. *The World in a Frame*. Garden City, N.Y.: Anchor Press.

Caputi, Jane. 1993. American Psychos: The Serial Killer in Contemporary Fiction. *Journal of American Culture*. 16, 4:101–111.

Caputi, Jane, and Diana E. H. Russell. 1990. Femicide: Speaking the Unspeakable. *MS*. September/October 1990: 34–37.

Carr, Jay. 1990. Why Is Hollywood Bashing Woman? *Boston Globe*. March 25: B30.

Carroll, Noël. 1988. *Mystifying Movies: Fads and Fallacies in Contemporary Film Theory*. New York: Columbia University Press.

Cavell, Stanley. 1981. *Pursuits of Happiness: The Hollywood Comedy of Remarriage*. Cambridge, Mass.: Harvard University Press.

Cawelti, John G. 1970. *The Six-Gun Mystique*. Bowling Green, Ohio: Bowling Green University Popular Press.

———. 1979. *Chinatown* and Generic Transformation in Recent American Films. In Barry Keith Grant, editor, *Film Genre Reader II*. Austin: University of Texas Press, 227–245.

Chodorow, Nancy. 1978. *The Reproduction of Mothering: Psychoanalysis and the Sociology of Gender*. Berkeley: University of California Press.

Citron, Michelle, Julia Le Sage, Judith Mayne, B. Ruby Rich, Anna Marie Taylor, and the editors of *New German Critique*. 1978. Women and Film: A Discussion of Feminine Aesthetics. *New German Critique*. 13:83–107.

Clover, Carol J. 1992. *Men, Women, and Chainsaws: Gender in the Modern Horror Film*. Princeton: Princeton University Press.

Conlon, James. 1989. The Place of Passion: Reflections on *Fatal Attraction*. *Journal of Popular Film and Television* 16, 4 (Winter).

Crane, Diana. 1992. *The Production of Culture: Media and the Urban Arts*. Foundations of Popular Culture, vol. 1. Newbury Park: Sage.

de Lauretis, Teresa. 1984. *Alice Doesn't: Feminism, Semiotics, Cinema*. Bloomington: University of Indiana Press.

Doane, Mary Ann. 1982. Film and the Masquerade: Theorising the Female Spectator. In Gerald Mast, Marshall Cohen and Leo Braudy, editors, *Film Theory and Criticism: Introductory Readings*. Fourth edition. New York: Oxford University Press, 758–772.

———. 1984. The 'Woman's Film': Possession and Address. In Mary Ann Doane, Patricia Mellencamp, and Linda Williams, editors, *Re-Vision: Essays in Feminist Film Criticism*. Frederick, Md.: The American Film Institute/University Publications of America, 67–80.

———. 1987. *The Desire to Desire: The Woman's Film of the 1940s*. Bloomington: Indiana University Press.

Doctorow, E.L. 2000. *City of God*. New York: Random House.

Douglas, Susan J. 1994. *Where the Girls Are: Growing Up Female with the Mass Media*. New York: Times Books.

Drexler, Rosalyn. 1973. There's a Cop-Out in the *"Sandbox." New York Times*. January 21, II, 13:6.

Dubino, Jeanne. 1993. The Cinderella Complex: Romance Fiction, Patriarchy and Capitalism. *Journal of Popular Culture* 27, 3:103–117.

Eco, Umberto. 1987. *Travels in Hyperreality*. Translated by William Weaver. New York: Harcourt Brace Jovanovich.

———. 1989. *The Open Work*. Translated by Anna Cancogni. Cambridge, Mass.: Harvard University Press.

Elsaesser, Thomas. 1973. Tales of Sound and Fury: Observations on the Family Melodrama. In Barry Keith Grant, editor, *Film Genre Reader II*. Austin: University of Texas Press, 350–380.

Faludi, Susan. 1991. *Backlash: The Undeclared War Against American Women*. New York: Doubleday.

Feuer, Jane. 1977. The Self-Reflexive Musical and the Myth of Entertainment. In Barry Keith Grant, editor, *Film Genre Reader II*. Austin: University of Texas Press, 441–455.

Fiske, John. 1987. *Television Culture*. New York: Methuen.

———. 1989. The Jeaning of America. In John Fiske, *Understanding Popular Culture*. Boston and London: Unwin Hyman, 1–23.

———. 1992. British Cultural Studies and Television. In Robert C. Allen, editor, *Channels of Discourse, Reassembled: Television and Contemporary Criticism*. Second edition. Chapel Hill: University of North Carolina Press, 284–326.

Fiske, John, and John Hartley. 1978. *Reading Television*. London: Methuen.

French, Philip. 1973. *Westerns: Aspects of a Movie Genre*. New York: Viking Press.

Frye, Northrop. 1970. *Anatomy of Criticism: Four Essays*. New York: Atheneum.

Gabler, Neal. 1998. *Life: The Movie: How Entertainment Conquered Reality*. New York: Vintage Books.

Gallagher, Tag. 1986. Shoot-Out at the Genre Corral: Problems in the "Evolution" of the Western. In Barry Keith Grant, editor, *Film Genre Reader II*. Austin: University of Texas Press, 246–260.

Geduld, Harry M., and Ronald Gottesman. 1973. *An Illustrated Glossary of Film Terms*. New York: Holt, Rinehart and Winston.

Gehring, Wes D. 1986. *Screwball Comedy: A Genre of Madcap Romance*. New York: Greenwood.

Gledhill, Christine. 1984. Developments in Feminist Film Criticism. In Mary Ann Doane, Patricia Mellencamp, and Linda Williams, editors, *Re-Vision: Essays in Feminist Film Criticism*. Frederick, Md.: The American Film Institute/University Publications of America, 18–45.

Goldman, Robert. 1992. *Reading Ads Socially*. New York: Routledge.

Goldman, William. 1983. *Adventures in the Screen Trade*. New York: Warner Books.

Goodman, Ellen. 1999. Remember Forgotten Women. *New Orleans Times-Picayune*. December 21: B7.

Grant, Barry Keith, editor. 1986. *Film Genre Reader*. Austin: University of Texas Press.

———, editor. 1995. *Film Genre Reader II*. Austin: University of Texas Press.

Hall, Stuart. 1980. Encoding/Decoding. In Stuart Hall, D. Hobson, A. Lowe, and P. Willis, editors, *Culture, Media, Language*. London: Hutchinson, 128–138.

———. 1986. Cultural Studies: Two Paradigms. In Richard Collins, James Curran, Nicholas Garnham, Paddy Scannell, Philip Schlesinger, and Colin Sparks, editors, *Media, Culture and Society: A Critical Reader*. Newbury Park: Sage, 33–48.

Harvey, James. 1987. *Romantic Comedy in Hollywood from Lubitsch to Sturges*. New York: Knopf.

Heath, Stephen. 1978. Difference. *Screen* 19, 3 (Autumn 1978): 51–112.

Henderson, Brian. 1978. Romantic Comedy Today: Semi-Tough or Impossible? *Film Quarterly* 31, 4 (Summer 1978): 11–23.

Henry, Sherrye. 1994. *The Deep Divide: Why American Women Resist Equality*. New York: Macmillan.

Henslin, James. M. 1999. *Sociology: A Down-to-Earth Approach*. Fourth edition. Boston: Allyn and Bacon.

Hochschild, Arlie. 1990. *The Second Shift*. New York: Avon Books.

Horkheimer, Max, and Theodor Adorno. 1955. *Dialectic of Enlightenment*. Translated by John Cumming. New York: Continuum.

Jamesen, Frederic. 1992. *Signatures of the Visible*. New York: Routledge.

Johnson, Kathleen. 2000. *Understanding Children's Animal Stories*. Lewiston, N.Y.: The Edwin Mellen Press.

Kaminsky, Stuart M. 1974. *American Film Genres: Approaches to a Critical Theory of Popular Film*. Dayton, Ohio: Pflaum.

Kaplan, E. Ann. 1983. *Women and Film: Both Sides of the Camera*. New York and London: Methuen.

Kemp, Alice Abel. 1990. Estimating Sex Discrimination in Professional Occupations with the *Dictionary of Occupational Titles*. *Sociological Spectrum*, 10, 3: 387–416.

Klinger, Barbara. 1984. "Cinema/Ideology/Criticism" Revisited: The Progressive Genre. In Barry Keith Grant, editor, *Film Genre Reader II*. Austin: University of Texas Press, 74–90.

Kuhn, Annette. 1985. *The Power of Image: Essays on Representation and Sexuality*. London: Routledge.

Lacan, Jacques. 1977. *Ecrits: A Selection*. New York: Norton.

Lazarsfeld, Paul, and Robert Merton. 1957. Mass Communication, Popular Tastes and Organized Social Action. In Bernard Rosenberg and David Manning White, editors, *Mass Culture: The Popular Arts in America*. Glencoe, Ill.: The Free Press.

Lemert, Charles. 1997. *Postmodernism Is Not What You Think*. Malden, Mass.: Blackwell Publishers.

Levi-Strauss, Claude. 1949. *The Elementary Structures of Kinship*. Translated by Rodney Needham. Boston: Beacon Press.

———. 1963. *Structural Anthropology*. New York and London: Basic Books.

———. 1977. *Structural Anthropology*, vol. 2. London: Allen Lane.

MacDonald, Dwight. 1957. A Theory of Mass Culture. In Bernard Rosenberg and David Manning White, editors, *Mass Culture: The Popular Arts in America*. Glencoe, Ill.: The Free Press.

Marchetti, Gina. 1986. Subcultural Studies and the Film Audience: Rethinking the Film Viewing Context. In Bruce A. Austin, editor, *Current Research in Film*. vol. 2. Norwood, N.J.: Ablex Publishing, 62–79.

———. 1989. Action-Adventure as Ideology. In Ian Angus and Sut Jhally, editors, *Cultural Politics in Contemporary America*. New York: Routledge, 182–197.

Martin, Steve. 1991. A Side Order of Steve Martin. *Los Angeles Times/Calendar*. February 3: 7.

Mast, Gerald, Marshall Cohen, and Leo Braudy; editors. 1992. *Film Theory and Criticism: Introductory Readings*. Fourth edition. New York: Oxford University Press.

Mayne, Judith. 1993. *Cinema and Spectatorship*. New York: Routledge.

McCluhan, Marshall. 1964. *Understanding Media: The Extension of Man.* Second edition. New York: McGraw-Hill.

McConnell, Frank D. 1976. *The Spoken Seen.* Baltimore: John Hopkins University Press.

McRobbie, Angela. 1984. Dance and Social Fantasy. In Angela McRobbie and Mica Nava, editors, *Gender and Generation.* London: Macmillan, 130–161.

Mellen, Joan. 1978. Hollywood Rediscovers the American Woman. *New York Times.* April 23: II, 1:1.

Merkin, Daphne. 1990. Prince Charming Comes Back. *New York Times Magazine.* July 15: 18.

Metz, Christian. 1974. *Film Language: A Semiotics of the Cinema.* Translated by Michael Taylor. New York: Oxford University Press.

———. 1975, English translation 1982. *The Imaginary Signifier: Psychoanalysis and the Cinema.* Translated by Celia Britton, Annwyl Williams, Ben Brewster, and Alfred Guzzetti. Bloomington: Indiana University Press.

Mitchell, Edward. 1976. Apes and Essences: Some Sources of Significance in American Gangster Films. In Barry Keith Grant, editor, *Film Genre Reader II.* Austin: University of Texas Press, 203–212.

Monaco, James. 1981. *How to Read a Film: The Art, Technology, Language, History, and Theory of Film and Media.* New York and Oxford: Oxford University Press.

Morley, David. 1980. *The 'Nationwide' Audience: Structure and Decoding.* London: British Film Institute.

———. 1992. *Television, Audiences and Cultural Studies.* London: Routledge.

Mukerji, Chandra, and Michael Schudson. 1991. *Rethinking Popular Culture: Contemporary Perspectives in Cultural Studies.* Berkeley: University of California Press.

Mulvey, Laura. 1975. Visual Pleasures and Narrative Cinema. *Screen* 16, 3 (Autumn): 6–18.

———. 1981. Afterthoughts on "Visual Pleasures and Narrative Cinema" Inspired by *Duel in the Sun. Framework* 15–17:12–15.

———. 1989. *Visual and Other Pleasures.* Bloomington: Indiana University Press.

Nachbar, Jack. 1973. Riding Shotgun: The Scattered Formula in Contemporary Western Movies. In Jack Nachbar, editor, *Focus on the Western.* Englewood, N.J.: Prentice-Hall, 101–112.

O'Barr, William M. 1994. *Culture and the Ad: Exploring Otherness in the World of Advertising.* Boulder, Colo.: Westview Press.

Penley, Constance, editor. 1988. *Feminism and Film Theory.* New York: Routledge.

———. 1989. The Lady Doesn't Vanish: Feminism and Film Theory. In Constance Penley, editor, *Feminism and Film Theory.* New York: Routledge, 1–24.

Postman, Neil. 1985. *Amusing Ourselves to Death: Public Discourse in the Age of Show Business.* New York: Viking Press.

Prince, Stephen. 1993. The Discourse of Pictures: Iconicity and Film Studies. *Film Quarterly.* 47, 1:16–26.

Pristin, Terry. 1993. How *Sleepless in Seattle* Slew 'em. *Los Angeles Times*. July 2: F4.

Propp, Vladimir. 1968. *The Morphology of the Folktale*. Translated by Laurence Scott. Austin: University of Texas Press.

Radford, Jean. 1986. *The Progress of Romance: The Politics of Popular Fiction*. London: Routledge.

Radway, Janice. 1984. *Reading the Romance: Women, Patriarchy, and Popular Literature*. Chapel Hill: University of North Carolina Press.

Rapf, Joanna. 1993. Comic Theory from a Feminist Perspective: A Look at Jerry Lewis. *Journal of Popular Culture*. 27, 1:191–201.

Raymond, Diane. 1995. Feminists on Thin Ice: Re-Fusing Dualism in the Narrative of Nancy and Tonya. In Cynthia Baughman, editor, *Women on Ice: Feminist Essays on the Tonya Harding/Nancy Kerrigan Spectacle*. New York: Routledge, 122–147.

Reskin, Barbara F., and Heidi I. Hartmann. 1986. *Women's Work, Men's Work: Sex Segregation on the Job*. Washington D.C.: National Academy Press.

Riesman, David, with Nathan Glazer and Reuel Denney. 1969. *The Lonely Crowd: A Study of the Changing American Character*. Abridged edition. New Haven, Conn.: Yale University Press.

Rothman, Ellen K. 1984. *Hands and Hearts: A History of Courtship in America*. New York: Basic Books.

Saussure, Ferdinand de. 1916, reprint 1974. *Course in General Linguistics*. London: Fontana.

Schatz, Thomas. 1977. The Structural Influence: New Directions in Film Genre Study. In Barry Keith Grant, editor, *Film Genre Reader II*. Austin: University of Texas Press, 91–102.

———. 1981. *Hollywood Genres: Formulas, Filmmaking, and the Studio System*. New York: Random House.

Schwartz, Richard A. 2000. *Woody, From Antz to Zelig: A Reference Guide to Woody Allen's Creative Work, 1964–1998*. Westport, Conn.: Greenwood Press.

Seiter, Ellen. 1992. Semiotics, Structuralism, and Television. In Robert C. Allen, editor, *Channels of Discourse, Reassembled: Television and Contemporary Criticism*. Second edition. Chapel Hill: University of North Carolina Press, 31–66.

Shumway, David R. 1991. Screwball Comedies: Constructing Romance, Mystifying Marriage. In Barry Keith Grant, editor, *Film Genre Reader II*. Austin: University of Texas Press, 381–401.

Silverman, Kaja. 1983. *The Subject of Semiotics*. New York: Oxford University Press.

———. 1988. *The Acoustic Mirror: The Female Voice in Psychoanalysis and Cinema*. Bloomington: Indiana University Press.

Sobchack, Thomas. 1975. Genre Films: A Classical Experience. In Barry Keith Grant, editor, *Film Genre Reader II*. Austin: University of Texas Press, 102–113.

Squire, James, editor. 1992. *The Movie Business Book*. Second edition. New York: Simon & Schuster.

Starr, Paul. 1978. Hollywood's New Ideal of Masculinity. *New York Times*. July 16: Section 2, 1:1.

Stone, Philip J., and Robert Philip Weber. 1992. Content Analysis. In *The Encyclopedia of Sociology*. New York: Macmillan, 290–295.

Strinati, Dominic. 1995. *An Introduction to Theories of Popular Culture*. London: Routledge.

Studlar, Gaylyn. 1985. Masochism and the Perverse Pleasures of the Cinema. In Gerald Mast, Marshall Cohen, and Leo Braudy, editors, *Film Theory and Criticism: Introductory Readings*. Fourth edition. New York: Oxford University Press, 773–790.

Thompson, Kristin. 1988. *Breaking the Glass Armor: Neoformalist Film Analysis*. Princeton: Princeton University Press.

Traube, Elizabeth G. 1992. *Dreaming Identities: Class, Gender, and Generation in 1980s Hollywood Movies*. Boulder, Colo.: Westview Press.

Tudor, Andrew. 1973. Genre. In Barry Keith Grant, editor, *Film Genre Reader II*. Austin: University of Texas Press, 3–10.

Turner, Graeme. 1990. *British Cultural Studies: An Introduction*. Boston: Unwin Hyman.

Walkerdine, Valerie. 1986. Video Replay: Families, Films, and Fantasies. In Victor Burgin, James Donald, and Cora Kaplan, editors, *Formations of Fantasy*. London and New York: Methuen, 167–199.

Warshow, Robert. 1971. Movie Chronicle: The Westerner. In *The Immediate Experience*. New York: Atheneum, 35–54.

Weber, Robert Philip. 1990. *Basic Content Analysis*, second edition. Newbury Park, Calif.: Sage.

Wexman, Virginia Wright. 1993. *Creating the Couple: Love, Marriage, and Hollywood Performance*. Princeton: Princeton University Press.

Whitehead, Alfred North. 1985. *Adventures of Ideas*. Glencoe, Ill.: The Free Press.

Whiteley, Sheila, editor. 1997. *Sexing the Groove: Popular Music and Gender*. London: Routledge.

Wiley, Mason, and Damien Bona. 1993. *Inside Oscar: The Unofficial History of the Academy Awards*. New York: Ballantine Books.

Williams, Linda. 1984. When the Woman Looks. In Gerald Mast, Marshall Cohen, and Leo Braudy, editors, *Film Theory and Criticism: Introductory Readings*. Fourth edition. New York: Oxford University Press, 561–577.

Williams, Raymond. 1977. *Marxism and Literature*. Oxford: Oxford University Press.

———. 1982. *The Sociology of Culture*. New York: Schocken Books.

Williamson, Judith. 1978. *Decoding Advertisements: Ideology and Meaning in Advertising*. London: Marion Boyars.

Woolf, Virginia. 1929, reprint 1990. *A Room of One's Own*. New York: Harcourt Brace.

Wright, Judith Hess. 1974. Genre Films and the Status Quo. In Barry Keith Grant, editor, *Film Genre Reader II*. Austin: University of Texas Press, 41–49.

Wright, Will. 1975. *Sixguns and Society: A Structural Study of the Western.* Berkeley: University of California Press.

Yakir, Dan. 1991. Steve Martin's Lifework Is Also an *L.A. Story. Boston Globe.* February 3: A35.

Yant, Monica. 1993. It's What It Isn't that Charms Fans. *Los Angeles Times.* July 5: F1.

Zeitlan, Irving M. 1986. *Ideology and the Development of Sociological Theory.* Englewood Cliffs, N.J.: Prentice-Hall.

Zipes, Jack. 1989. *Don't Bet on the Prince: Contemporary Feminist Fairy Tales in North America and England.* New York: Routledge.

———. 1997. *Happily Ever After: Fairy Tales, Children, and the Culture Industry.* New York: Routledge.

Index

About the Author

MARK D. RUBINFELD is an Assistant Professor of Sociology at Loyola University New Orleans, where he specializes in popular culture.